Merry Christmas
2004
with love

from Mark & Shirley

BLOOD AND WHISKEY

Also by Peter Krass

Carnegie
The Book of Business Wisdom
The Book of Investing Wisdom
The Book of Leadership Wisdom
The Book of Management Wisdom
The Book of Entrepreneurs' Wisdom
The Little Book of Business Wisdom
The Conference Board Challenge to Business

More information about Peter Krass and his books is available at www.petekrass.com.

BLOOD AND WHISKEY

THE LIFE AND TIMES
OF JACK DANIEL

Peter Krass

WILEY

John Wiley & Sons, Inc.

This book is printed on acid-free paper. ∞

Copyright © 2004 by Peter Krass. All rights reserved

Published by John Wiley & Sons, Inc., Hoboken, New Jersey
Published simultaneously in Canada

Photo credits: Pages 61, 131, 152, and 163, courtesy of the Tennessee State Library and
Archives, Nashville, Tennessee; pages 73 and 196, courtesy of Brown-Forman; page 139, courtesy of the Moore County Library, Lynchburg, Tennessee; page 147, the White Rabbit Saloon,
and page 148, the Silver Cornet Band, appear courtesy of Jack Daniel's Properties, Inc.

JACK DANIEL'S is a registered trademark of Jack Daniel Properties, Inc.

For general information about our other products and services, please contact our Customer
Care Department within the United States at (800) 762-2974, outside the United States at
(317) 572-3993 or fax (317) 572-4002.

Wiley also publishes its books in a variety of electronic formats. Some content that appears in
print may not be available in electronic books. For more information about Wiley products,
visit our web site at www.wiley.com.

Library of Congress Cataloging-in-Publication Data:

Krass, Peter.
    Blood and whiskey : the life and times of Jack Daniel / Peter Krass.
        p.   cm.
    Includes bibliographical references and index.
    ISBN 0-471-27392-9 (acid-free paper)
        1. Daniel, Jack, 1846–1911. 2. Whiskey–Tennessee–Lynchburg–
History. 3. Distillers–Tennessee–Lynchburg–Biography. I. Title:
Life and times of Jack Daniel. II. Title.

    TP591.D36K73   2004
    663′.52′092–dc22

                                                        2003019103

Printed in the United States of America

10 9 8 7 6 5 4 3 2

Quickly, bring me a bottle of whiskey, so that I may wet my mind and say something clever.

—A Tennessee Aristophanes

For Diana

CONTENTS

✣·✣

ACKNOWLEDGMENTS

A special thanks to my editor, Hana Lane, for her continued support and tolerance; my agent, Ed Knappman, for his purveyance of this and that; Aaron Sathre and Christine Pyrdom, for diligent research; Joe Mas, for being an inquisitive father-in-law; my brother, Kurt, just because; June and Francis Tucker, for fine biscuits and stories; Lynne Tolley, for a lovely twenty-minute interview; Roger Brashears, for a few sound bites; Jana Markle, for some photographs; various librarians in Lynchburg, Tullahoma, Fayetteville, and Nashville, for their dedication; Diana, for kicking my butt; Pierson, Alex, and Julia, for needing to be clothed and fed; the Hill people, for cold beverages and mind purges; and sundry musicians and bands like the late Johnny Cash, Eric Clapton, the Cowboy Junkies, Fleetwood Mac, Dave Matthews, and the Red Hot Chili Peppers, for gettin' the juices flowing. If they only knew. Peace.

INTRODUCTION

⊹·⊰

"There was a real Jack Daniel?" friends ask me, often adding, "Jeez, I thought he was invented for marketing the whiskey." Well, there was indeed a flesh-and-blood Jack Daniel. United States census and tax records, among other documents, prove that he lived from 1849 to 1911, his entire life spent in the Lynchburg, Tennessee, environs. The much harder question to answer is "Who was Jack Daniel?" The man lies buried under a rapidly growing legend perpetuated by the marketing-savvy Jack Daniel Distillery, which has inflated him to mythic proportions to sell its whiskey. Another impediment to uncovering the real Jack Daniel is that unlike the very public titans of his age—Andrew Carnegie, J. Pierpont Morgan, John D. Rockefeller—he didn't bequeath us volumes of letters and business documents that would allow us to easily pry into his life. Probably a wise move on his part.

Regardless of the challenges in reconstructing the life of Mr. Jack or Uncle Jack, as he is affectionately called in Tennessee, I became obsessed with exploring this ghostly character in American lore. My interest was first piqued a number of years ago when I was working on a book on classic entrepreneurs in American history and my editor asked me if I had anything on Jack Daniel. I didn't, nor was there anything of substance readily available. The gauntlet was thrown down, and my obsession with Jack evolved rapidly. Truth be known, my relationship with him actually dated back to high school, when one of the preferred drinks was Jack and Coke. Unfortunately, we Krass kids weren't allowed soda in the house, but my mom did stock

1

that foul-tasting Tab for herself, so, in raiding dad's liquor cabinet and mom's soda stash, I was a closet imbiber of Jack and Tab. A painful admission. Not to fear, I redeemed myself. Shortly after departing those sordid teenage years, I started drinking Jack straight up.

As for researching Jack's life and times, the easiest starting point is the liquor store, where you can find Jack Daniel's No. 7, Single Barrel, and Gentleman Jack, all three labels worthy of sipping. However, I quickly realized that no matter how much Jack Daniel's I drank, no matter what quantity of spirits I poured into my bloodstream, his spirit would remain elusive. This was going to take sober, diligent research, which meant starting from scratch, which meant digging into church records, cemetery records, tax assessment lists, deed books, and anything else I could lay my greedy hands on. First stop: Lynchburg, Tennessee, Jack's old romping ground and home to the distillery.

WITH LYNCHBURG ALMOST seventy miles southeast from Nashville as the crow flies, the journey from the host city of the Grand Ol' Opry to the Jack Daniel Distillery begins on Interstate 24 to Murfreesboro, where the bloody Civil War Battle of Stones River took place. There you leave behind the highway for scenic Route 231 and then Route 82, which take you through Shelbyville, the verdant landscape defined by expansive horse farms, many home to the renowned Tennessee walking horse, and white rail fences cutting starkly through the green fields. There is a sense of peace rolling through this gently undulating countryside, with the pace of life slowing considerably. Once in Moore County's quaint, tidy Lynchburg, built around a central square, the pace slows to a point to where you think you're traveling backward– backward in time, anyway. Here, the locals stretch one-syllable words into three or sometimes even four syllables, if they're particularly skilled in elocution. At a popular eatery, conversation admirably centers on coon hunting and crappie fishing, not on the latest cell phone technology. In fact, the best day to hunt bullfrogs is marked on the Moore County calendar.

On my trips to Lynchburg, I always stayed at the Tucker Bed & Breakfast in the village of Lois, five miles to the southwest and just a bottle's throw from Stillhouse Creek, where Jack first learned to make whiskey. June and Francis Tucker, whose roots go back to the area's pioneers, exude southern hospitality, and their establishment typifies the pervasive Baptist mores: a prominent sign declares no alcohol or drugs allowed under their roof. No booze, a tough decree in J.D. country. However, their breakfasts make up for it; these are always a feast and include biscuits, of course—the recipe refined by their son. One of Francis Tucker's first questions for me was, Why? Why would an author hailing from New Hampshire be interested in writing a book on a Tennessee distiller? Uh-oh, I thought, he's got me there. The easy answer would have been that I like to drink Jack Daniel's, and this gives me a great excuse to overindulge. Of course, any royalties would most likely wind up going toward dialysis—then again, it would be a tax write-off, wouldn't it? But now was not the time to be flip. I explained the challenge of tackling such a murky character and the plain, good ol' fun of writing about whiskey and moonshine and other colorful topics associated with Jack Daniel. After a couple of evening bull sessions around the kitchen table, the Tuckers adopted me as one of the family and shared their knowledge of local lore with me, which proved invaluable.

HOT ON THE TRAIL of Uncle Jack, my first stop on official business in Lynchburg was the office of Lynne Tolley, an official Jack Daniel's ambassador, who happens to be Jack's great-grandniece. A beautiful southern belle who plays hostess to perfection, she is one of those who can indeed get four syllables out of "y'all." She is also a shrewd businesswoman—not much different from Uncle Jack. When not traveling extensively to promote the company's products and propounding on how to taste whiskey, she manages Lynchburg's renowned Miss Mary Bobo's Boarding House, an eating establishment that features a regional menu, including excellent fried chicken and okra, washed down with freshly brewed iced tea. Because Ms. Tolley is the only Daniel family member in Lynchburg, I was hoping she might have a handle on archived material pertaining to her legendary great-granduncle. Although she told me she had whiskey in her blood, she had no records in her possession.

It was on to Roger Brashears, the unofficial company historian and media relations man, whose office was in the old Lem Motlow home, a white Greek Revival house adjacent to the distillery. With close-cropped silver hair, a gravelly voice, and a drinker's gut and nose, he appeared to be the epitome of a hard-drinking distillery man. Roger, whose brain—in his own words—tended to go out to dinner, was certainly adept at telling a string of distillery stories in a stream of consciousness that blunted any questions I had. As for archived material, again no luck. Of course, this was coming from a marketing man who claimed to have never seen a marketing plan for Jack Daniel's products.[1]

Next stop was a distillery tour in the "Hollow," where crisp, clean water flows from a cave. My guide's name was Junior, who, in jeans and a flannel shirt, with his name burned into his leather belt, was a chip off Roger's block. Junior was equally skilled at telling stories, one of his favorites clearly being the joke that many a distillery taster is forced to become a tour guide because he can't help but swallow the whiskey—a career-ending no-no for tasters. It is just too criminal to spit out good whiskey, says Junior. Who can argue with that? At the tour's conclusion, I was met by the greatest of disappointments: Instead of a shot of Jack Daniel's, they served lemonade. Lynchburg, along with the county it's in—Moore—is dry. So, in addition to the whiskey being missing, there were no Jack Daniel archives to be found in Lynchburg or elsewhere.

Many papers had been lost, I was told, when the town burned to the ground in both 1883 and 1892. In addition, ten years prior to the enactment of national prohibition in 1919, the company moved from Lynchburg to St. Louis, and then back again in the 1930s, which served to further destroy any paper trail or historical records. However, not all was lost. Most fortunately, the Moore County Library, as well as the public libraries in nearby Fayetteville and Tullahoma, contains a treasure trove of both oral family histories that had been recorded and newspaper articles that detailed Jack's life. And then there was the State Library in Nashville, which has detailed genealogical information, including tax, deed, and court records involving Jack, among other useful documents. In these places, the master distiller came to life.

AFTER TEN DAYS RETURN TO
JACK DANIEL
JACK DANIELS HAND MADE LYNCHBURG TENN.
JACK DANIELS SOUR MASH LYNCHBURG TENN.
JACK DANIELS WHISKEY LYNCHBURG TENN.
DISTILLER OF
PURE-SOUR-MASH-LINCOLN CO.
WHISKEY,
LYNCHBURG, TENN.

LYNCHBURGH TENN. JAN 27 1891

W B Martin C&M
Fayetteville Tenn

Most of the Jack Daniel Distillery records were destroyed, but here is one of Jack's few surviving personal letters.

Jack Daniel,
DISTILLER OF
PURE-SOUR-MASH-LINCOLN CO.
WHISKEY.

Lynchburg, Tenn Jan 26 1891

Mr W B Martin Clerk & Mas
Fayetteville

Dear Sir
Your Kind remittance
to hand Thanks
my claim against the
Estate was $48.00 and same
cost would mail this interest
make it more than $53
for it has been an interest
a long time
Respectfully
Jack Daniel

5

So now it's time to kick up your feet and read the book while sipping a refreshing drink, preferably whiskey. After all, whiskey is the one unique spirit that symbolizes America's fiery spirit. It has been rightly called as American as baseball or jazz. From California to Maine, whiskey has raised barns, has cleared fields of stone and tree, has fought wars, and has killed men in cold blood. This brown liquor's magnetism and charisma are not limited to the United States, however. When U.S. forces invaded Iraq in 2003, a *New York Times* reporter asked a rather pleased citizen of Najaf what he hoped the Americans would bring. The man replied, "Democracy. Whiskey. And sexy!"[2] Even in this dry desert climate of the Middle East, American whiskey is a preferred thirst quencher. And everybody looks sexy after a few belts.

As for Jack's whiskey adventure (really, his love affair with sour mash), the poignant questions surrounding his myth—again, much of the myth perpetuated by the Jack Daniel Distillery—are answered in these pages. Did he run away from home before reaching age ten? Did he first start distilling during the Civil War as a moonshiner? Was he the first to register his distillery in 1866, as the company claims? Why did he call his flagship brand simply No. 7? Until now, the Jack Daniel Distillery's official position on the latter question has been, "We don't know the source of the name." No longer. Read and ye shall discover these truths and more, about a flashy, charismatic American legend who started with nothing but dirt, who fought temperance-crazed preachers and corrupt government officials on his way to earning the coveted title of distilling the world's best whiskey.

1

THE CURSED CHILD

⚜

Freedom and whisky gang thegither.
> —Robert Burns, Scottish poet

Jasper "Jack" Newton Daniel was the cursed child. The youngest and by far the smallest of ten children born to Calaway and Lucinda Daniel, he was the neglected runt of the family. His mother had died shortly after he was born in 1849—most likely, from complications in childbirth. His stepmother had never taken to him. And now his father was dying. It was the winter of 1863–1864. The Civil War raged on. The family's once-productive Middle Tennessee farm lay raped and wasting; the avaricious Union invaders had long pillaged their livestock, their produce, their grain, and their wood; Confederate soldiers on the run had begged for any remaining scraps; and bandits continued to raid indiscriminately. Perhaps Jack's four older brothers could have protected the family land—perhaps—but Robert and James had removed themselves to Texas, while Wiley and Lemuel had enlisted in the Confederate army. There was nothing young Jack could do as his father lay stricken with pneumonia in their drafty, dank, wood-frame house. Soon, the fourteen-year-old boy would be left to his own means, forced to become resilient and self-reliant. Fate was apparently against him.

Calaway was a broken man; the Civil War and the subsequent plundering of his farm had shattered him. It was a humiliating end for a man whose brazen ancestors had fought in both the Revolutionary War and the War of 1812. The Daniel blood, a mix of Scotch-Irish and Scottish, was the right kind of "blude" for soldiers, for pioneers on the American frontier, and for distilling robust whiskey. The family's most prominent ancestor and hero was Jack Daniel's grandfather, Joseph "Job" Daniel, an adventurous immigrant. Through the bloodline, Job bequeathed to his grandson a fierce desire for independence and a fighting spirit.

Joseph's nickname said it all. In the book of Job from the Old Testament of the Bible, God severely tested Job's faith by allowing Satan to inflict indignities and pain upon him. His oxen, asses, and camels were stolen; his servants killed; and a windstorm struck down his son's house, killing all of his children. As a final affront, Satan "afflicted Job with loathsome sores from the sole of his foot to the crown of his head."[1] Despite these rather brutal calamities, Job eschewed Satan and never lost his faith in God. Eventually, he was rewarded. Our Job Daniel also suffered, only under a would-be god—the king of England.

Job's plight began in Northern Ireland, where he was a member of the oppressed Scotch-Irish enclave. This ethnic recipe had been concocted in the early 1600s, when, after ruthlessly suppressing a rebellion in Northern Ireland, the British crown had granted land there to Scottish lairds, on the condition that they recruit thousands of their minions to settle the region. Promised more freedom and liberal leases on land, they did so. King James I hoped these Scottish emigrants, or royal colonists, would prove relatively domesticated and would rub off on their wild Irish peers. Thus was born the Scotch-Irish, an opportunity-seeking and freedom-loving people. Among them were the ancestors of Job.

More poignant to the Jack Daniel story, in the ensuing years, the Scottish settlers, who were practiced in the art of distilling single malt scotch, shared their respective trade secrets with the native Irish whiskey distillers—secrets that would eventually make their way to American shores. Both traditions use barley, one of the few crops easily grown in the harsh Irish and Scottish soils, but from there the respective recipes take different courses. The Scots relish the earthy peat flavor created when they add decomposing vegetable matter to their fires while toasting their barley during the malting process, whereas the Irish prefer their whiskey unpeated. Debate over the respective recipes, however, played second fiddle to arguments over which land started distilling whiskey first. As many a Scot says, "Aye, the Irish may've invented the stuff. But, by Jings, man, we were the ones who perfected it."[2] What's known for certain is that by the 1490s, single malt was being produced by one Friar John Cor for King James IV of Scotland, who, like any good gluttonous king, had a royal taste for the intoxicating spirit.

PEACE IN NORTHERN IRELAND didn't last long. It began to disintegrate as early as the 1640s, when England and Scotland passed excise taxes on "all strong waters and aqua-vitae"—cultured terms for whiskey.[3] So much for promised freedoms. The dogged excise man, who represented the despicable monarchy, became a hunted animal and met with increasing violence, as distillers refused to pay taxes on what they considered a basic necessity. Not until the 1700s would the tension climax, brought on by economic deprivations that created calamitous conditions. Expensive food, discriminatory trade policies on the part of the English, and the collapse of the linen industry in the early 1770s compounded the Scotch-Irish financial woes. Particularly galling to the Scottish settlers was "rack-renting." This devious practice was executed by the native landowners, who unjustifiably inflated rental costs to force the Scotch-Irish from their homes so that pure-blood Irish could reoccupy them. Between the 1750s and the 1770s, rent doubled.[4] Another indignity: the native Catholics and members of the Church of England persecuted the settlers for being Presbyterian, the Protestant sect that dominated Scotland. The time was ripe to move on—namely, to the New World. Joseph "Job" Daniel was among the throng of Scotch-Irish immigrants who arrived in America just prior to the Revolutionary War.

Several attractive options were open to Job, in deciding his destination. In particular, there was Pennsylvania, which had a tradition of religious tolerance dating back to the days of William Penn, a Quaker who founded the colony. A popular port of entry was Philadelphia, from which immigrants pushed west to Pennsylvania's Allegheny Mountains, some choosing to breach the mountains while others turned southward, racing each other down the Shenandoah Valley via the Great Wagon Road in search of fertile land. Immigrants migrating south also poured through the Cumberland Gap, a mountain pass close to where the borders of Virginia, Kentucky, and Tennessee converge. Here, the premier trailblazer Daniel Boone, clad in buckskin, created the Wilderness Road and founded Boonesville, Kentucky, in 1775, thus accelerating migration. The Scotch-Irish refused to be hemmed in as they scrambled for property and freedom. Their sentiment: "I hain't a goin' to rent. I'll own some land if hit's only a house-seat."[5] Another popular destination was the Carolinas, which boasted acres of cheap, sometimes free, frontier land. Southern ports of entry included Charleston, South Carolina, and New Bern, North Carolina, the latter a major seaport strategically located at the confluence of the Neuse and Trent rivers.

After weighing his options, Job Daniel booked passage to New Bern, where he would settle. The insidious passage from Northern Ireland to North Carolina was typically a long nine weeks, barring headwinds or no winds. Few ships had portholes for ventilation and light, and the crowded deck space was stuffy. Disease and pestilence, privateers and pirates, and shortages of food and water always threatened to make for a more brutal odyssey. Adult passengers were promised seven pounds of beef, seven pounds of bread, one pound of butter, and fourteen quarts of water weekly; however, the cost of food cut into the captain's profits, so you can be certain he didn't overstock.[6] A high mortality rate was about the only thing the captain guaranteed.

To ease the suffering, rum was sold on board. West Indies rum, plentiful and cheap, was the liquor of choice in the Americas; corn whiskey had yet to make its grand entrance. Rather than taking a liking to this cheap dark liquor, which was valuable for bartering and trading slaves, the Scotch-Irish came with a thirst for good whiskey, an essential ingredient for survival in a foreign land where, as far as they were concerned, the quality of water was suspect. Even though fresh water in America would be the least of their problems, still houses sprung up as quickly as log homes. As one pious Pennsylvania doctor observed of the settlers, "The quantity of rye destroyed and of whiskey drunk in these places is immense, and its effects upon their industry, health and morals are terrible." It was commonly acknowledged, "Where there's smoke, there's bound to be whiskey."[7] Such was the case in New Bern, where the frontiersman—known as "the meaner sort"—would come into town and "there remain Drinking Rum, Punch, other Liquors for Eight or Ten Days successively," a physician wrote, "and after they have committed this Excess, will not drink any Spirituous Liquor, 'till such as they take the next Frolick, as they call it, which is generally in two or three Months."

While New Bern was the North Carolina colony's capital from 1765 to 1778 and a major seaport, it was hardly a booming metropolis, with a mere 150 dwellings when Job arrived. It had been founded by a native of Switzerland but became a particularly popular destination for the Scotch-Irish after a former citizen of Ulster, Arthur Dobbs, became the governor of the North Carolina colony in 1754. In addition, the colony offered vast tracts of land without fencing where livestock could roam, and farmers could simply clear new land as the fertility of old land was exhausted. As for the social scene, New Bern offered the aforementioned binge drinking, as well as card playing, hunting, fishing, cockfighting, and hand-to-hand competitions.[8]

JOB DANIEL HAD HARDLY settled into his new life as a North Carolina farmer when the tyrannical British crown—a vicious dog clinging to America's coattails—again threatened his freedom. King George III's coffers were empty after the Seven Years War, which had engulfed Europe's colonial powers from 1756 to 1763, and the French and Indian War, which had been waged in North America from 1754 to 1763. As his greedy eye swept the landscape, he determined that the resource-rich American colonies were ripe for taxing. It began with the Sugar Act of 1764 and culminated with the British Tea Act of 1773, the latter resulting in the Boston Tea Party on December 16, 1773, during which Bostonians disguised as Indians threw tea into the harbor in protest. Because they had no voice in the royal court or in the British parliament, the colonists' rallying cry became "No taxation without representation." The next year militia groups—the Minutemen—formed. Tension built between the patriots and the loyalists. The Revolutionary War exploded on April 19, 1775, when the Minutemen engaged the British on the Lexington Green in Massachusetts.

Devoutly loyal to their new homeland, the Scotch-Irish volunteered in droves to fight the despised redcoats. Job Daniel was in a quandary, however. He had just married Elizabeth "Bettie" Calaway, an adventurous lass who had emigrated from Scotland. Born circa 1757 to wealthy parents, Bettie forsook any dowry and, at age fifteen, eloped with the family's coachman. They then made the voyage to America, and she never spoke to her family again.[9] Not long after, due to either death or disenchantment, she lost her first husband. Subsequently, Bettie swooned for Job. Bettie was the romantic in the Daniel family, a young woman with a zest for life, who lived to be an old woman with vinegar, surpassing the ninety-year mark. From Bettie, her grandson Jack would inherit a romantic streak; he would gain quite a reputation as a light-footed dancer and for having an eye for the ladies.

Despite his recent marriage, Job volunteered to fight for the patriots when Captain Charles C. Pinckney of the 1st South Carolina Regiment was in New Bern, North Carolina, recruiting men for the cause. Pinckney was a Charleston native, who in 1775 served as a member of the first provincial congress and would become an aide to George Washington. In 1804 and again in 1808, he would run for president of the United States unsuccessfully. Yet his charisma could not be ignored. Job Daniel enlisted on November 4, 1775, and served at least until December 31, 1776, but possibly until May 16, 1777.[10] In describing the rugged patriot soldiers drawn from the pioneer ranks, the historian Robert Leckie wrote, "No breed of frontiersmen existed in America hardier than these settlements of mostly Irish and Scots-Irish. . . . Fiercely independent, hunters, Indian fighters, deadly shots with those rifles to which they had given such names as 'Sweet Lips' or 'Hot Lead,' they could campaign for days on their horses with no other equipment than a blanket, a hunting knife and a bag of parched corn sweetened with molasses or honey."

The journalist and social critic Irvin S. Cobb further perpetuated the Scotch-Irish reputation, observing that they were "self-reliant, high-tempered, high-headed, high-handed, high-talking folk who would be quick to take offense and quick with violent force to resent it; a big-boned, fair-skinned, individualistic breed, jealous of their rights, furious in their quarrels, deadly in their feuds, generous in their hospitalities. . . . a breed of lovers of women, lovers of oratory and disputation, lovers of horses and card-playing, lovers of dogs and guns—and whiskey."[11] Jack Daniel would be imbued with these characteristics, too. The Scotch-Irish love of whiskey was a key card to be played in winning the war, and George Washington was all too cognizant of it. In 1777, he wrote to the Continental Congress, "Since our imports of spirits have become so precarious, nay impracticable, on Account of the Enemy's Fleet which infests our Whole Coast, I would beg leave to suggest the propriety of erecting Public Distilleries in different States. The benefits arising from the moderate use of strong Liquor, have been experienced in All Armies, and are not to be disputed."[12] Yes, a belly full of whiskey made for a courageous soldier.

Job and his regiment were active in defending Charleston, South Carolina, in late June 1776, when a fleet of nine English ships took up positions there. The English pounded modest Fort Moultrie—strategically located in Charleston's harbor—with heavy cannon, but the men held. With unerring accuracy, the patriots raked the ships, eventually driving them off. Still, Charleston would fall to the English in 1780, and their forces would turn northward, wreaking havoc in the Carolinas. Years later, Bettie Daniel regaled her grandchildren with stories of the war. Her favorite was from when Job was home on furlough. A band of Tories hunting for patriot soldiers—that is, traitors—was approaching their property, so Bettie hid Job in the fire pit of a large oven in the yard. Her cool actions saved his life.[13] With Tory leaders like the homicidal Colonel Banastre Tarleton, who allowed the massacre of over a hundred effectually unarmed Continentals at Waxhaw, roaming the Carolinas, had Job been discovered, he would clearly not have been taken prisoner. Even after Job left the army, his life was in danger, as the Tories continued their raiding, looting, burning, and murdering. Retaliation by the rebels was equally bloodthirsty. The war effectively ended when General Charles Cornwallis surrendered his army at Yorktown on October 19, 1781, and it was officially concluded with the signing of the Treaty of Paris on September 3, 1783.

Without the strong Scotch-Irish and a few wee drams of whiskey, the American Revolution would have been lost.

Now Bettie and Job could focus on having a family, which would eventually include at least five boys, two of whom would fight in the War of 1812, and an untold number of girls. One of the youngest boys and the father of the future sour mash whiskey king, Calaway Daniel, was born in 1800 in New Bern. Before he reached age ten, his parents decided to move to Tennessee, a reputed land of milk and honey. Not only was the land fertile and cheap, but the threat of frontier violence had greatly diminished since 1796, the year Tennessee was granted statehood, with George Washington himself signing the bill. Subsequent *peace* treaties with the Chickasaw and Cherokee tribes in the early 1800s further opened the land to settlers. On the heels of these developments, pioneers, including Job and Bettie, breeched the Appalachian Mountains, with their family treasures loaded in oxcarts, and tumbled into Tennessee. Members of the Daniel family settled in Franklin County, located in Middle Tennessee, where they purchased fertile land at the head of Coffee Creek.[14]

In Tennessee, with its great geological diversity, the land truly shapes the human experience. The east is defined by the Cumberland Plateau and the Appalachian Mountains, the middle by the Central Basin, while the west gravitates toward the Mississippi River. The Central Basin, where Jack was born and bred, is an expansive, elliptical area of gently rolling plain, surrounded by the Highland Rim, a ring of hills rising several hundred feet.[15] Plateaus, ridges, and spurs shoot out into the plain like the coast jutting into the sea, while ravines in the forest-crowned hills dive three hundred feet or more. The dramatic folding and the sensual swooping of the earth create a beautiful sylvan landscape. The rich soil here is spread across a limestone table, from which clean, cool water percolates and rushes, filling the air with a fresh scent. These gurgling springs emerging from clefts in the land are ideal for feeding whiskey distilleries.

When the Daniel family members and their fellow pioneers arrived in Middle Tennessee, they discovered a lush, heavily forested land— the hill slopes were dense with groves of yellow poplar, oak, chestnut, and walnut, with underbrush of pawpaw, dogwood, and canebrake several feet high. There were no trails or road signs to guide them.

While the soil was rich, frontier life remained perilous, challenging, and arduous. Fortunately, these men were not soft aristocratic plantation owners; they were toughened yeomen, many of them Revolutionary War soldiers, who owned few slaves and were well prepared for the challenge. These men cleared their own land by the sweat of their brow.

Although they encountered plenty of wild game—bear, deer, and turkey—farming quickly became more crucial to their survival than was hunting. Corn, planted in fields and on hillsides, became not only the foundation of their daily diet but integral to their culture. Corn was made into hoecakes and provided hominy for the settlers; it was used to feed hogs and horses; the husks made fine stuffing for bed mattresses; and, most significant of all, it was the base for making their aqua-vitae—corn whiskey. It was indeed aqua-vitae, the elixir. The very word *whiskey* evolved from the Gaelic word *uisgebeatha,* or *usquebaugh,* which translates as the "water of life," but the word was reduced over time to *uisge* and then *whiskie.* The simplification of the word made sense, with *whiskie* much easier to pronounce than *uisgebeatha* when under the influence. Corn whiskey was key to survival, as it not only soothed aches and pains but was medicinal. Like wizards and witches over their caldrons, the pioneers mixed whiskey with yarrow tea to cure colds, with a poultice of beeswax and black pepper to combat pneumonia, and with honey and hot water to ward off chills. A good snort of whiskey also alleviated the psychological stress of being on the frontier.

Whiskey raised many a log cabin and barn, too. As one frontiersman recalled, "When we had a corn-shuckin', a log rollin', a house-raisin', or any such frolic, the whiskey just sloshed around like water. . . . Whiskey! I should say so!"[16] Often, there were open tubs of whiskey, with gourd dippers for slurping it down. In Tennessee they deservedly drank their share, as these pioneers were attempting to cultivate a land where Cherokee, Chickasaw, Creek, and Shawnee Indians once roamed but never settled, land where English and French traders had ventured into over a hundred years earlier but had built no communities.[17] Carving out a piece of civilization in the unforgiving wilderness killed many men, women, and children. Job knew he was in no Garden of Eden as he hewed logs for a cabin, chinked and daubed the walls, then turned to building a corn crib, a smokehouse, and a barn. He plowed the fields with two mules and a bull-tongue plow, the beam made of yellow locust wood. For Elizabeth, it was no easier, as she cooked the game he killed; made cornbread, hoecakes, and mush; collected berries; hauled drinking water from the stream; sewed cloth; bore children; and served as a midwife. Women married as young as age thirteen; they were old and worn out by thirty.

These small farming communities were extremely tight-knit, with families relying on each other for survival. During hog killing season—farmers might kill a hog or two for meat that would last the year—together, neighbors butchered the meat; salted it down in the salt box; hung hams, shoulders, and bacon to cure in the smokehouse; and ground sausage and rendered the lard. During wheat thrashing, they also joined together, and afterward, each farmer hosted a big dinner to show his appreciation. At any time, if one man fell sick and behind in his field work, the others came to his aid. This spirit of cooperation continued in Jack Daniel's time. And this sense of community was imbued in Jack, who, despite his success, would never leave his home of Lynchburg, Tennessee, for such glitzy towns as Nashville.

The only cultural activity with any semblance of leisure in their small community was the quilting dinner, a popular event that brought families together and usually featured a plump gobbler for dinner.[18] Perhaps, after a social dinner, one of the men might pull out a fiddle and strike up "Billy in the Wild Woods" or "Jenny, Put the Kettle On," among other tunes that celebrated frontier life. One of the favorite folk songs among the children was "Buffalo":

> Come to me, my dear, and give me your hand
> And let us take a social ramble to some far and distant land
> Where the hawk shot the buzzard and the buzzard shot the crow
> And we all ride around the canebrake and shoot the buffalo.[19]

Book reading was another matter. In stark contrast to upscale neighborhoods in New York City, there were no literary clubs; most pioneers were illiterate and spoke in a rich folk idiom, merrily using nouns as verbs, verbs as nouns, and adjectives as nouns or verbs. Isolated in their "hollers"—that is, hollows—they produced such beautiful colloquialisms as "My mind went a-rambling like wild geese in the West," "I've got them weary dismals today," and "Granny's standing on the drop-edge of Yonder and we'll soon be laying her down in her silent grave."[20]

As for Job, he lasted a half dozen years in Tennessee and then, as related by Bettie to her grandchildren, he "died two years after the big shake."[21] The big shake was the earthquake that ripped through the region in late December 1811 and early January 1812, sending the earth reeling, the aftershocks reverberating for two weeks, and rupturing the land to create Reelfoot Lake in western Tennessee. Jack's father, Calaway, was just a thirteen-year-old boy who was now forced to be a man. Jack would find himself in precisely the same situation fifty years later.

LIKE HIS FATHER, Calaway was a yeoman, a modest farmer who rode in a buck wagon pulled by mules, a far cry from the fine horse-drawn surreys paraded around Nashville by plantation owners living in Greek Revival mansions. Once he established himself, in 1822 Calaway married a seventeen-year-old Irish girl, Lucinda Cook, daughter of James Watson Cook and Mary Riddle. Lucinda proved as fertile as the land, bearing ten children—split evenly between boys and girls—over a span of twenty-seven years. About the time of the arrival of their fourth child in 1835, Calaway moved the family from Franklin to Lincoln County, where he bought land about five miles southwest of Lynchburg and seventy miles south of Nashville. Even though Lynchburg was on the main road—the pike—running between the towns of Fayetteville and Tullahoma, there was very little traffic. Nor were there railroads or navigable rivers. This land was in the middle of nowhere, which would have both its advantages and its disadvantages when the Civil War broke out.

The Revolutionary War soldiers John and Mark Whitaker first settled in the area in the early 1800s.[22] Other families and former soldiers of the patriot's army followed in 1809 and 1810, the names including Taylor, Motlow, and Crawford, among others. Not long after came the Waggoners, the Calls, the Tolleys, and the Daniels—all of these families were considered pioneers. Prior to the Daniels' arrival,

Lynchburg had been christened under somewhat grisly circumstances. Moses Crawford, who settled in the area in 1809, recalled for the editor of the *Lynchburg Falcon* "that after the war of 1812 closed, a clan of thieves was found in and about the present town of Lynchburg. And that in the neighborhood of Barnes Clark, a blacksmith three or four miles southeast of Lynchburg, stealing was as common as going to church. A member of this clan by the name of Woods, or something else, was lynched till he told of or showed the cave or warehouse of stolen goods."[23] Because there was no organized law, vigilante citizens used the same tree on the village green to administer justice to other offenders, sometimes tying them to it for a good whipping, other times hanging them, with "Judge Lynch" presiding. In a sentimental fit, Lynchburg was named in honor of the lynching tree.

More than just the lynching tree brought the community together. By the 1820s, a number of stills had sprung up, providing the men with places to congregate discreetly and shoot the breeze while they passed the jug. Another spirit bringing people together was God. One of the more prominent local churches was the Mount Moriah Primitive Baptist Church, established in 1816 and located on a stream suitable for full immersion baptisms a few miles from the Daniel farm. It was not only a place of worship but a social center for exchanging news and arranging marriages. Primitive Baptists had broken away from the main Baptist church in the 1830s, due to disagreements over embracing missionary work and other initiatives, arguing that they wanted to maintain strict traditions. The Scotch-Irish Presbyterians, including the stoic Daniel family, were naturally drawn to the rigid Primitive Baptists, who did not overindulge in exhibitions of emotion that marked revivals. More appealing, Baptists were concerned about protecting freedom of speech, as well as freedom from civil authorities. With an endearing sense of equality, Primitive Baptists decreed that their ministers required no special education—anyone could be called by God to be a minister. All of this was quite attractive to frontier settlers, which explains why the Baptist church rapidly took root in the rural South and still enjoys a strong presence.

Members, some traveling an entire day, gathered one Sunday a month to hear the elders preach with full-throated passion. "Primitive Baptists will drive the furtherest to hear the least" is a favorite aphorism for those with a cynical streak.[24] Indeed, the preaching lasted for several hours but was often quite entertaining. The sin-bustin', Bible-thumpin' preachers put on a better show than dancehall girls, the best sermons coming from vagabond Whiskey Baptists. "Ef you're elected you'll be saved," they would cry, "ef you a'n't, you'll be damned. God'll take keer of his elect. It's a sin to run Sunday-schools, or temp'rince s-cieties, or to send missionaries. You let God's business alone. What is to be will be, and you can't hender it."[25]

The Daniel family joined Mount Moriah, the church a very simple wood-frame structure with side-by-side doors, one for women, one for men, who sat on opposite sides. They listened to the chanting style used by church elders; they joined in unaccompanied hymn singing; and they participated in the traditional foot washing. Using tin pitchers and bowls, members washed their pew neighbors' feet, mimicking Christ washing the feet of his disciples during the Last Supper, as recounted in the Gospel of John, chapter 13. It is not just symbolic of a spiritual cleansing but is also a demonstration that one man is no greater than another. It ends with handshaking, embracing, and sometimes weeping. Even though the Primitive Baptists were relatively informal and democratic in their practices, to Jack the church was still too gloomy and too sober concerning how one's life should be conducted, and once of age, he would leave the church. Jack Daniel was a free spirit.

BY THE TIME JACK WAS BORN in January 1849, Lynchburg was established and prospering.[26] Downtown boasted a livery stable, a saddlery shop, a blacksmith shop, a dentist, a doctor, and several spacious residences. On the immediate outskirts of town—on the very land where Jack Daniel would one day locate his distillery—was a gristmill. Also near the future distillery was a carding factory, where wool and cotton rolls were made, to be used for spinning thread for blankets, socks, and other clothing. Two horses walking around a big, flat wheel powered the machinery.[27] Mules were the most important beasts of burden, however, and Lincoln County was considered the Mule Capital of the South. In nearby Fayetteville, on the first Monday of each month, men gathered in the square to trade or sell mules, as well as horses, hogs, sheep, turkeys, crops, and sundry merchandise. In time, Lynchburg would become a mule-trading center. Mules were far more suitable than horses for the area's steep terrain. They were more even tempered and more durable, didn't bolt at the first sign of trouble, and, unlike their equine compatriots and human owners, ate only what they needed to eat. When the sun is low in the Lynchburg sky, casting shadows, it is still possible to see the furrows, the paths left by mules cutting diagonally across the hills from the days when they were ploughed for planting corn. Also along the hillsides and through the meadows thousands of sheep and cattle grazed, as livestock was the area's greatest export.

Considered a pillar of the community, Calaway Daniel prospered, owning several slaves and a couple hundred acres of land, his personal assets valued well above those of his neighbors.[28] The family appeared blessed, with not one of their ten children dying in infancy. But then, shortly after Jack's birth, his mother, Lucinda, died.[29] The diminutive boy would grow up with the haunting stigma of wondering whether he had directly caused his mother's death. There would be little comfort from his father, who spent his waking hours working the farm. Later, their relationship was largely limited to a father teaching his son the ways of the land, of planting and harvesting, and of managing livestock. An earnest backwoods boy knew well, "When it comes to farming, I'd sink down to beggar-trash in no time if I didn't know the things I learnt from my daddy and he learnt from his daddy about farming. Suppose you plant potatoes near onions. Well, onions will put their eyes out. I've never seen a garden that throve good unless it was planted in the full of the moon. . . . Always plant peppers when you're good and mad at your wife and give your gourd seeds a hard cussing or they wont come up."[30] And on went the folk superstitions of farming.

Including Jack, there were still eight children at home when his mother died. There was also Calaway's feisty old mother, Bettie, who relished spinning yarns for her grandchildren but was suffering from dementia and was useless around the house. A desperate Calaway shipped Bettie off to his sister Anne and actively searched for a second wife to care for his brood. Although considered a kind and indulgent father, he wasted no time; on June 26, 1851, he married thirty-year-old Matilda Vanzant, who was from a relatively prosperous farming family in nearby Franklin County, his old hunting ground. Over the next six years they had three children, one boy and two girls, the boy dying in 1858. With Matilda more attentive to her own children than to her stepchildren, little Jack—or Jackie Boy, as he was called—became lost in the porch cracks. Also, by all family accounts, Matilda was not a particularly loving mother, to put it kindly.[31] Legend has it that Jack ran away from home for good when he was only six years old to escape his evil stepmother, but the truth is, he endured and was living at home in 1860, on the eve of the Civil War. He even managed to attend school for a year. Book learning was a luxury, however; in 1860, less than half the white children in Tennessee were enrolled in school.[32]

TONGUES HAD BEEN WAGGING about war for ten years, as people complained about how the North was attempting to violate the Constitution of the United States by restricting slavery or even ending it; how the North was making a mockery of states' rights; how the federal government was behaving like a dictatorial ogre. For those who read the four-page *Fayetteville Observer*—$2 for a year's subscription, if they were willing to pay upfront; otherwise, a total of $2.50—they encountered emotional editorials as early as 1851: "We led the way into this Union; we remain faithful to its Constitution and its laws; we shall never desert the Union; if you choose to rebel or secede, go, but we abide!" Editorials on southern slaves enjoying better living conditions than the northern poor were also standard fare, as were runaway Negro lists. However, the bigger concerns for farmers like the Daniels remained the market prices for cotton and flour, a new-fangled corn-shelling machine, and the size of one's manure heap—you didn't want unused manure to dry because it would burn and become waste.[33]

The Lynchburg citizens couldn't understand all the hoopla over slavery—partly because, measured by slave ownership and land ownership, Lincoln County was the third-poorest county in Middle Tennessee in 1860. Just 28 percent of family heads owned slaves, whose average value was pricey at over $800, and just 59 percent owned the land they farmed.[34] Slaves just weren't that prevalent, with one voting district in Lincoln County having none.[35] Although slaves could be bought in Fayetteville–even in 1863, with the war raging–a distant Nashville was the closest major slave-trading market. Out of sight, out of mind. In general, Tennesseans were relatively lenient toward their slaves; however, at the same time, according to the prevailing public opinion in Tennessee, abolition was simply not practical. Freed slaves wouldn't be able to sustain themselves, they weren't prepared for citizenship, they needed to be nurtured and civilized. This view on abolition was accepted by the freedom-loving Primitive Baptists, who believed slavery was morally and spiritually right. Some ministers preached that abolitionism was no different than theft.

Tennesseans did begin to take a harsher attitude toward their slaves in 1856, when there were rumors of a slave insurrection. Panic swept through large swaths of Middle Tennessee, but the rumors were indeed just "loose talk." In 1860, a rash of mysterious fires in Middle Tennessee was blamed on blacks, prompting one Middle Tennessee planter to declare that "a servile rebellion . . . is more to be feared now than [it] was in the days of the Revolution against the mother country. Then there were no religious fanatics to urge our slaves to deeds of rapine, murder, & c.–now the villainous hounds of Abolitionism will glory in gloating in the blood of the 'Slave Drivers' and turn loose upon us the very worse material in our midst." In Lincoln County, the editor of the *Fayetteville Observer* argued for a patrol system: "While we do not learn of any misgivings as to continued quiet hereabouts, yet the news that is frequently reaching us of attempted insurrectionary movements elsewhere, are a warning."[36]

In the summer of 1860, the war of words between the North and the South moved closer to becoming a bloody war. Democrats, who held their national presidential convention in Nashville, once again chastised Republicans for desiring to curtail slavery and for attacking both the rights of states and the constitutional rights of the South. The election of Republican Abraham Lincoln, who received less than 40 percent of the popular vote, was the final provocation. Two days after the November election, South Carolina called for a convention and on December 20 voted to secede. The states of Texas, Mississippi, Georgia, Florida, Louisiana, and Alabama quickly followed suit, in that order. Tennessee, as well as Arkansas, North Carolina, and Virginia, was not yet ready to take such a radical step, however; Nashville and Memphis newspapers carried editorials that supported trade with northern states and pointed out the monetary benefits. Tennessee, a border state, felt that the Deep South was leaving it on a sinking ship.[37] In February 1861, delegates from the seven secessionist states met in Montgomery, Alabama, and organized a new nation, drafting a temporary constitution and electing a provisional president, Jefferson Davis. When he was introduced to the cheering crowd, Davis declared, "The South is determined to maintain her position, and make all who oppose her smell Southern powder and feel Southern steel."[38] In that spirit, their sharpened eyes immediately turned on Fort Sumter, located on an island just off Charleston, South Carolina, and home to an enemy garrison. A delegation from South Carolina attempted to negotiate for the fort, but, unwilling to lose face, Lincoln refused to capitulate and even attempted to resupply the federal troops. The Confederates took matters into their own hands.

On April 12, 1861, the Confederates attacked Fort Sumter with a heavy bombardment, signifying that the war for southern independence was on. Two days later the garrison was forced to surrender, and the Confederate Stars and Bars was raised over the fort. The very next day Lincoln called for all states to supply troops to put down the insurrection, forcing Tennessee to choose sides. It was difficult for the people of idyllic Lynchburg to fully comprehend what their choice meant, to measure the weight of consequence. They could only imagine the carnage of a real war, as the stories of the Revolutionary War and the War of 1812 were too romanticized and distant. The only local disasters to date that had caused any amount of grief were a vicious storm that hit in February 1851, known as "the storm," which killed a number of people, and the cholera epidemic of 1854. In June of that year, cholera had raged through the area, forcing Lincoln County businesses to close. Church bells hung motionless in their cupolas, as citizens—including the preachers—fled towns, taking refuge in the fresh air on surrounding ridges. More than thirty died in the county. Fortunately, the highland ridges around Lynchburg and the surrounding villages were healthy places to live; typhoid was virtually unknown, and during the cholera epidemic, the area was largely unaffected.[39] More recently, in the summer of 1860, the people in the Lynchburg area had suffered a drought that brought a poor harvest and empty barns; therefore, in the spring of 1861, the farmers of Middle Tennessee were more concerned with rain than with war. Yet after Fort Sumter, attitudes changed quickly, and the people of the Lynchburg area were irrevocably pro-secession, wholly committed to their southern brothers.

At the outbreak of the war, public meetings were immediately organized in Lynchburg–each speaker more grandiloquent than the last–with the people voicing almost unanimous support for the Confederacy.[40] Momentum to join the fight picked up quickly. In May 1861, the nearby village of Boone Hill organized a home guard; its motto: "He who is not for us is against us"–a rallying cry still used almost 150 years later to galvanize the country and the world against *evil doers*.[41] In June, Tennessee voted to secede in a statewide referendum, the eleventh state to do so. Volunteer companies mustered and marched in training camps. In Fayetteville, boys too young to join the Confederate army formed their own companies for training purposes and paraded like peacocks. Jack's two older brothers still at home, Wiley and Lemuel, announced their determination to volunteer, even though the crops required tending. The Civil War would tear the Daniel family and its community apart; Jasper "Jack" Newton Daniel would be left with nothing.

EVERYTHING GONE
BUT THE DIRT

I like it; I always did, and that is the reason I never use it.

—General Robert E. Lee, on whiskey

The cannons roared and the gunfire crackled, coming ever closer to the Daniel farm, as the Union troops invaded Middle Tennessee in February 1862. Boys still too young to fight paraded more fervently, while impatiently waiting for their turn to join the slaughter—about 260,000 southerners would die.[1] Wiley and Lemuel Daniel continued to march as well, only back and forth across their fields, planting and harvesting the crops on their out-of-the-way farm. Their father had convinced them to remain; however, that situation would soon change, as a noose of Union forces began to fall around Lynchburg.

After the fall of Fort Sumter, much of 1861 had been a series of trials and errors, as both armies learned the art of killing their fellow countrymen, their brothers. In July 1861, the Confederates did score an early victory at Manassas, Virginia, partly aided by confusion over uniform colors. Not all Johnny Rebs had settled on gray and not all Billy Yanks on blue, and, at a pivotal moment, a Yankee artillery battery mistook an enemy regiment to be friendlies. It paid the price.

Following this disgraceful loss for the North, there was much inactivity in the Virginia theater, as Union generals counted and recounted their troops and bickered. It was a different matter in the western theater, where Brigadier-General Ulysses S. Grant was intent on raising hell along the Mississippi and the Tennessee Rivers.

While the South had yet to lose a major battle, in the winter of 1861–1862, its situation was bleak. The army lacked enough weapons to arm its soldiers; those soldiers who had enlisted for a year's duty—nearly half the force—were near the end of their commitment; the economy was in tatters, with inflation running as high as 10 to 15 percent a month; and then Union forces finally started pushing toward Richmond.[2] It appeared that the Confederacy was on the verge of collapse; however, in the ensuing months, a peculiar-looking man, dressed in an old army coat from the Mexican War and a broken-visored V.M.I. cadet cap, emerged as an unlikely hero. Once nicknamed "Old Tom Fool" because of his eccentricities, Thomas "Stonewall" Jackson displayed battlefield brilliance, using his philosophy of "always mystify, mislead, and surprise the enemy." Over a two-week period in May 1862, he marched his men 160 miles, confounding and wreaking havoc on Union troops in the Shenandoah Valley and ultimately thwarting their drive to Richmond. He brought both morale and strategic victories. Meanwhile, in the western theater, which included Middle Tennessee, a contrasting story was unfolding.

IN THE FALL OF 1862, it became apparent that the odious Federals, the damn Lincolnites, were preparing to push toward Murfreesboro, Tennessee, just fifty miles to the north of the Daniels' home. Nothing, including a father's wishes, could restrain his boys now. Wiley, age 20, and Lemuel, age 18, joined Company E of the 23rd Tennessee Battalion the day it formed in Lynchburg, on November 8, 1862, under Captain Tazewell Waller Newman.[3] It was a beautiful time of year: the sugar maple leaves had turned a glorious red, the autumnal air was crisp, and horses frolicked in the fields. Yet sadness reigned, as the Daniel men, looking smart in their gray uniforms and forage caps, marched down the pike. Their departure left Calaway, age 58, and

Matilda, age 43, short-handed. Jack's oldest brothers, Robert and James, had moved to Texas in the 1850s, a natural migration point for local would-be ranchers, due to a wagon train station not far north of Lynchburg; his sisters Louisa, Caroline, Elizabeth, and Adeline were married off, the latter having recently betrothed a Dr. William T. Baldwin, who had been boarding with the family. The only children remaining in the roost were 12-year-old Jack, his 16-year-old sister Finetta, and his stepsisters Sena, age 6, and Belle Thada, age 4.[4] It would be a physically grinding fight to keep the farm from falling into disrepair.

Other Lynchburg-area families faced similar crises as their boys left home to fight an enemy in violation of the U.S. Constitution and threatening their way of life. Back in March 1861, Felix W. Motlow, who intended to marry Finetta, volunteered and was made a corporal in Company E of Turney's 1st Tennessee Regiment.[5] Other local Johnny Rebs intent on killing Billy Yanks joined Company K of the 8th Tennessee Infantry Regiment, formed April 24, 1861, at nearby Mulberry Station. A Daniel family neighbor, Felix W. Waggoner, and Jack's friend William Riley ("Button") Waggoner would later be recruited to fill the depleted ranks of Company H of the 8th Tennessee Infantry Regiment. And still other Daniel neighbors joined up with the legendary cavalryman Nathan Bedford Forrest.

Forrest cut a dashing, romantic figure, with his high cheekbones and chiseled face, mustache and goatee, and hair swept back to expose narrow, intense eyes. Prior to the war, Forrest had been an ambitious slave trader—one of the most prominent in Memphis—importing slaves from Virginia, Georgia, South Carolina, and Kentucky. By the late 1850s, he was selling a thousand or more slaves a year, sometimes selling free blacks back into slavery, and earning about $100,000 annually.[6] Once hostilities commenced, Forrest enlisted in the cavalry as a private, but his political connections quickly secured a field command for him. He set about recruiting his own men with the simple incentive, "Come on, boys, if you want a heap of fun and to kill some Yankees."[7] An imaginative risk taker who was fearless as he charged into the enemy's ranks, Forrest embodied southern chivalry. His courage belied death. Yet even with such men rampaging through the frontlines, the Yankees were still able to push into Tennessee.

The fight for Jack's home state would have a great impact on the outcome of the war. Consider that Tennessee produced more pig iron and bar, sheet, and railroad iron—all crucial to the war machine—than any other Confederate state. More important, Chattanooga was the gateway to the Deep South. Before Atlanta could be captured, first Chattanooga had to fall. Middle Tennessee—Jack's backyard—provided the most direct route to Chattanooga and points beyond. As further evidence of the state's importance, except for in Virginia, more battles would be fought in Tennessee and six armies would eventually clash here, including two divisions of Robert E. Lee's Army of Northern Virginia, dispatched by President Jefferson Davis to assist in the defense of Tennessee. The ability of the top brass to repel the invaders was in doubt from the start, however; as the historian Steven E. Woodworth noted, "The Army of Tennessee's high command was a tangled mass of bitterness, jealousy, and hatred."[8] And the Daniel family would pay dearly for it.

THE INVASION OF TENNESSEE had been initiated on February 6, 1862, when Fort Henry, on the Tennessee River, fell to General Ulysses S. Grant, the loss threatening the Confederates' forward line along the Kentucky border. Ten days later, Grant, marching with speed and power, captured Fort Donelson, another key Tennessee defensive point near the Kentucky border—15,000 Confederate troops surrendered, a devastating blow. Nathan Bedford Forrest refused to capitulate, emphatically telling his men, "Boys, these people are talking about surrendering, and I am going out of this place before they do or bust hell wide open."[9] He and his men escaped to Nashville, which, for some insanely logical reason, had not been fortified. Forrest saved what valuable supplies and ammunition he could, then distributed or destroyed the remainder.

With word out that Donelson was in enemy hands, a Confederate officer recalled, "The whole city of Nashville was in an uncontrollable panic, people were rushing madly about with their most valuable possessions in their arms.... It was a supreme pandemonium."[10] It was a madcap exodus, with even the Tennessee governor fleeing to Mississippi. Nashville fell on February 19, 1862. The women, clearly braver than their political leaders, held their noses as the Union troops passed by. On the heels of this disaster, the entire state, except the Union stronghold in the eastern section, was horrified when the Lincolnites appointed Andrew Johnson as their military governor. Johnson, the senator from Tennessee who refused to go along with the secession, had been branded a traitor long ago. His despicable reputation would be tainted further in the coming months, as he ordered Baptist and Methodist publishing houses closed for alleged disloyalty; he jailed clergymen for pro-Confederate sermons; and he imprisoned public officials who didn't take oaths of allegiance, known as Johnson's "damnesty oath."[11]

On the war front, the federal commander William S. Rosecrans hesitated to push the attack beyond Nashville, and, while Lincoln fumed at the delay, the Confederates gathered themselves. Back on the Tennessee River, however, Grant remained an angered hornet. In April 1862, he won the Battle of Shiloh, located over a hundred miles west of Lynchburg, further tightening the screws on Middle Tennessee. It was a disconcerting loss for the Confederates, because they had won early victories during the battle but then failed to capitalize on these late in the day. Forrest, who was itching to press the attack, observed, "We'll be whipped like hell tomorrow."[12] And they were. That month Federals also occupied Huntsville, Alabama, not that far south of the Daniel home. The noose was falling around Lynchburg's neck, and tension mounted dramatically in the Daniel neighborhood.

The month after Jack's brothers joined the war, Rosecrans finally prodded his military monster forward. He engaged Braxton Bragg, the commander of the Army of Tennessee, at Murfreesboro—the Battle at Stones River—a bitter fight lasting from December 31 to January 2, 1863. Prior to the shattering cannonades, acrid smells of gunpowder, and blood running in the water, Stones River had been a tranquil setting with trees that overhung the meandering river. On the eve of the battle—the holiday season—both sides had bands playing music within listening distance of each other. To celebrate Christmas, the soldiers held foot races and wrestling matches. And then, New Year's Eve brought the real fight. Over the next three days, the 8th Infantry Regiment, which included many Lynchburg men, suffered 306 casualties of 474 engaged, a small portion of the more than 23,000 total casualties on both sides. It would be known as the Bloody Winter, the ground decorated in holiday red.[13] By all measures, the battle was a draw, but Bragg, once described as looking like "an old porcupine," elected to withdraw to Shelbyville, thus earning the moniker "Great Retreater."[14] Now the Confederate line was less than twenty miles from the Daniel farm. The family waited anxiously for any news from Wiley and Lemuel, but there was none. For Lynchburg area residents seeking news of loved ones, there was plenty of gossip and information exchanged at the Call general store, located on the pike, a natural meeting point to share any word coming from Fayetteville or Tullahoma. The proprietor, Daniel H. Call, had joined Forrest's Escort, while his wife, Mary Jane, struggled to keep the store open.

Under mounting pressure from Rosecrans, Bragg continued to fall back, making headquarters in Tullahoma, just twelve miles east of Lynchburg. Hoping that high ground would win him the day, Bragg positioned his infantry along the Highland Rim, which looked out over Jack Daniel's homeland. However, fearful of being flanked, Bragg had extended the front fifteen miles, which, with his defense stretched thin, made him vulnerable. Rosecrans took advantage of the lapse, seizing two weakly guarded passes in the Highland Rim and then marching on Tullahoma. Once again Bragg decided to retreat; on June 30, 1863, he issued orders to withdraw toward Chattanooga. An ungodly rainstorm pummeled the men's backs and heavy mud clung to their boots—a humiliating punishment.

With federal troops taking Tullahoma and Fayetteville, the latter town a mere ten miles to the southwest of the Daniel farm, the cry went up in Lynchburg to hide everything of value. Any still houses in operation were shut down; the only thing worse than a sober Yankee was a drunk one. To feed the Billy Yanks liquor was traitorous and had become a major problem in the bigger cities like Nashville, where prostitutes and liquor abounded. The *Nashville Dispatch* railed against "a whiskey shop on College Street, where the poison is dealt out to soldiers at all hours of the day and night."[15] Intoxicated soldiers were inclined to break into houses, steal whatever caught their fancy, fire off their guns, and generally wreak havoc. As far as the southerners were concerned, the draconian Yanks, who drank more than the Confederates for the simple reason that they had more money, simply

The cemetery at the Battle of Stones River, where the headstones are like an expansive crop field, is a grim reminder of the Civil War.

couldn't handle their booze. Also aware of this weakness, the federal army's high command had officially discontinued daily whiskey rations as far back as 1830, permitting only army doctors to prescribe whiskey for treating rheumatism, neuralgia, fevers, syphilis, gonorrhea, and measles, among other ailments. Despite the policy, field commanders used their discretion in doling out strong drink; some were more liberal than others, depending on their beliefs and their need to fabricate bravery.

The Confederates had trouble holding their liquor, too. When one group of officers bought their Tennessee boys a barrel of whiskey for Christmas to cheer them up, the camp erupted into chaos. As one soldier later reported, "We had many a drunken fight and knockdown before the day was closed." But then there is the charming story of the Confederate soldier who carried his jug right into battle—cradled in his arms—because "there wasn't no safe place to set it down."[16] A more temperance-minded Robert E. Lee said of whiskey, "I like it; I always did, and that is the reason I never use it." In stark contrast, Lee's opponent, Grant, was a renowned imbiber. After the

Mexican war, Grant had served at dreary frontier posts, where whiskey made life bearable, and rumors of his excessive drinking made the rounds. During the battle of Shiloh, he was accused of partaking in a jug. Apparently, Old Crow was Grant's favorite; he could toss off a big goblet without a wince. When Henry T. Blow, a representative of Congress from Missouri, complained to Lincoln about Grant's drinking habit, the president cut him short with the whimsical remark, "I wish I knew what brand of whiskey he drinks. I would send a barrel to all my other generals."[17] As for Lincoln, he told the Washington Temperance Society, "The making of liquor is regarded as an honorable livelihood. If people are injured from the use of liquor, the injury arises not from the use of a bad thing but from the abuse of a very good thing."[18] Certainly, the wily politician couldn't come any closer to endorsing a healthy snort.

No doubt, on Independence Day of 1863, Braxton Bragg could have used a belt of Old Crow when, completely unobstructed, Rosecrans's army crossed the Tennessee River, near Chattanooga, that fateful gateway to Atlanta, and Middle Tennessee was now wholly in the Federals' possession. Rosecrans wrote in his report: "Thus ended a nine day's campaign, which drove the enemy from two fortified positions and gave us possession of Middle Tennessee, conducted in one of the most extraordinary rains ever known in Tennessee at that period of the year."[19] As Union confidence soared, Confederate morale sank. One deserter from Georgia wrote, "There is no use fighting any longer no how for we are done gon up the Spout."[20] But one great battle remained—Chickamauga—the Daniel brothers' first engagement. Not yet having been brought forward to fight, Wiley and Lemuel's 23rd Tennessee Battalion was stationed in Chattanooga, from where they would be thrown into the fray at Chickamauga.

In preparation for the final push to seize Chattanooga, Rosecrans stockpiled supplies, which meant that the pillaging of Middle Tennessee was conducted in earnest. As federal troops closed in on the town, Lemuel Daniel fell gravely ill, as did thousands of other soldiers in the cramped, unsanitary quarters. On August 6, he died at the age of eighteen—having not fired on a single Yankee—a terrible blow for Calaway, who was already suffering mightily at the hands of federal foragers.[21] Less than two weeks later, the bloodiest battle in the western theater was instigated when enemy patrols clashed west of Chickamauga Creek. It was September 19, 1863. In an attempt to turn the Federals' left side, Bragg ordered vicious attacks, but minimal ground was gained. On day two of the Battle of Chickamauga, General James Longstreet, with his veterans of the Army of Northern Virginia, who had been ordered to Tennessee to strengthen Bragg's hand, punched through a gap in Rosecrans's line. Panic on the Union side ensued, as its troops were flanked. Rosecrans beat a hasty retreat to Chattanooga, where his men immediately began reforming the line. Longstreet and Forrest begged to press the fight; however, for Bragg, the horrific sight of dead men lying thick on the ground was overwhelming. When he surveyed his casualties— 20,000 killed, wounded, or missing, including 10 generals, which amounted to 30 percent of his effectives—he refused to force the fight into a third day. As information slowly filtered back to Lynchburg, the Daniel clan waited anxiously for news. The family held little hope. Wiley Daniel's company suffered 51 casualties of 145 engaged, but Wiley was one of the lucky ones who survived the carnage. He would be made a corporal, and his battalion would be consolidated with the 45th Tennessee Infantry Regiment under Colonel Anderson Searcy.

Rosecrans paid for his failure at Chickamauga with his command; Grant replaced him and that autumn drove Bragg from the field— the gateway to Atlanta was now open. The next year Union General William T. Sherman's notorious march to the sea would commence, his scorched earth policy leaving behind a wide swathe of blackened devastation. All the while attempting to turn back the barbaric Federals, Wiley's harried regiment would be tormented—enduring bravely under the weight of futility—as its men were beaten across Georgia, from Resaca to Atlanta, and then northward into the Carolinas.

LEMUEL DANIEL'S CROSSING of the river was not the only hardship endured by the family, because the pillaging of the Daniel farm intensified. When the Federals seized Fayetteville in 1862, the Lincoln County government shut down. If the patronizing soldiers in blue weren't enough, crime immediately became rampant without local law enforcement. Private citizens called meetings to denounce the "lawless persons," and they organized posses to hunt them down.[22] A more respected lawless breed consisted of guerrilla fighters wreaking havoc on the Yankee garrisons. These freedom fighters were generally small bands operating in rural areas. They cut telegraph wires, tore up railroad tracks, sniped from the woods, and ambushed the enemy. Villages like Lynchburg were particularly difficult for the Federals to control. As Union Brigadier-General James S. Negley wrote on July 30, 1862, "The country is swarming with guerrillas."[23]

One of the most notorious guerrilla episodes occurred in December 1863, when local vigilante rebels captured a group of five Yankees, including a lieutenant, foraging not far from Lynchburg. They took their now-helpless prisoners deep into the woods near Elk River, tied their hands behind their backs, and fired on them. Miraculously, the lieutenant was not hit—strongly suggesting that our vigilantes must have been drinking—and he threw himself into the river. He escaped. The other four were thrown in the river after him. Three were still alive, but one drowned, while the other two loosened their hands from the ropes and escaped. For retribution, the Union army demanded $30,000 total from the neighbors living within ten miles from where the men were captured.[24] By punishing the citizens, the federal authorities hoped to curtail the guerrilla activity. In retaliating against another heroic bushwacker, Thomas Carrick, Union troops burned his grandfather's house and killed his father. Even in isolated Lynchburg, there was enough Yankee harassment that the respectable Parks family moved from its fine main street house to a log home more than two miles into the woods to escape attention.[25]

Yankee foraging and food shortages inflicted a living death on Middle Tennesseans, as their rich farmland served as the enemy's breadbasket, with the raiding parties confiscating horses, mules, pigs, cattle, cotton bales, cornmeal, and even fencing for their fires. To alleviate suffering, the smuggling of food and medicine by both southern men and women was rampant—even coffins were packed with valuable items. Also, the Confederate command, realizing the dire need for food, granted furloughs to soldiers at planting and harvesting times. Regardless, much land, particularly in occupied areas, fell into disuse—partly because no self-respecting southerner wanted to inadvertently support the Yankee cause by sowing the fields. Compounding the dire food situation, slaves refused to work; in fact, 20,000 blacks from Tennessee alone would enlist in the Union army. Prices for coffee, sugar, salt, and other basic foodstuffs were ridiculously inflated, with salt alone skyrocketing from $2 to $60 a bag.[26] Both Tennessee's economy and its land were ripped up and ravaged.

In Murfreesboro, a Mrs. Bettie Ridley Blackmore wrote that she was "surrounded by a desperate, insolent, unscrupulous, but victorious foe."[27] *Insolent* and *unscrupulous* certainly described one unforgiving Yankee soldier, who wrote his wife, "It does us good to distroy the greesey belleys property when some of the boys get holt of any property of any kind belonging to the rebels they distroy it as fast as they can and then say dam him he was the coss of bringing us here."[28] A more compassionate Yankee cavalryman, riding through the Tennessee countryside, wrote home, "It is really sad to see this beautiful country here so ruined. There are no fences left at all. There is no corn and hay for the cattle and horses, but there are no horses left anyhow and the planters have no food for themselves."[29] Such was the scene at the Daniel farm. Even though the Daniel family members escaped the presence of a permanent federal garrison, in some respects, they, as did many in rural areas, suffered more than their urban counterparts did. Isolated on their farms and in their hollows, they were at the complete mercy of the roving Yankee foragers and bandits. At times fearful of being killed, they were forced to hole up inside their homes for weeks and face the possibility of starvation. For two years Calaway was barely able to provide sustenance for his family, let alone make any kind of profit. Their farm was stripped of everything, which included Wiley's prized horse—one of the few symbols of pride and prosperity the family had been able to hold onto.

Calaway Daniel's spirit broke in the winter of 1863–1864; pneumonia took hold, and even wearing asafetida—a foul-smelling resin derived from carrots—as suggested by a folklore remedy, didn't improve his health. Calaway Daniel became increasingly gaunt and skeletal, and, on January 21, 1864, one of the area's pioneers died.[30] For this Scotch-Irishman, whose blood burned for freedom after generations of oppression, the indignities suffered under federal occupation were too severe. He had been stripped of every vestige of property. For Jack to watch his father die a slow death was an agonizing experience—it was as though his gut had been ripped open by a Union bayonet. Of all the Daniel boys, Jack would be the only one to remain on the hallowed ground cleared by the Lynchburg area pioneers, to honor his father, to honor the past.

THE CIVIL WAR HAD DOMINATED Jack's life, his own existence made completely insignificant. As a boy he had full cheeks, accentuating his luminous baby face, and a mop of brown hair that cascaded over a high forehead. His nose was straight and his eyebrows were naturally arched, inquisitive, and playful. Once-sparkling eyes now smoldered like burning coals as the fifteen-year-old realized he was an orphan. He had his first serious decision to make: whether to stay with his brusque stepmother or wander into the wasteland. Matilda was planning to remain on the farm but immediately set her eyes on a new husband to support her and her two young children. She would marry the Lincoln County resident Wilson Hinkle and move to his farm.[31] Jack, who had no desire to remain with her, decided to take his chances in the madness around him and hotfooted it to the home of his neighbor Felix Waggoner.

Felix's father, Jacob, a German immigrant, had fought in the War of 1812 under "Old Hickory" Andrew Jackson and then settled in the Lynchburg area.[32] By 1850, Jacob was one of the largest landowners, his family's home situated near the confluence of East Mulberry and Louse Creeks. Now, Felix, who had coal-black hair and lived off hog meat—for breakfast, lunch, and dinner—was in his mid-forties and well established and was respected as a civic-minded man, so it was natural that Jack turned to him. Uncle Felix—as he was known—subsequently agreed to become Jack's legal guardian. He felt sorry for the pint-sized boy, who had but a quilt and a couple of other items valued at a grand total of $9 to his name.[33]

Jack, who scurried about performing what chores there were in this time of deprivation, was hoping he could remain indefinitely with Uncle Felix; however, the Waggoners were diligently procreating and could ill afford to feed another mouth during this time of destitution. Married for twenty years, Felix and Huldah already had four children of their own—including a six-year-old named Jasper, in honor of their favorite little neighbor—as well as two boarders working the farm.[34] Not wanting to forsake Jack, Uncle Felix knew of a family in need of a sprite young man—the Call family, which lived in the nearby village of Lois and owned the general store down on the pike. Dan Call, a sinewy, long-legged fellow with a scarecrow figure who walked with the hint of a strut, had joined Forrest's Escort, leaving his twenty-year-old wife, Mary Jane, to manage their farm and general store while raising three children—they would eventually produce an astounding eighteen offspring.[35] Although married by age sixteen and quite independent, Mary desperately needed help, especially with the general store to look after. Jack, Felix knew, would make a great chore boy and handyman to have around. The young man was small—he would reach only 5 foot 2 inches as an adult—but sturdy. He never walked anywhere; he always always seemed to be at a trot, as if running from something.

IT WAS COMMON PRACTICE for neighbors to care for orphaned children and, because her husband, Dan Call, himself had been orphaned and adopted by his aunt and uncle, Mary Jane agreed to take Jack in.[36] For the young man, it was the start of a journey very much in the tradition of Huckleberry Finn. In Mark Twain's masterpiece *The Adventures of Huckleberry Finn,* our boy-hero Huck bolts from the cozy home of Widow Douglas, who had taken him in. Although he had some affinity for her, Huck just couldn't tolerate her treating him like a lost lamb or her desire to civilize him. In Lynchburg, what remained to be seen was whether Jack would rebel against or accept his Widow Douglas—that is, Dan Call—when this very conservative and pious man returned from the war.

In addition to being a farmer, Call was a lay preacher in the evangelical Union Lutheran Church of Lois, a church more rigid than the Primitive Baptists Jack would forsake. The Union church was well known in the county—there weren't too many Lutherans kicking around—and once a year it held a "protractive meeting," which lasted a week or more.[37] Services had been held in German and English, but as fewer Germans migrated south, English came to dominate.

This development suited Dan, who was all Anglo and no Saxon and was interested in becoming a deacon. The Civil War, however, was a troubling, not so insignificant affair, that challenged his and many a Lutheran's faith.

Prior to the war, Lutherans permitted slaves to worship in the same church—albeit in their own section—at the same time as their owners, and black children were baptized just as the masters' children were. Lutherans, who on the whole owned relatively few slaves, believed it was their duty to christianize these heathens.[38] In the early 1800s, there were even some antislavery grumblings among the southern Lutherans, and in the 1820s, the church's Tennessee leadership declared slavery a great evil but failed to offer any means for eliminating it. Some Germans in Tennessee went so far as to uproot themselves and migrate north to escape this ethical dilemma.[39] By 1861 attitudes changed. Now, God and the Bible sanctioned slavery, and the southern Lutheran newspaper railed against "nasal-twanging, abolition-bred rats."[40] The Lutheran clergy viewed the war as romantic and divinely right and felt that God favored the southern states, signified by the abundant harvest in 1861 and the early Confederate victory at Manassas, Virginia, in July of that year.[41] Having preached the righteousness of the war so fervently, many clergymen left their pulpits for the battlefield.[42] Dan Call, who treated his slaves so decently that as freedmen they remained on his farm, was another who felt compelled to fight. This apparent paradox of treating slaves kindly, yet fighting for the right to own slaves, was not unusual or contradictory; after all, Dan was ultimately defending against the tyranny of the federal government that wanted to abolish the rights of individual states.

When Captain Nathan Boone of West Mulberry, a large, stalwart man who was the kind of leader soldiers would follow into the jaws of hell, had recruited men to join Nathan Bedford Forrest's Escort in the fall of 1862, Dan Call answered. So did other prominent names in the community: Dance, Eaton, Enochs, and Parks. The men supplied their own mounts and arms, with pistols and shotguns highly recommended as the most suitable for the close-quarter fighting Forrest anticipated. Call's first engagement was on December 18, 1862, at Lexington, Tennessee, followed by a New Year's Eve battle at Parker's

Crossroads, both raids into Union lines designed to delay Grant's advance. Although Forrest suffered heavy casualties at Parker's Crossroads, of all the raiders, Grant feared Forrest the most because he struck quickly and savagely.

The courage and the grit demonstrated by Forrest's men, including Dan Call, made for great stories told by the men who congregated at the Calls' general store to swap war news. One of the better yarns involved Captain Jack Eaton, of the Escort, who would eventually become one of the larger distillers in the Lynchburg area. During one particular battle, it was said, Captain Eaton shot eleven Yankees "in short order." Some folks thought they must have been like sitting ducks in a row, but not so, according to the storyteller Sergeant James Smith:

> Some were runnin' off, others were runnin' at him, and some were tryin' to hide in a ditch. The Captain had two Navy pistols loaded and he fired them with both hands.
>
> "Hey," said a bystander. "The Navy Pistol holds six bullets and two pistols had 12 bullets. Jackie must have missed one," the bystander goaded the Sergeant.
>
> "Nope, not at all," Smith answered in a hurry. "They tell me the captain had to hit one Yankee twice."[43]

Call rode through hell with Forrest, as well as through Tennessee, northern Georgia, northern Alabama, and northern Mississippi, descending on Union troops like yellowjackets, stinging them again and again, mercilessly. The one black mark on Forrest's war exploits was the Fort Pillow episode. On April 12, 1864, when the Confederates captured Fort Pillow, strategically located on the Mississippi River, Forrest and his men were accused of slaughtering the Federals, black soldiers in particular, who were trying to surrender. The evidence against Forrest was circumstantial and suspect itself, but rumors died hard.

IN DECEMBER 1864, while Jack prepared for his first Christmas without family, Confederate forces under John Bell Hood made one last valiant attempt to take back Middle Tennessee with a brazen campaign launched from Mississippi. It failed, utterly shattering morale.

The loss of life was appalling; Middle Tennessee soldiers deserted; and citizens took the allegiance oath by the thousands. It was only a matter of time before the South succumbed to the North's superior troop numbers and Grant's relentlessness.

As the war drew to a close in early 1865, Forrest set up quarters down the pike from Felix Waggoner's homestead and then, as a soldier, took one of his last meals there.[44] On April 9, 1865, Lee surrendered. The bloody maelstrom—more than 620,000 Americans died—had finally blown itself out.[45] There was one more casualty for the scroll: Lincoln was assassinated that April, thus elevating the despised and now Vice President Andrew Johnson to the presidency, another stab to Tennessee's heart. A good bit of news reached Jack Daniel, when he heard that Wiley Daniel and other survivors of Company E, who had been captured in the waning days, were paroled at Greensboro, North Carolina, on May 1, 1865. Yet southern despair and anger would linger an infernal long time, for, as one soldier noted, he arrived home to discover "everything gone but the dirt."[46] Devastation throughout the South was so complete that in Jack's neighborhood, for one, resentment against Yankees lingers almost 150 years later.

WHEN DAN CALL MADE his joyfully distressed return, he took an immediate paternal liking to Jack, who, at age sixteen, was fifteen years his junior. Dan was also pleasantly surprised to discover that Mary Jane, along with Jack and the few loyal slaves who had chosen to remain, had kept the farm in relatively good shape. Fortunately, it was tucked at the base of a hollow a couple miles south of the pike and therefore off the beaten path. In the coming years, the Call family would prosper, and Dan would transform their simple wood-frame farmhouse into a large Greek Revival home. Still, it took a great deal of sweat, as Jack and he toiled to repair fences and outbuildings while planting the crops. Together they slopped the hogs and milked the cows that had been hidden from foragers up in the dark hollow. Jack was paid a moderate sum and received room and board—in the warmer months, he preferred the barn, a sanctuary from the growing multitude of crying children that blessed the Call home.

Out there alone in the barn, the young man, having lost his parents and having witnessed the countryside ripped open by the war to reveal Satan's underworld, was disillusioned, angry, and quite capable of self-destructing or lashing out at everyone around him. He trusted no establishment, a grievous lesson from the war. Not the church—it had done little to ease suffering during the war. Not the political leaders—their miserable failures had resulted in hundreds of thousands of deaths. In fact, despite his own future success, Jack would forever eschew politics at all levels. He certainly gave little thought to the Yankees' grand Reconstruction, which was designed to aid blacks and refugees but brought more resentment and violence; besides, it offered no help to a sixteen-year-old orphan. More so than ever, the young man was determined to be self-reliant. However, matters would soon become more complicated when his father's farm was sold in 1867; the estate was tied up in court for several years, as the Daniel children fought over how to divide the spoils.[47] In this hellish landscape, the diminutive, apprehensive, and poverty-stricken Jack Daniel desperately needed a guiding hand, a mentor who would instill in him confidence and direction.

3

LEGEND OF THE BOY
DISTILLER

The making of liquor is regarded as an honorable livelihood. If people are injured from the use of liquor, the injury arises not from the use of a bad thing but from the abuse of a very good thing.

—Abraham Lincoln

The Calls labored to save Jack from becoming a heathen, with Dan Call proving to be the perfect mentor. He was obviously compassionate, considering that he was a religious man and his former slaves had chosen to remain with him. He was broad-minded, having seen a good piece of the country during the war, and was educated, one of the few in the community who could read and write. He also had an excellent grasp of business beyond merely farming, thanks to the savvy uncle who had adopted him after his father's and his mother's premature deaths. A relatively sophisticated investor, compared to his peers, Uncle D. H. Call had been a stockholder in the Nashville & Chattanooga Rail Road Company, which kept his family, including Dan, well attuned to a marketplace beyond trading mules in Fayetteville.[1] Such knowledge was imparted to Jack, who absorbed everything. And when there was time, Mary Jane taught him arithmetic, spelling, reading, and writing.

Even though Jack was bound to the soil by family tradition, he comprehended early on at the Call homestead that he was not cut out for farming. Not only was he lacking the physical stature required to become a durable, productive tiller of soil, but he suffered from occasional bouts of white swelling, a skin disease that resulted in open sores and turned the hair on those sores white. Heat and sweat made it all the more irritating. More significant, Jack desired something grander for himself than a toilsome farm life. "Anyone could work if they had to, if they had grit," his grandmother Bette had been fond of saying in describing her pioneer days.[2] Such was the case now; Jack had her grit, he was eking out a living, but he had brains and vision, too. Backwoods folklore suggested that because Jack was a tenth child, he was destined to be a preacher, but that wasn't likely. Going by his physical traits—his physiognomy—to determine character and destiny, Jack's stubby fingers were the key. A man with stubby fingers, according to folklore, "masters his way through the world and he's bull stubborn."[3] Jack was indeed stubborn, as well as imbued with raging curiosity, and something the inquisitive young man had discovered on the Call property captured his unrelenting interest: a whiskey still. As circumstances would have it, Dan Call, also of Scotch-Irish descent, was a lay preacher and a distiller of whiskey—a curious, yet understandable, blending of spirits. As young Jack mulled over the contraption, he quickly grasped that whiskey was a means to escaping poverty. He became determined to learn the noble art of distilling.

LEGEND HAS IT THAT Dan Call taught Jack Daniel the art of distilling in the late 1850s. It has been claimed that during the Civil War, Jack became renowned in the Lynchburg area as the boy distiller, smuggling his whiskey to Huntsville, Alabama, a booming marketplace. If true, Jack would have been a traitorous criminal in the eyes of the Confederacy. He was no traitor. Not this Scotch-Irish boy, with two brothers risking their lives for the southern cause, not with friends and neighbors sacrificing theirs. But let the policies and the facts ingrained in history settle the dispute.[4]

Prior to the war, alcohol had not been regulated. As a major ingredient in both southern and American society, it was plentiful; those who didn't distill their own could buy a gallon of whiskey for less than 25 cents. But during the war, attitudes changed dramatically as millers, who supplied the army with valuable flour and meal, competed with distillers for coveted grain and corn. As one Confederate soldier declared in a letter to the Georgia governor Joseph E. Brown, "I don't think they [distillers] ought to be considered true loyal citizens that will in these times of distress take corn out of the women's and children's mouths and distill it to kill their husbands and sons."[5] In Florida, Georgia, South Carolina, and Texas, either legislation was passed to strictly control distilling or the stills were shut down all together.

The Confederate War Department also stepped in. To better control the flow of alcohol among its soldiers—ultimately, a futile effort—beginning in October 1862, war officials made contracts with individual states and distillers to purchase specific quantities at fixed prices. One year later the black market price of whiskey had shot up to an astronomical $6 a gallon.[6] While Tennessee may not have passed legislation to shut down stills and the inflated price was a most-enticing situation to take advantage of, no true southerner, including Jack Daniel, would have taken corn from the mouths of soldiers, women, and children. Besides, he was too young; he didn't leave home until 1864; Dan Call was a wee bit occupied dodging bullets to be instructing on the art of distilling; and it was far too dangerous, between federal troops and bandits, to consider smuggling whiskey all the way to Huntsville. Jack's exploits as a bootlegger would come in due time, however.

AS DAN DIVULGED HIS prewar distilling activities, the notion that this was a way out of the drudgery of farming further crystallized in Jack's mind; it was a way to maximize profits from the corn harvest. Consider that a mule could carry only 4 bushels of raw grain, weighing 240 pounds, but could transport what amounted to more than 32

Jack's mentor Dan Call, seated center with his wife, Mary Jane, was enthralled by both temporal and heavenly spirits.

bushels when that grain was converted into two 8-gallon kegs of whiskey.[7] Not only did the whiskey sell for a superlative profit, but it never spoiled on the way to market, as corn might. For farmers in isolated Lynchburg, it was a very simple matter of economics: corn whiskey was the money crop.

While there was money to reap, relatively few had the right constitution for distilling on a large scale. You had to have spunk, fiery determination, and creative intuition. You even had to have a shade of the criminal, a piece of Mollie Miller or Betsy M., two notorious Tennessee moonshiners. Mollie was "a young athletic woman of great nerve and presence of mind, she was a fine rifle and revolver shot, and rode a beautiful sorrel horse." She once sent an informant who had attempted to infiltrate the local moonshiners back to the U.S. marshal in a coffin. As for Betsy, she was a generous tartar reportedly weighing in at six hundred pounds, who dispensed whiskey to any visitor, including government men—there was no point in arresting her, she couldn't be moved.[8] Jack had these ladies' infectious enthusiasm for the business; he had the fire and the charisma for becoming a great distiller.

Because many distillers had gone out of business during the war—either they were killed or hopelessly wounded or their property was destroyed—it was an auspicious time to enter this dashing industry. Distilling remained a brisk business and had been almost from the day pioneers settled the area; after all, drinking whiskey was as natural as drawing water from a well. Alfred Eaton, the father of the local Civil War hero Jack Eaton, was reputed to be one of the first to build a still in the area in about 1825, located in the very hollow Jack Daniel would make famous. Other prominent local stillers included Samuel Isaacs and John Silvertooth, who jointly erected a still on East Mulberry Creek in the 1820s; Calvin Stone, who built one on West Mulberry Creek in 1852; and the Spencer family, one-time neighbors of the Daniels, who built one on Farris Creek near Lois in the 1850s.[9] One of the more popular locations for stills was upstream from where the Call farm lay on Louse Creek, which ran through a deep hollow before cutting across the Calls' front yard.

Behind every name, there is at least one story; behind legendary Louse Creek, there are two. One version has it that a doctor was riding along the creek when he saw a mother picking lice from her child's head, and he commented that the water must be a louse breeding ground. The other version is that Louse Creek got its name during the War of 1812, when an army officer stopped alongside the creek with his troops. It was muddy after a rain, prompting the officer to say, "This is a lousy creek," which was turned into Louse. It was hardly lousy, however, with the clear stream of water fed by springs running from a hollow at a perfectly cool temperature. It was ideal for distilling. In addition to Dan Call's still, which was located a few hundred yards from the house, at times there were as many as thirteen modest stills.[10] A more apt name was the stream's nickname: Stillhouse Creek. How could Jack ignore the glorified distilling culture?

After the bullheaded sixteen-year-old pleaded his case relentlessly, Dan agreed to take him into the business. Considering that the young man was essentially penniless, Dan had little choice. There were strict rules, however, that were grounded in his Lutheran temperament. Even though God-fearing Dan didn't mind indulging in spirits more temporal in nature, Lutherans, who tended to shun circuses, theaters,

The famous Stillhouse Creek was in the hollow to the right of the Dan Call farm.

dancing, and even fancy dresses and novels, were not big drinkers. In other words, at the Call table, three whiskeys and a chaw of tobacco did not make for a decent breakfast. And there was no dancing around the still while singing the jingle:

> Mush-a-ring-a-ring-a-rah!
> Whack fol'd the dady Oh!
> Whack fol'd the dady Oh!
> Thar's whiskey in the jug![11]

In fact, Dan forbade drinking on the Call farm or at the general store. There'd be no getting pickled or blossom-nosed, no getting drunk as a boiled owl or so drunk that you opened your shirt collar to relieve the bladder. Dan abided by the belief that whiskey could be your medicine or your master and that whiskey was like fire: it could warm you on a cold winter night or it could burn you alive. It was a matter of discipline, and in Dan, a lay preacher and a Civil War veteran, Jack had the perfectly disciplined instructor. He learned to greatly respect whiskey. Coolness under fire, courage in the face of the enemy, and defending your turf were other qualities Jack would absorb from his mentor.

ON THE CALL FARM, there was another instructor who not only taught Jack everything about distilling but infused in him a love for culture. It was Dan's master distiller Nearis Green, a former slave in his mid-twenties who also worked the farm. Living with Nearis in his former slave quarters was his wife, Harriet, and two little boys, Lewis and George—seven more children were to come.[12] Echoing Uncle Remus of the Brer Rabbit tales, he went by Uncle Nearis—clearly, in the hollows no one went simply by his or her given name. And like the fictional Uncle Remus, he imparted life's lessons and wit. Jack would spend many an evening, sitting in the gathering dusk, in the company of Uncle Nearis, who taught him to live close to the land, who filled his soul with music and stories.

A mean country fiddler, Uncle Nearis played hoary tunes that sprang from backwoods life and sun-scalded fields, that erupted from oppressive slavery and economic depravity. These field songs, hollers, and chants, which were short and lyrical and reflected their daily lives, included "Turkey Bone Buzzer," "Possum Pie," "Slop the Hogs," "The Boll Weevil," "The Coon-Can Game," and "My Father Gave Me an Acre of Land." At village square dances, Uncle Nearis provided the foot-stompin' music, while Dan called out the numbers, opening with, "Salute your partner! Let her go!/Balance all and do-si-do!" Other tunes relied on calls and responses: "Oh, where you runnin' sinnah," followed by the response of "No hidin' place down here!" Well, not everyone came to the dances; some thought the fiddle to be the devil's snare.

As for the southern spirituals Uncle Nearis sang, they were powered by his religious fervor and his dream of salvation. These spirituals would win national attention during Reconstruction, with the Jubilee Singers from Nashville's Fisk University even traveling to England to sing "Swing Low, Sweet Chariot" for Queen Victoria. Such themes as conversion and being saved struck basic emotional chords, all the more powerful as Uncle Nearis moaned in the darkness:

We'll stem the storm, it won't be long,
The heav'nly port is nigh;
We'll stem the storm, it won't be long,
We'll anchor by and by.

Eventually, the spirituals and the Delta chants would evolve into the blues, heartbreaking songs of lamentation.

Uncle Nearis entertained Jack with folk stories, too. One of the favorite subjects among the boys was the Tennessee hero Davy Crockett, himself a great yarn spinner whose exploits as a bear hunter, a marksman, a lover, and a drinker were celebrated.[13] There was the classic story of Davy Crockett passing through Little Rock, on his way to meet his maker at the Alamo, when he stopped for some refreshment. In one swallow he polished off a horn of "Green Whiskey" that was so hot, he claimed, he didn't have to have his food cooked for two months: "The grub was cooked afore it got settled in my innards."[14]

WHILE JACK LEARNED TO appreciate music and storytelling, he also absorbed every shard of whiskey-distilling wisdom thrown his way, which included a rich tradition, from its evolution to distinct techniques. Although today's Tennessee whiskey enjoys its own unique U.S. government classification as Tennessee Whiskey, in Jack's time it was simply known as bourbon, sour mash, or corn liquor, among other variations. And the bourbon tradition, with a Lincoln County twist, was what he learned from Uncle Nearis. Bourbon, by definition and law, must be made from at least 51 percent corn, a marked difference from the barley used by Jack's forefathers in Ireland and Scotland, and then aged in virgin, charred white oak barrels. Making whiskey from corn—Indian maize, technically speaking—was discovered by the Episcopalian missionary Captain George Thorpe, who, in the early 1600s, was based at the Berkeley Plantation on the James River, where corn grew in prodigious amounts. He wrote a friend that he was distilling "so good a drink of Indian corn as I protest I have divers times refused to drink good strong English beer and chosen to drink that."[15] Indian scalpers, drunk on his corn liquor, killed

Captain Thorpe on March 27, 1622—Good Friday—a perfect twist of fate in the noble captain's life.

Through the 1700s, this new drink called corn whiskey wasn't aged; it was either served au naturel—that is, with a throat-burning kick otherwise known as being filled with mule heels—or it was colored with caramel so that it resembled a more sophisticated brandy, thus fooling the imbiber into thinking he was sipping a smooth refreshment. In 1798, whiskey took a vital turn for the better. That year is widely recognized as the historical marker for the creation of civilized bourbon, the year when the Reverend Elijah Craig, a Baptist preacher, allegedly stumbled across the process for making it. He had migrated from Virginia to Kentucky, where he built a gristmill at Royal Spring—not in Bourbon County, incidentally, for which this new corn whiskey would be named. After a bountiful corn harvest, Craig used excess corn mixed with some soothing rye for his mash. He then stored his whiskey in uncharred oak barrels, as was the custom. But then, according to the myth, one day Craig became distracted while heating the oak staves for a barrel and burned them. A frugal man, he used them anyway. When he later tapped that barrel, he discovered that the charred oak had given the whiskey an amber color and had drawn out impurities, making for a smooth, oak-flavored bouquet. The veracity of this story is suspect, as is any story involving liquor, especially when told by those indulging in liquor. In fact, whiskey and fish have a lot in common when it comes to storytelling.

One alternative story credits Daniel Boone's cousin Wattie with inventing this process for making bourbon. And there are a number of alternative myths concerning the discovery of using charred oak barrels. Some say it was an act of God: lightning struck a barn and charred a barrel, turning the whiskey red and improving its flavor. Others say a farmer ran out of crocks for his whiskey, so he used a barrel that had been charred in a fire. When he poured out an amber red liquid, he feared it was poison, so he offered his slave his freedom in exchange for tasting it. A more likely scenario is that the insides of the barrels were purposefully burned to clear rough edges and splinters, as well as to purify them, and more than one stiller recognized the difference between the whiskey that came from charred oak barrels and that which didn't. Word then spread like firewater. "Gentle-men exchanged private systems for reducing the shock to the palate," the whiskey raconteur Jonathan Daniels explained, "which extended all the way from the introduction of dried fruits into the liquor to advanced chemical procedures. Sometimes they succeeded. But at their worst, corn liquor and monkey rum were concoctions taken stoically, with retching and running eyes. There was certainly a democracy in drinking then. Rich and poor drank with the same gasping."[16] It was an honest manifestation of America's heralded but sometimes dubi-ous democracy.

By the 1840s, Craig's or cousin Wattie's brand of corn whiskey was made mainly in Bourbon County, Kentucky, and, recognized as a regional product, thus acquired the bourbon name. This link with French aristocracy–Bourbon County was named after the royal Bour-bon family–immediately perpetuated an arrogant attitude among the Kentucky whiskey makers. They derided other corn whiskeys as yak-yak bourbon. Of course, Uncle Nearis and Jack didn't share that sentiment.

IN ADDITION TO THE CHARRED BARRELS, another key ingredient is the water. The better the water, the smoother the whiskey. And it's claimed that there's more pure water in the Lynchburg area alone than in any other in the state in the Union, thanks to the prodigious springs that percolate through a limestone shelf. The limestone acts as a filter, removing the iron, which would otherwise make the whiskey bitter and black. "Limestone in bourbon," bourbon authorities will ex-plain, "lets you wake up the next morning feeling like a gentleman."[17] As opposed to a hung-over louse. It was also important that the water was between 56 and 60 degrees, which many of the springs bubbling up around Lynchburg were (and are), including Louse Creek, which cut through the Calls' property. The cool water both chilled his milk house and fed his condenser, while providing consistent quality.

Together Uncle Nearis and Jack would hike into the hollow, where Dan's still was nestled among the trees and thick underbrush. Like other operators, Dan owned a pot still with about an 8-gallon capacity that made whiskey a batch at a time, versus the continuous process introduced later. Made of copper, courtesy of the local blacksmith, who charged anywhere from $15 to $30 for a pot still, and set in a home-made furnace built with stone, the still was shaped like a tea kettle—a giant, Alice-in-Wonderland kettle—topped with a head from which a long, tapered neck protruded, linking it to a second crucial component, the condenser.[18] The condenser was a spiral of copper tubing, nick-named the worm—or the snake, by ill-humored, teetotaler preachers—immersed in a tub filled with circulating cold water. Next to the still were the barrels for making the mash and the still house, a shed with a mud floor, in which sundry supplies and equipment were locked.

Like an old woman enamored with baking, Uncle Nearis described the distilling process as he set about cooking a batch. These back-woodsmen didn't rely on chemical equations; here, intuition played the main role and each stiller had his own unique method. As one old timer put it, "When six men start to make moonshine, they're like six women making a cake. No two work exactly the same. Every man has his own recipes for making whiskey, just like every woman has her own recipes for cake."[19] And some of those recipes were dead secret, dating back to the old country.

The first step was to cook the mash, from which the whiskey would ultimately be distilled. Uncle Nearis hauled a sack of cornmeal from the shed, which he scalded and then mixed with water in a big kettle. As beads of sweat gathered on his forehead, he explained that the quality of the corn is crucial. It couldn't be too moist and it couldn't smell bad; in other words, it couldn't be like Jack and him. Next, this simple mixture was cooked over an even fire and stirred with wooden paddles to avoid scorching. Once it was a puddinglike texture, they poured it into the wooden barrels and added barley malt, which con-tains an enzyme that converts starch to sugar. (Uncle Nearis probably didn't talk enzymes.)

The mash was now ready for fermentation, but there was a menu choice to make: sweet or sour. Sweet mash involves adding only yeast, it being the wonderful catalyst that turns the mash to alcohol—into what would essentially be beer at this stage, technically speaking. However, sweet mash was branded with a scarlet letter, as vulgar corn whiskey that was too sweet and unsophisticated for the palate. Uncle Nearis preferred a more refined recipe: the sour mash method.

Instead of using only fresh yeast every time, sour mash uses a portion of the previously fermented mash, or spent beer, as it's called—this technique is known as yeasting back or slopping back—to which some fresh yeast is also added to jump-start the fermentation. Because the spent beer has no sugars left, it has an acidic flavor; it's sour, resulting in a more full-bodied whiskey. Just as important, the concept behind slopping back is to maintain some continuity, some greater uniform-ity in the whiskey, to keep the natural bacteria in the fermentation process under control. Rolling his eyes to heaven, Uncle Nearis would declare that the sour mash method renders the soul of the grain eternal.

The wooden barrels or tubs filled with mash were covered and left to ferment for three to five days, depending on the strength of the spent beer and the outdoor temperature. October to June were prime months, the summer too hot. As the sugar turned into alcohol, the liquid roiled and bubbled, both a frightening and a beautiful thing, which mesmerized Jack. The wafting smell of beer, accompanied by a hint of sweet roasted corn, intoxicated him. To fully understand the fermentation process, Jack tasted the liquid periodically, discovering that on day one it tasted sweet, on day two a little sour, and on day three much like flat beer. When they took the cover off the barrel, unleashing the trapped fumes, it was Uncle Nearis's duty to warn Jack, "Don't go breathin' it! It'll knock your head off."[20]

Once satisfied with the strength of their beer, they moved on to the distillation phase, which involved three basic steps: heat, vaporization, and condensation. Uncle Nearis poured the beer into the giant teapotlike chamber, which was heated to vaporize the alcohol that would then pass through the worm immersed in cold water and become condensed. From the moment the fire was lit under the teapot, matters took a dangerous turn. "In the first place," one early distiller noted in his diary, "the Distiller must be an Industrious man, a Cleanly Sober, Watchful man."[21] Watchful, indeed, because if the fire weren't monitored with strict attention, if the temperature shot up, the still would blow up, shooting deadly shrapnel like canister fired from a Union cannon. Controlling the makeshift stone furnace was an art itself, Jack learned, as the heat needed to be damn close to 173 degrees, alcohol's vaporizing point. "After a while—it don't take too long—your furnace is good and hot," a stiller explained, "you'll see a little steam look like comin' out the worm. Next thing you'll see directly a drop, maybe two or three drops. Then it'll piss just a little."[22] How sweet it was for young Jack—his round, luminous face glowing and his playful eyebrows arched with delight—to draw off the whiskey into earthenware jugs.

To achieve a pure-enough white dog—a fine breed and the name for the whiskey before it went into the casket for mellowing—Uncle Nearis and Jack put their animal through a second distillation. First time around, the alcohol content was at 55 to 60 percent; the second time, it was over 60 percent and needed to be cut with some water, the goal being 50 percent or 100 proof. An old method for testing if the alcohol content was correct involved mixing equal amounts of gunpowder and whiskey, a seemingly volatile concoction. If the powder wouldn't burn when a flame was put to it, the whiskey was too weak. If it burned brightly, it was too strong. A slow, even burn with a blue flame signified perfection; it was 100 percent perfect or proved; in other words, 100 percent proof. In another method to test the strength of this homespun whiskey, the stiller studied the bead. He'd shake the whiskey in a glass, and if the bubbles were about the size of No. 5 shot, the proof was good. If the bubbles were big and loose—known as rabbit eyes or frog eyes—then it was too weak.

For Lincoln County distillers like Dan Call and Uncle Nearis, there was one more absolutely crucial step: before the whiskey was poured into the wooden kegs, it was filtered through pulverized charcoal made from the sugar maple tree. This became known as the Lincoln County Process. Some distillers had been sweetening their whiskey with maple sugar, but at some point someone decided to experiment with sugar maple wood charcoal, both to filter out any impurities and to capture a hint of sweetness—just a hint, because the charcoal itself has no distinct flavor. According to legend, it was the Lynchburg pioneer Alfred Eaton who invented the process in the 1820s, potentially another fish story—or, to use a fancier word, apocrypha. Others say this signature technique was handed down by slaves who distilled whiskey in the hills. The most important piece of lore, for big drinkers, is that this mellowing process magically takes the hog tracks—the hangover—out of the whiskey.

As the whiskey trickled through the charcoal, Uncle Nearis and Jack poured some into charred barrels for aging and some into jugs for immediate consumption. A portion of the spent stillage was saved for the next batch, while the remainder went to the pigs and the cattle. This beer served as excellent stock feed. Old geezers hanging around the still houses always got a hoot out of watching the pigs stagger about and squeal after gluttonously inhaling the feed with a kick. And a kick was what Dan Call and Jack Daniel wanted to give their customers, too; their whiskey would become renowned for being a big bruiser, a whiskey in which delicious flavors of maple, malt, rye, and, of course, corn did battle.

JACK WAS IN LOVE. He was in love with Dan Call's still, a great companion to an orphaned young man. The taste of the burning maple on his tongue, the smoke filling his lungs and giving him substance, the sour mash tempering the sweetness, and even the sharp sting of the white dog all created an experience he immersed himself in. Jack was embarking on a noble adventure, rooted in traditions handed down by his forefathers in Ireland and Scotland. Whiskey distilling was a symbol of their fight against oppressive governments–on both sides of the Atlantic. Whiskey distilling was a means for Jack, who embodied that independent fighting spirit of his ancestors, to recapture the glorious past.

While Uncle Nearis remained in command of the still, the charismatic sixteen-year-old Jack became the quintessential salesman. In contrast to Dan, who had been content to sell the whiskey at his general store alone, his protégé was obsessively intent on expanding their market. Jack would load the jugs into a mule-drawn wagon and peddle their whiskey to stores and individuals in the surrounding villages of Lois, Lynchburg, Mulberry, and County Line, among others. Although always quick to greet customers with a friendly wave and a joke, inside Jack was burning to break out of the backwoods. As he traveled around the county, he witnessed many who had prospered before the war now struggling in comparative poverty and mired in much bitterness and apathy, to which he didn't want to fall prey. He discovered that he wanted more for himself than what this rather modest market would yield. The boy distiller, as he'd soon be known, due to his diminutive stature and youthful looks, set his sights on the big city. If Jack could peddle enough whiskey, he could buy his own farm, build a superior distillery, and live the good life.

From discussions with Dan Call, Jack comprehended that there was a great expanding market, as Americans marched westward to where money could be made in barrelfuls. Emblematic of this ballooning opportunity was the construction of America's first transcontinental railroad, which would be completed with the glorious driving home of a golden–and final–spike at Promontory, Utah, in May 1869. It was said that this railroad was "annihilating distance and almost outrunning time"–a sentiment echoed again and again over the years, as new technologies wooed the nation.[23] Even before the railroad crisscrossed the countryside, whiskey trading was big business all the way to the north and south plains of the American West, especially on the Whoop Up trail in northwest British territory, where Indians craved firewater.[24] Always the first to arrive in the frontier settlements were the missionaries and the whiskey peddlers. Even in the most remote mining towns, saloons sprung up as though planted by Johnny Appleseed. One story that always evoked a chuckle involved a St. Louis whiskey peddler who was making his way across the plains. Completely spent, the ox pulling the man's prairie schooner dropped dead, so the man unloaded his whiskey for display, right there in the middle of nowhere. He painted *Saloon* on a board and nailed it to a nearby tree, and, as a result, overnight a town sprouted around him.

But some of the whiskey being sold was hardly whiskey. The liquor sold to the Indians was cut with whatever was handy–burnt sugar, oil, paint, Jamaican ginger, red pepper, and patent medicines– all for the effect of coloring, flavor, and profit. One firewater recipe included:

> One barrel of Missouri water.
> Two gallons of raw alcohol.
> Two ounces of strychnine to make them crazy.
> Three twists of 'baccer to make them sick,
>   cause Injuns won't believe it's good
>   unless it makes them sick.

Five bars of soap to give it bead.
1/2 pound of red pepper to give it a kick.
Broil with sage brush until brown.
Strain through barrel.
Wall, that's yer Injun whiskey.[25]

The true test of firewater was to throw some on a fire, of course, and see if it flamed skyward.

"I never knowed what made an Injun so crazy when he drunk till I tried this booze . . . ," Charles Russell, a frontier artist, wrote. "With a few drinks of this trade whiskey the Missouri looked like a creek and we spur off in it with no fear." Even though this whiskey was a putrid concoction, the traders couldn't afford to be left with empty kegs or they would pay with their lives. By 1881, the situation had so deteriorated that the commissioner of Indian Affairs wrote, "The history of all our troubles with the Indians proves conclusively that if whisky and bad men had been kept away from them thousands of lives and millions of money would have been saved to the Government."[26] Whiskey and the fact that the white man wanted all their land.

NOW, WHILE JACK WASN'T PEDDLING ROTGUT, Red Dynamite, Skull-bending Lightning, Coffin Varnish, or Kickapoo Jubilee Juice, among dozens of other variations on the name for strong water, to Indians, untold dangers lurked where he intended to venture with his whiskey: Huntsville, Alabama. A good fifty-mile journey south, on the strategic Tennessee River, it was an expanding marketplace wallowing in sin—a city where men drank whiskey one-half of the time and fought the other half. When a Huntsville Baptist minister declared he would preach against liquor, a crowd attacked his church. That was 1848 and not much had changed by the latter 1860s. It was perfect.

In the years immediately after the war, according to the historian Edward Chamber Bette, the city was rife with transgressions. "After the close of the war and military discipline was relaxed," Bette wrote, "conditions became unspeakable depraved. Huntsville and her citizens suffered 'depredation, robbery, murder, arson and rapine' at the hands of marauding hordes of 'tories,' 'scalawags' and federal and Confederate 'deserters.' The county was overrun with this scum of humanity, the flotsam and jetsam of ignominy itself." There was a plethora of women of easy virtue; bloody violence committed against private citizens was a daily affair; there were carpetbaggers from the North; and Huntsville was a hotbed of anti-Yankee sentiment and racial tension, the Ku Klux Klan soon to have a strong presence. However, Bette acknowledged, the city was ideal for dealing whis-key: "For a great while the local traffic in whiskey was enormous. The streets were crowded with the drunken and debauched, and lawlessness stalked abroad unbridled."[27] So, in spite of the dangers, Jack hatched a plan to distribute whiskey among the "scum of humanity."[28]

Huntsville was indeed an ideal market for distributing goods. Ever since Alabama had been admitted to the Union in 1819, Huntsville had been a center of commerce—a big cotton-gathering center, in particular. The city was well situated in the cotton belt, flat boats and barges lined the Tennessee River, and the railroad arrived in the 1850s. There was money in the area, too, mostly thanks to the large garrison of Union soldiers. Even though Union troops had burned Huntsville and the state's general assembly had petitioned President Johnson to remove them, they remained en force to maintain some semblance of order. Away from their loved ones, the soldiers were great patrons of the local grocers and the saloons, buying vast quantities of whiskey. Jack envisioned both the Billy Yanks hoisting his jugs and steamboats ferrying his whiskey westward. To aid in this improbable adventure, Jack recruited one of his boyhood friends, William Riley Waggoner, known as Button to his kinfolks and friends. Considering that Button had volunteered to fight in the Civil War, even though he was not of age, he was the perfect companion for this foolhardy exploit.

In addition to the Sodom and Gomorrah–like conditions in Huntsville, the two young men faced a host of other looming threats: guerrilla warfare against federal soldiers continued bravely onward; federal soldiers unilaterally punished suspected troublemakers; starving marauders roamed the countryside for victims; a select number of blacks were seeking vigilante justice; and the Ku Klux Klan had been birthed in Pulaski, Tennessee. The South may have lost the war, but many were unwilling to capitulate, determined to impede and sabotage Reconstruction, which sometimes resulted in innocent casualties.

WITH THE OLD RELATIONSHIP between master and slave destroyed, the new social order was difficult to accept. The local newspapers perpetuated the upheaval and the violence rippling through the countryside. "We believe social equality a humbug and an impossibility," the *Lincoln County News* opined. "The area of usefulness which nature has fitted Sambo for, is a very limited one. As a field hand, with some white man to do the thinking for him, he is useful; as a house servant to a degree he may be serviceable; as a leading working man, a 'boss,' he is, and ever was a failure." The *Fayetteville Observer*—the most influential paper in the Lynchburg area—warned, "The negroes of this State have done all in their power to forfeit the good opinion of the white race, and, as a consequence, their day of trouble is just dawning. . . . They will have their reward." In Memphis they had already been given their reward—at least forty-six of them, anyway. The worst case of antiblack violence had erupted there on May 1–2, 1866, when minor friction between white policemen and discharged black soldiers escalated to white mobs attacking black communities. After two days of riots, 46 blacks and 2 whites lay dead; 5 black women raped; and 91 homes, 12 schools, 9 churches, and the Freedmen's Bureau office burned.[29]

In Jack's neck of the woods, the *Fayetteville Observer* did little to soothe tensions. When whites lynched a black man accused of raping a white woman, the newspaper defended their actions, determining that such retribution was necessary for the "safety of society." In nearby Shelbyville, a black church and a school were burned; in adjacent Franklin County, armed whites attacked a group of black political marchers, climaxing with a shootout; and in nearby Giles County, a Freedmen's Bureau agent made the obvious observation, "The idea of Negroes getting justice before the magistrates of this county is perfectly absurd." At the same time, a Freedmen's Bureau agent in Lincoln County noted that blacks were as well off, sometimes even better off, than poor whites.[30] There were plenty of situations where blacks had amicable relations with their former owners—as was the case at the Call farm.

And then there was the KKK.

Lynchburg was not immune to the Ku Klux Klan, which had been founded in Pulaski, Tennessee, not too far to the west. Facts surrounding the Klan's early history are sketchy, as its members shrouded themselves in mystery, but sometime in the spring of 1866 six Confederate Civil War veterans—bored with small-town life—organized what would become a sociopolitical monster. They were Captain John C. Lester, Major James R. Crowe, John B. Kennedy, Calvin Jones, Richard R. Reed, and Frank O. McCord. In its infancy, the Klan was not a violent political machine; it was modeled after a college fraternity. It was a club, with its members' amusement—hazing and practical jokes—centered on inducting new members. Masquerading was all the rage, thus the costumes, the Halloween-like masks, the high caps and faces covered with veils. As a historian observed, "On one crucial point all the early members who later had anything to say about the matter were unanimous: the Klan was designed purely for amusement, and for some time after its founding it had no ulterior motive or effect. All the evidence supports this."[31]

By the spring of 1867, this so-called club was widespread in Middle Tennessee; Lincoln County was one of five counties in Tennessee in which the Klan was particularly active.[32] Such secret orders had been around for a hundred years or more, so the Primitive Baptists in Jack's neighborhood didn't object.[33] But then the Klan went through a sudden and violent metamorphosis. Pranks and silent visits that were intended to spook the victim escalated into whippings and lynchings. A radical element within the network of Klan chapters realized that its members could influence public officials and the outcome of the elections through the threat of force and, indeed, assault and murder. Here was a chance to give the South back to loyal Confederates.

In Middle and Western Tennessee, many outrages were committed—not just by the Klan—against unionists, freedmen, and, in particular, the Freedmen's Bureau. The bureau had been created to protect blacks, disburse relief funds to both blacks and whites, and aid with Reconstruction initiatives, such as taking jurisdiction over abandoned land and issuing food, clothing, and shelter to refugees and freedmen.

Most Lynchburg-area Civil War combatants did not survive to old age, unlike John B. Kennedy, who cofounded the Ku Klux Klan.

Perhaps not so obvious to the policy makers in Washington, in the South there was popular support for just about any rebellion against federal machinations, including against the well-intended Freedmen's Bureau. Editorials in southern newspapers resounded with spite; the Jackson, Mississippi, *News* reported, "Nearly every Southern gentleman with whom we have latterly conversed, concurs in the opinion that the Freedmen's Bureau is doing incalculable harm throughout the South, and particularly in Tennessee and North Alabama, where it is under the control of a General Fisk, who seems to think that it is his chief duty to annoy and insult in every way that he can the late owners of Freedmen, whom he was appointed to assist."[34] In fact, in Tennessee, a number of subordinates of Brigadier-General Clinton B. Fisk, who was appointed the assistant commissioner in charge of handling Tennessee, Kentucky, and Northern Alabama, were charged with fraud, misappropriation of funds, malfeasance in office, neglect of official duties, and abuse of whites, as well as rape and adultery.

Quite a laundry list of constructive accomplishments. Now, who could question the paramilitary response?

To suppress the inflamed violence, by February 1867, the Tennessee governor William G. Brownlow was preparing to organize the state militia and use it wherever necessary to uphold the law. He ordered federal troops in from Louisville, Kentucky, with one squad to be stationed in volatile Pulaski, where the situation had deteriorated to a point where the Freedmen's Bureau agent, along with his wife and children, was forced to live in his office because no one would board them. To impose more control over those using the Klan for their own nefarious purposes and to head off a showdown with Brownlow, Klan chieftains called for a reorganization meeting at the lavish Maxwell House hotel in Nashville in the spring of 1867. Shortly thereafter, the Civil War hero Nathan Bedford Forrest joined the Klan and was elected as Grand Wizard, in hopes that his strong leadership would exert order and suppress violence. It had the opposite effect, as Forrest's uncensored rhetoric inspired the men as though they were making another brazen charge into enemy lines. According to a Huntsville politician, "He [Forrest] said that Brownlow was drilling his negro militia all over up there, and bad white men, and they had organized for the protection of the society in Tennessee."[35] Indeed, Brownlow now considered the Klan a "dangerous organization of ex-rebels."[36]

After the Nashville meeting, the Klan started to spread rapidly, chapters taking root in Columbia, Franklin, and Shelbyville, Tennessee. Violent behavior escalated precipitously in early 1868–the leaders lost control–due to the burning desire to influence the impending fall elections. In towns around Lynchburg, Klansmen dragged blacks and pro-Unionists from their houses and then beat, whipped, lynched, or shot them.[37] In nearby Fayetteville, the state senator William Wyatt, age sixty-five, was taken from his house, beat over the head with pistols, and left unconscious. Also in Fayetteville, the Klan broke into the sheriff's house and, in another escapade, killed two men.[38] Meanwhile, the *Fayetteville Observer* noted cheerfully that in Nebraska City, when a "nigger" crowded a Texan off the sidewalk, the Texan pulled his gun and crowded the "nigger" into "t'other world."[39] On the eve of the November 1868 elections, Klan violence reached a crescendo;

like Confederate guerrilla fighters, Klansmen moved in small groups—after dark—set pickets around their target, and attacked. Brownlow ordered federal troops to Middle Tennessee to protect the electorate, and, in February 1869, he mobilized the State Guard, declaring martial law in nine counties.

Even bucolic Lynchburg—always on the periphery—had its secrets when it came to the KKK. One respected community member in their midst who was a Klansman was the nephew of the Daniel family's doctor, S. E. H. Dance.[40] It was Maize Alexander Lafayette Enochs, who had served as a private in Forrest's Escort during the war and was studying medicine. As he trained to be a doctor under his oblivious uncle, Enochs also participated in Klan activities. But then, one morning, Dr. Dance arrived at the office to discover his nephew stashing away a long white robe. A stern lecture followed, with the doctor—who had served as a surgeon during the war but who had no sympathy for the Klan—strongly recommending that Enochs mend his ways or he would find himself out of the medical profession. Although young Enochs forsook the Klan, clearly, anyone was suspect.

Amid the violence wreaking havoc in the first years of Reconstruction, the topping cherry on this damned prune pudding was a cholera epidemic that swept through the South in 1866–1867 (peaking in August and September of 1866) and inflicted widespread suffering. Meanwhile, Jack was expecting to transport whiskey to distant Huntsville via mule-drawn wagon? He would have to ride through a veritable gauntlet. How was a physically modest young man expected to survive such an odyssey? With a quick wit and deception.

4

THE NOMAD

Whiskey has been blamed for lots it didn't do. It's a bravemaker. All men know it. If you want to know a man, get him drunk and he'll tip his hand.

—Charles Russell, cowboy artist

The madcap Huntsville trips would become the stuff of family lore, as Jack regaled his nephews and nieces with stories of the arduous journey, which he prepared for with the slyness of a Rebel smuggler.[1] The first order of business was to procure two red mules capable of making the trip and a high-bodied wagon. After padding the wagon bed with straw, he and his chum Button loaded the jugs of whiskey. Now, to hide their valuable cargo, the two young men bought cured meat from local farmers and placed the slabs across the jugs. On top, another layer of straw. While on the road—the old Winchester Road from Fayetteville—if they found any loose fence rails, they loaded those in the wagon, too. So, by all appearances, Jack and Button were just two cocksure boys on their way to market to peddle cured meat and some wood they'd come across. Although Jack's pint size and baby face—he looked more like ten years old than he did sixteen—worked to his advantage in protecting him from a criminal element that was less likely to attack a boy, he was certainly exhibiting personal mettle, the kind of courage that was in his patriot grand-

64

father's blood and in the Civil War veteran Dan Call's, because the dangers Jack faced were all too real. In addition to marauders and unscrupulous federal soldiers, there was the revenue man—or the reve-nooer, the derogatory name for government tax collectors—to contend with. Yes, Jack's diligent camouflaging of the whiskey strongly sug-gested that he was hiding it from not just landlocked pirates but also from the excise taxman, who had made an ignominious return.

In 1862, the Lincoln administration had imposed an excise tax on a number of goods to pay for the war and created the office of the Commissioner of Internal Revenue to oversee collection efforts; it was wholly dedicated to ensuring that people paid their obligation to the government. It was the public's patriotic duty to ante up. Subse-quently, the country was divided into collection districts, managed by assessors. In the field, assistant assessors inspected the targeted busi-nesses and calculated the taxes due, while the collectors attempted to actually collect. Once the Civil War concluded, the tax was lifted on most products, with the exception of tobacco and alcohol. There remained a $2 per proof gallon levied on liquor, which amounted to an astounding 1,000 percent on the manufacturing cost. This excise tax was naturally extended to the southern states, where the oppres-sive atmosphere thickened with yet another federal intrusion. Right from the get-go, southern stillers evaded the revenuers; after all, laws were meant to be broken, and due to the high tax, the black market boomed. The widespread resistance was unexpected, and, compound-ing the trouble, the tax collection system was inefficient and, in some districts, corrupt. A government consultant at the time, the economist David A. Wells recalled, "Under the strong temptation of large and almost certain gains, men rushed into schemes for defrauding the revenue with the zeal of enthusiasts for new gold fields."[2]

So, one of the great mysteries surrounding Jack Daniel—consider-ing the "strong temptation" to defraud the federal government—is whether he, along with Dan, was indeed a moonshiner in the first years after the war. More specifically, when did Jack actually first reg-ister a distillery with the government, whether it was his own or one jointly owned with Dan? Was he first in line to register in 1866 when the federal tax revenue officers came calling, as legend has it? Some would claim that the definitive answer was destroyed long ago or buried in a box deep inside a government archive. However, the answer is a resounding *no;* neither Jack nor Dan had a registered distillery in the years immediately following the war. Just consider Jack's diligent preparation for the Huntsville trips. Consider that the federal government essentially killed Jack's bother Lem and his father, Calaway. Consider that the Internal Revenue Service epitomized the broader role the authoritarian federal government took in the postwar years. The tradition of distilling–of moonshining–far outweighed any laws. And the most definitive piece of evidence: their names do not appear in meticulously kept county court records that noted legitimate business activity, including the local distillers. In the Reconstruction years, many a southern whiskey maker was sorely tempted to rebel once again, albeit as a moonshiner, and Jack counted himself among these rebels with pride and honor.[3]

Moonshiners developed the most ingenious hiding places for their operations, from caves under riverbanks to basements under their homes, the latter preferred by a renowned imbiber of both heavenly and earthly spirits, the Baptist minister Baylus Hamrick, whose story made the *New York Times*.[4] For those inhabiting the inaccessible backwoods and hollows, it was hardly necessary to conceal the stills. These wildcat distillers were not completely united against the federal government, however; there was plenty of infighting in the tradition of the Hatfield-McCoy feud. In close proximity to Lynchburg was the village of County Line, christened the "Bloody District," due to the abundance of moonshine-inspired violence. The Purdom family, which settled in this district, proudly recalled the gun battle their ancestor R. W. Purdom was involved in. Not long after the Civil War ended, he angered some fellow moonshiners, who, in the dead of the night, broke into his house and fired on his wife and him, both lying in bed. The attackers must have been pickled because they missed, allowing Purdom to seize his pistol and kill one, while wounding others.[5] The Wild West, epitomized by Tombstone, had nothing on the Tennessee backwoods. Truth be known, even metropolitan New York City and Philadelphia were rife with moonshiners and corrupt federal officers, so corrupt that a congressional investigation conducted in 1866–1867 concluded that "the frauds in those cities are so universal and gigantic; the morals of manufacturers have become so tainted; confidence in the local officers of internal revenue has become so shaken it is manifest that frauds cannot be practiced so generally and so openly without either connivance or gross inefficiency on the part of a large number of revenue officers."[6]

Although revenue laws were not strictly enforced immediately after the war—the government was more concerned with Reconstruction issues—the importance of the excise tax to the federal government could not be underestimated; it would soon contribute 50 percent of total tax revenue to the Yankee government's coffers.[7] Not until 1868 did the federal government begin to turn its attention to improving the enforcement of the whiskey excise tax. That year the tax was reduced from $2 per proof gallon to 50 cents, in hopes that the lower levy would encourage the proliferating moonshiners to go legit. (The license for making whiskey was $100 a year and for brandy $50 a year.[8]) To better monitor individual distilleries, the federal government created the positions of gauger and storekeeper. Operating at the distillery site, the gauger tested and recorded the alcohol content of every barrel, while the storekeeper recorded other aspects of the operation, such as how many bushels of corn were used per gallon of whiskey. Also, to prevent internal fraud and improve overall management, Congress created another layer within the revenue department: supervisors, who were watchdogs over several tax districts. Despite the heavy-handed federal involvement, President Johnson's administration remained mired in accusations of incompetence and corruption.

UNDETERRED BY GOVERNMENT machinations and threats, every couple of weeks or so, Jack, with or sometimes without Button, made the Huntsville journey. These escapades continued right through winter, when it became necessary to break the ice forming on streams they had to ford. In the bitter cold, Jack would crack the ice so that the mules could wade safely through the water without the wagon teetering. This young man, living the nomadic life, was as tough as a hardened soldier. Once on the outskirts of Huntsville, Jack would wait to enter the city until after midnight—after the sheriff's men, who would either be looking for a bribe or to throw him in jail, had gone off duty. He sold to steamboat captains stocking their ships and to saloons, eating establishments, grocery stores, and the federal soldiers, who had rolls of greenbacks. Only after all the jugs were gone, did he peddle the meat to butchers. Jack proved himself a natural-born salesman. Who could resist his boyish face and impish charm? He even captivated a landlady at a Huntsville boarding house, who adopted him as her own and provided him with a safe haven. Not yet twenty years old, Jack's sense of drive, resolve, and courage was evident. Jack embodied a favorite local aphorism of the era: "If you don't take care of your future, nobody else will do it for you."

Jack desperately wanted a grand future, but perilous trips to Huntsville and cavorting with scalawags weren't destined to be part of it. The prodigious money he imagined making didn't materialize. He needed a larger operation with a more efficient means of distribution. But that meant going legit—not a bad move, considering that the Internal Revenue Service had reduced the excise tax to 50 cents a gallon in 1868, thus depressing the black market. Also, following the abhorred Ulysses S. Grant's election to the presidency that year, the government was more avidly persecuting small illicit distillers. Rather than register their still and expand operations, Dan Call preferred to call it quits for the moment. So, it was time for Jack the nomad to leave the shelter of his mentor's home to search for new opportunities. Also of weighty, if not audible, consideration, in 1868 Dan Call had five children under his roof, ranging from one to eight years old, with another babe on the way, creating familial chaos that Jack, almost twenty years old, was quite ready to escape.[9] His next move would bring the boy distiller into close contact with two other strong-willed Civil War veterans who would further strengthen his character.

A DISTILLER LIVING IN LYNCHBURG proper appeared to offer Jack greater opportunities and thus more money: Colonel John Mason Hughes, a Civil War hero and a respected Lynchburg businessman. He was shipping his whiskey to nearby Tullahoma, which, as the 1860s came to an end, offered a far more convenient point for distribution, with its expanding railroad depot and burgeoning trade. Hughes, who was self-possessed and exuded coolness, was a stout but athletic man. He was bigger than life; like Bedford Forrest, he had courted peril during the war; and he was said to have been a man who shot from the saddle, killing more than 250 Yankees.[10]

At the seasoned age of twenty-nine, Hughes had enlisted in the 25th Infantry Regiment, Company D, at Livingston, Tennessee, on August 1, 1861, and was elected as captain the next year, then as colonel in 1863.[11] Like the ranks of all southern regiments, its ranks were decimated, including a 36 percent casualty rate of the 336 men engaged at Murfreesboro, where Hughes was severely wounded. Refusing to retire, the obstinate colonel fought at Chickamauga, where his regiment witnessed a 39 percent casualty rate of the 145 engaged. Yet they distinguished themselves, capturing valuable Yankee ordnance and sweeping their enemy from the field. Toward the end of the war, Hughes found himself in the Petersburg trenches, which, for a time, valiantly prevented the Union army from taking Richmond, and, finally, he was at the Appomattox Courthouse, where Lee surrendered.

When Hughes returned to Tennessee, he discovered his plantation in ruins—it seemed that everything needed reconstructing—so he, along with his wife, Sarah, and five children, moved to Lynchburg, intent on rebuilding his life.[12] Like many other returning war heroes, Hughes knew that one of the quickest means to regain fortune was through whiskey. So, while he operated a saddlery shop on the second floor of his residence, he aggressively pushed his way into the local distillery scene. To ingratiate himself in the community, he quickly befriended Jack Eaton, a fellow Civil War hero and a son of the renowned distiller Alfred Eaton. In April 1869, the two veterans leased property belonging to Mary "Grandma" Green of Lynchburg proper "for the purposes of Distilling." Hughes also partnered with Ben Tolley; in March 1869, they leased property jointly owned by Dan Call and his older brother William that included a deliciously cool spring, perfect for distilling purposes.[13] It was through Dan that Jack became acquainted with Hughes and, wanting to join this elite group of distillers, decided to go work for him.[14]

JOINING HUGHES IN LYNCHBURG to distribute whiskey via Tullahoma raised a quandary for Jack: he still didn't have a penny to his name and needed a place to live in the village. He wasn't going to find a home with Hughes, however, who already had a gaggle of kin under his roof. Fortunately, Jack's sister Finnetta–called Nettie by friends and family–offered to board him at her Lynchburg home. Nettie had recently married Felix Motlow, yet another Civil War veteran whose family had deep American roots. The Motlow family could trace its genealogy back to 1666, the year the family's ancestor John Motley emigrated from England to settle in Virginia.[15] One of his descendents, also a John Motley, and his wife, Tabitha, moved to North Carolina in the late 1750s and then to South Carolina in the mid-1760s. There, a band of Indians massacred the entire family, except for one daughter, Susanna, and one son, John, whose young bride lay among the victims. For undisclosed reasons, John, who fought for the 5th South Carolina Regiment in the Revolutionary War, changed his surname to Motlow. He also remarried and was, in time, Felix's grandfather. After John died in 1812, his wife, Agnes, and their children migrated north and were among the first settlers in the Lynchburg area.

Like his grandfather, Felix was a fighter. Once the Civil War erupted, he enlisted in Company E, 1st Tennessee Confederate Infantry, in April 1861, and the next month his company departed for Virginia. Company E was an integral part of General Robert E. Lee's vanguard when he made the bold strike into Pennsylvania. Then, on the first day of the Battle of Gettysburg, July 1, 1863, Felix's company was ambushed–all were forced to flee, were killed, or were captured, the latter being Felix Motlow's fate. He remained imprisoned until hostilities ceased but returned a hero.

Felix's honeymoon with Nettie had hardly ended when twenty-year-old Jack arrived to board with them at their 140-acre spread on the outskirts of Lynchburg. Along with Frank Taylor and Murry Baxter, two farmhands also boarding, he received a modest wage for helping around the farm, as time would permit.[16] Jack was, after all, dedicated to becoming a master distiller and making sales trips to Tullahoma, among other area towns and villages. Also joining the Motlow household–in 1869–was Felix and Nettie's first child, Lemuel. Lem would have a major influence on Jack Daniel's legacy and would become a renowned distiller in his own right.

* * *

PEACE DID NOT REIGN in the Daniel family while Jack boarded with his accommodating sister. Calaway's farm and accompanying land had been sold for $7,537.80 in 1867, the proceeds to be divided among his surviving heirs; however, a dispute immediately arose as to how to do so fairly. The quarreling became ever more acrimonious, and, in 1869, the family went to court, where the battle would be fought over the next few years.[17] It pitted the younger Daniel children against the older, with Wiley Daniel leading the charge for the younger set. After the war, he had married Susan Elizabeth Waggoner, a daughter of Felix and Huldah Waggoner, and then settled in Mulberry, not quite ten miles southwest of Lynchburg.[18] Igniting his own civil war, he filed suit against the older siblings, including Louisa Daniel, the eldest, and her husband, Samuel, who was executor of the estate. The issue was this: Wiley didn't want the farm sale proceeds divided equally among all of them because the older children had, prior to their father's death, already received money, heirlooms, and household items, amounting to hundreds of dollars–the eldest son, James, had been given $500 and Louisa a slave and a filly–and they stood to benefit most if an even distribution took place. Wiley argued that the previous gifts should be included in the pot, and therefore, those who received little in the way of prior material gain would now receive more from the farm sale.[19] For Jack, who languished with nothing to his name, the outcome was crucial. He stood to win as much as $1,000–an enormous windfall for a young man in Lynchburg.

EVEN A FEW HUNDRED DOLLARS was a good deal of money–enough to buy a modest piece of property, enough to support a family for over a year, and enough for a desperate man to kill for. These were tough times–every penny counted–as the people in the Lynchburg area continued to struggle to rebuild their devastated farms. Even in 1870 there were 15 percent less horses, 18 percent less mules, 22 percent less swine, and 37 percent less oxen than prior to the war. Corn output–the all-important staple–was down 21 percent.[20] To inspire the farming class of Tennessee, J. B. Killebrew, who served as the state's commissioner of agriculture, spoke before Farmers' Clubs and civic groups, exhorting, "It [farming] calls forth the most varied qualities of mind and body: patience and care, diligence and zeal; energy, industry and economy; tact to manage and skill to direct; fertility of resource; comprehensiveness of plan, with a knowledge of detail; looking forward through years, yet attentive to the business of to-day. Every latent faculty of the intellect, every dormant power of the muscle, every noble feeling of the heart is called into requisition by a successful farmer."[21] He certainly romanticized what was a grimy, wearisome, backbreaking life.

When Killebrew passed through Lincoln County in 1871 on his pants bottom–kicking tour, the natural splendors were not lost on him: "The beauty of the landscape, the delightful alternation of hill and vale, and swelling mountains clothed in perennial verdure, and pellucid streams gliding like threads of silver down the valleys, and vine-clad cottages surrounded with groves of cedar, and oak, and mulberry, and sugar tree, present to the traveler a scene which for beauty, and freshness, and variety is unsurpassed in the State." However, one of the problems the Lynchburg area faced was access to government services that would aid economic recovery. Because the county seat of Fayetteville–with its overpopulation of twenty-six lawyers versus just five blacksmith shops–was a relatively long distance by horseback, in 1871 it was decided to create a new county, Moore County, by carving out fringe portions of Lincoln, Franklin, Coffee, and Bedford Counties. It was named after General William Moore, an early settler of the region and a War of 1812 hero. For their county seat, the people selected Lynchburg, which would subsequently experience an economic boom–a boom relative to rural village standards. In a few short years there would be eight mercantile stores and two saloons, among other shops, around the graveled square. And a county courthouse found temporary quarters in Tolley & Eaton's Hall, owned by the two notable distillers, which was where the Daniel family case would now be settled.

The Daniel case dragged on, as the court assigned values to each item given to each child; meanwhile, from 1870 to 1874, Jack still had no property to his name.[22] Finally, the court finished its tally of all items and cash previously bequeathed, as well as the $7,537.80 from

Jack's signature outfit
included a wide-brimmed
plantation hat.

the sale of the farm, which totaled over $11,000. A settlement be-
tween all parties was reached in the summer of 1874.[23] Jack's take
was a bounty of $1,000, which, along with what he'd been able to
scrape together in savings, was enough to buy a modest farm and
launch his own distillery business. As a reporter for the *Lynchburg Falcon* recalled of Jack's early career, "When he had almost reached his
majority [age 21] he began to trade and after he had acquired some
means of his own, he went into business for himself."[24] At age twenty-
five he had that means.

So finally, after years of farm drudgery and peddling whiskey for
someone else, Jack could break away from Colonel John Mason
Hughes. The strong-willed colonel, after all, was not the kind of man
who would ever defer to Jack or give him a bigger piece of the business. On the other hand, Jack had learned from this man of action
how to start a respectable distillery from scratch and manage the

business aspects, from procuring large quantities of supplies to dealing with the revenue men to making contacts in Tullahoma, where Jack would eventually haul most of his whiskey. In a display of loyalty and as repayment to Colonel Hughes, a decade later Jack would hire the colonel's son Bill.

There was another impetus for change: a hailstorm ravaged Moore County in March 1875, ripping through Colonel Hughes's property and severely damaging his still and warehouse. The colonel reportedly lost 500 barrels of whiskey.[25] While God's creatures roaming his property may have enjoyed a good sousing, it was an awful tragedy. For Jack, there was not time to dally, as his competitors were wounded. Also, it had been a ten-year, step-by-step learning process, beginning with Uncle Nearis's soulful incantations on distilling to peddling for the colonel, so Jack was more than raring to go. Flush with cash and being a self-possessed young man, Jack left town on a surreptitious foray to whereabouts unknown; the result of this mission was to ultimately define his image. He returned decked out in a formal knee-length frock coat, a fawn-colored vest lined with silk, a broad tie, and a wide-brimmed planter's hat. As his signature daily uniform for the remainder of his life, it came to symbolize his identity—a classy southern gentleman. A country squire. And a man driven to attain wealth.

Like a Napoleon come of age, Jack surveyed the battlefield and considered his next move. A master distiller and well seasoned in all phases of running a whiskey business, he was absolutely determined to establish his own distillery. However, Jack couldn't have picked a more ominous time to thrust himself into his own business, especially the whiskey business.

5

REUNION AND CHALLENGE

⊱·⊰

As a cure for worrying, work is better than whiskey.

—Ralph Waldo Emerson

At age twenty-five, Jack was as vigilant as a fox, his survival instincts honed. His almond-shaped eyes were bright and inquisitive; he sported a full mustache that cascaded over his upper lip, flowing into a goatee; and his dark brown hair, thinning across his scalp, was neatly trimmed over the ear, lending him a professional look. Now at his fully matured height of 5 foot, 2 inches, Jack had anything but a Napoleonic complex. He was no bully. To the contrary, he comprehended that he needed an ally, a partner who would lend immediate credibility to his distilling business. Where did Jack turn? To his old mentor Dan Call, whom he persuaded to partner with him. It was a calculated move: Dan had the fields of corn, had the perfect water percolating into magical Louse Creek, and commanded the respect of fellow veterans and distillers, many of whom were at least ten years Jack's senior—they were of the forty-year-old Dan Call's generation. For the moment, although Jack was certainly accepted into the community, he was not yet part of their inner circle.

This time around, the two partners wouldn't be operating a modest 8-gallon pot still hidden in a hollow. No, this time it would be an operation employing a half-dozen men, including Uncle Nearis and his older boys, with a capacity of consuming 39 bushels of grain daily, or what would amount to making almost 100 gallons of whiskey. Assuming they distilled about nine months out of the year, their potential annual sales revenue would be a healthy $50,000 or so after federal taxes—yielding a sizable income for the day. Their markets were no longer village general stores but large grocers in a growing sphere that included Fayetteville, Huntsville, Winchester, Tullahoma, and Shelbyville, with their sights set on coveted Nashville. They named their company simply Daniel & Call, the partnership effective November 27, 1875—a date to be celebrated, for it officially marks a great whiskey legend's entry into the business as the owner of a distillery.[1]

Jack the nomad also settled down; he purchased a 140-acre farm from Mr. Polk Ellis, conveniently located on the pike between the town and the distilling operation on Call's farm. Not wedged in a hollow or perched on a rim, his verdant land undulated gently and offered two streams for watering his crops and livestock. East Mulberry skirted the farm for about three-fourths of a mile, while the Cam Floyd branch ran through it, making 5 acres fairly soggy and another 15 acres bottomland that was subject to flooding. But some 85 acres had rich, tillable soil. As for buildings, on one side of the pike there was a two-story frame house with ten rooms and porches in front and back, and the all-important outhouse, while on the other side of the road were the barns and other outbuildings. About three hundred yards from the main house was a small tenant house.[2]

After all the years of fighting the wolf of poverty, Jack could now begin to think of himself as a self-made man. Yet in the immediately ensuing years, he would have to contend with several looming obstacles that arose to cast dark shadows: he would have to steal market share from the older, more established firms; he would have to survive a national depression; he would have to fend off fire-breathing preachers and puckered-up, temperance-crazed women; and he would have to wrangle with both zealously patriotic and sinfully corrupt government men.

DESPITE THE IMPENDING CHALLENGES, it appeared that Jack's luck was changing for the better: he had won a sizable settlement from his father's estate, and Daniel & Call hadn't become operational until after the vicious hailstorm (a warning sign from God, as far as the prohibitionists were concerned). Incidentally, Colonel Hughes did survive the storm, as did the other distillers; in fact, Daniel & Call would find themselves up against more than a dozen legitimate players in Moore County alone. When the farming evangelist Mr. J. B. Killebrew had toured the county in 1873, he discovered twelve registered distilleries, with a total of seventy-two hands employed, averaging thirty barrels per day, eight months of the year. Large quantities of "Lincoln County" whiskey were being made, in his estimation, with the whiskey business paying 20 percent on the capital employed, a decent return.[3] The two top firms were Hiles & Berry and Tolley & Eaton, with both buying prominent display ads in the *Lynchburg Sentinel* to advertise their sour mash, log-distilled whiskey. With magazines just now becoming popular in the United States, advertising had yet to catch fire—it would be some time before marketers learned how best to entrap consumers with bodacious ladies. With time, Jack's natural genius for marketing would blossom. And as competition heated up, with the introduction of new technology for distilling and with better access to distant markets, he would position himself to seize the mantle of leadership.

The most aggressive of the bunch, Tolley & Eaton, continued to expand, recently building a mammoth shelter for the hogs being slopped at their distillery. While the livestock side of the business certainly bolstered profits, it was no highly efficient Chicago slaughterhouse, where thousands of animals passed through for a dressing and they used everything but the pig's squeal.[4] In fact, the average whiskey plant in the early 1870s remained a relatively crude affair, resembling a sawmill plunked down in the forest: There were open sheds with tools, boilers, and condensers; simply constructed barnlike warehouses, using ramps and pulley systems to move the barrels; and absolutely no frills—if there was an office, it was a shack. But by the close of the decade, technology leaped forward with the introduction of the semicontinuous process: the old pot still gave way to a three-chamber charge; and the batch process gave way to mass production methods, with the mash pumped into large wooden cisterns for fermenting and the beer flowing directly into the still. There was less grunt work and more instrument-controlled machinery measuring temperature and alcohol content to refine the process. Column-shaped stills reaching the height of four stories now towered over the old sheds. There were victims of this progress, as the small distillers struggled, some forced to shut down. In a respectful requiem, the *Lynchburg Sentinel* observed that many small hillside still houses in the area had passed away but pointed out with pride that Lynchburg was quite a whiskey-manufacturing place.[5]

With these advanced processes, however, came physical dangers. The monstrous boilers now used were prone to unleash massive explosions, if not carefully managed. In June 1875, a large tank at Tolley & Eaton exploded, blowing a hole through the roof, spewing hot beer, and sending huge pieces of wood flying. Luckily, no one was hurt by the scalding liquid and flying shrapnel.[6] In March of 1876–even with snow blanketing the ground from an eight-inch storm earlier in the week–the malt house at Tolley & Eaton's caught fire. "Wednesday night about 11:00," the *Sentinel* recorded, "the peaceful slumbers of our citizens were disturbed by the cry of 'fire.'"[7] In February 1877, it was Hiles & Berry's turn–they had a fire at their malt house, not the first.[8] To his credit, Jack ran a disciplined operation and stayed out of the newspaper. However, there were other, greater challenges than competition, explosions, and infernos.

THE DISTILLING BUSINESS ALWAYS ran in cycles, dependent on weather and corn crops. Consider that as of November 1875, the month Jack and Dan formed their partnership, the Moore County distilleries had been idle for months, due to hot weather and then the lack of corn; in December, they resumed production and were running full in April 1876, only to suspend operations for a few months beginning in July.[9] This cyclical madness was compounded to the nth degree when, in September 1873, a financial panic rocked the country and the subsequent depression sucked money from people's pockets, turning morally good Moore County citizens into criminals. It was precipitated by the collapse of one of the most prominent U.S. banking houses, Philadelphia-based Jay Cooke and Co., which had been attempting to keep the financially strapped Northern Pacific Railroad afloat. Like many railroads during the postwar boom, the company was afflicted by greed and overexpansion. Jay Cooke didn't succeed, obviously. On the heels of the Cooke disaster, the public panicked, fifty-seven other investment banks failed, the stock market crashed, and the New York Stock Exchange, for the first time ever, closed its doors on September 20, 1873. The thieving Wall Street Yankees even impacted little, out-of-the-way Lynchburg—another reason to despise the North.

Ever since becoming the county seat in 1872, Lynchburg had boomed. In a fit of cocky self-importance, the town petitioned the federal government "for a daily mail to this place. We hope it will meet with success, as better mail facilities is one of our greatest needs." The postmaster general respectfully declined the request.[10] In spite of the postmaster's denial, Lynchburg was the county's economic focal point. It soon became a mule-trading center, a lively affair that offered the men a chance to congregate on the corner of Main and Mechanic Streets. Here was Jack's domain, where salty characters haggled and swapped colorful jokes. It was no literary club like the one that met at the residence of Walten Hiles, a venerable distiller and a community father. Always desiring to better the town, he funded the construction of a brick sidewalk that ran the entire length of a newly built street in 1877, which was declared a "luxury, never before known in Lynchburg."[11] Certainly true, considering there would be no electric streetlights in Lynchburg for another seventy years. Meanwhile, J. Pierpont Morgan would have his Madison Avenue mansion wired by Thomas Edison in 1883.

Other prominent Lynchburg characters lending the town a genial, innocent atmosphere that rightfully should have been immune to the northern capitalists included the photographer Mr. Croley, who, according to the village resident and diarist Mary Motlow, "takes splendid pictures and would be pleased to have you give him a call if you are not ugly enough to break his apparatus." The wry diarist was also taken with Dr. S. E. H. Dance, the noted physician, even though "the Doctors have quit carrying their lancets about with them with which to bleed people, but bleed them altogether with their bills." And there was Mr. Shiver, owner of a livery stable. "He is always ready for a laugh or joke on anyone. He is the life of Lynchburg. This winter while he was south for his health, Lynchburg had the blues the whole time. Almost everyone had forgotten how to laugh when he came back." The village's two hotels, the Grand Central and the Metropolitan, impressed Mary, as "this massive pile of buildings may be seen rearing towards the sky."[12] *All three stories.* The very names—Grand Central and Metropolitan—suggested a small town with big city aspirations, despite the lack of regular mail service. Mary Motlow, in her brief memoirs, made no mention of Jack—or of any other distiller, for that matter. Not a surprise, considering her view of saloons: "I guess I had better say nothing of the drinking saloons of the town, of which we feel thankful these are but few in number." Even though whiskey was an acknowledged economic force, there was forever an underlying tension between the liquor men and the more devout Baptists.

As for entertainment in Lynchburg—typical small-town America—variety shows occasionally passed through, including The Great International Menagerie, Museum, Aquarium and Circus, with its two thousand curiosities, equestrians, acrobats, clowns, a petrified man, a woman with jaws of iron, and five hundred animals—all under three big tents.[13] It was the age of P. T. Barnum, who was either a brilliant entertainer or a humbug, depending on your point of view. At the time, New York City boasted P. T. Barnum's fantasmic museum of human curiosities, which featured a bearded lady, a mummified mermaid, shrunken heads, and midgets, among many other grotesque prostitutions of people and animals alike. Back in more modest Tennessee, the social scene included picnics in nearby Mulberry, at which the men played baseball and the good dames served a fine spread.[14] There were grand holiday balls held at Tolley & Eaton's Hall, with a flue band "so those of our young folks who delight in tripping the light fantastic should be certain to be on hand."[15] There were good ol' barn dances. Even with all the socializing, the *Sentinel* complained more than once that there were too many bachelors in Moore County. It was a safe bet that many a bachelor (and a married man) was nipping whiskey at the dances and the picnics to temper his needs.

* * *

BUT THEN THE 1873 PANIC HIT and rattled the citizens of Lynchburg. Money tightened, as an extended depression took hold. Times were still so hard in 1877 that in Lynchburg, the price of eggs plummeted from 20 cents a dozen to 8 cents.[16] The *Sentinel* newspaper was willing to take milk, eggs, butter, or other items for payment. Bartering became a way of life for the local merchants, as there remained a feeling of communal welfare–farmers aiding farmers–brought to the area by the pioneers. This spirit was in complete contrast to circumstances in eastern Tennessee, where the state's first extensive coalfields were being developed.

In 1876, the hardly paternal Knoxville Iron Company cut wages from a whole nickel per mined bushel of ore to a mere $2^1/_2$ cents, prompting the workers to call a strike. The company brought in convicts leased from the state as strikebreakers, initiating an ongoing battle that would last until World War II and would inspire such blues ballads as "Coal Creek Troubles." In big cities like New York, the effects of the depression were even more marked. One indicator was the plummeting price of property: lots near Fifth Avenue dropped from $100,000 to a mere $40,000–pity the poor developer. Meanwhile, $1,000 was more than enough to buy a hundred-acre farm in Moore County. Within a year of the panic, New York experienced 25 percent unemployment; bread lines wrapped around city blocks; the working class protested against the controlling moneyocracy; and, during a rally for the poor held in Tompkins Square, the mounted police beat seven thousand demonstrators into submission (the cops did manage to avoid a single fatality). While the Tompkins Square riot was negligible in terms of violence–consider that during the 1877 Pennsylvania Railroad strike, some forty men were killed–it served to widen the class divide and harden differences. To fend off beggars, the *New York Times* even advised its readers to "procure a large dog who understands how to insert his teeth where it will do the most good."[17] No such practical advice was found in the *Lynchburg Sentinel*.

It took a few years for the depression to take its toll on the Lynchburg area, but eventually, crime, still extremely modest by big-city standards, ran the gamut, as once-good citizens struggled to make ends meet. By 1876, stealing was infectious, a weekly affair, as orchard owners and vegetable farmers found themselves victimized on a regular basis. Snatching chickens was another favorite. In one exemplary act of desperation, robbers bored into the rear window of Evans and Roughton's saloon, removed the shutter fastenings, and proceeded to relieve the money drawer of it contents. Convictions for larceny, horse thieving, and assault increased dramatically. In 1875, thirty-seven men were prosecuted for packing pistols—evidence of their need to feel safe. A good night watchman was desperately needed, the newspaper wailed—to no avail. How debased did some people become? Consider that on May 15, 1875, the *Sentinel* ran four classified ads for curing opium addiction—hard drugs had made it to rural areas long before anyone suspected.[18]

Tension between whites and blacks also increased dramatically, as such economic downturns tended to exacerbate a host of social problems. Relatively minor crimes were exaggerated to a point of portending revolution, a rebellion by the blacks, who were still referred to as "former slave so and so." The local newspaper played up the case of four black men, including "Turkey Ben" Evans and Ned Waggonner, who would later go to work for Jack Daniel and who broke into Stanley Evans's smokehouse by loosening a large rock from the foundation and crawling in, then taking six choice pieces of meat.[19] On March 2, 1877, the *Lynchburg Sentinel* reported that three Negroes beat and robbed the favored citizen David Waggoner. The message between the lines was clear: blacks could not be trusted.

Intensifying the black-white tension in the South was the clarion call for the end of Reconstruction that emerged in the North. A prominent New York City lawyer and diarist, George Templeton Strong, reflected a view gaining in popularity when he wrote that southern governments were "nests of corrupt carpetbaggers upheld by a brute nigger constituency." Major northern newspapers and magazines began to depict Reconstruction as "a monstrous inversion of the natural order" that unfairly protected blacks at good white people's expense. Many Republicans, who had once supported Reconstruction, agreed. When Republican president Rutherford B. Hayes took office in March 1877, he swiftly abandoned Reconstruction and pulled the remaining federal troops out of the South.[20] Such sociopolitical uncertainties served to compound the dire economic situation.

IN ITS FIRST YEARS OF BUSINESS, the partnership of Daniel & Call faced a tough market. With money tight, securing a loan to buy a sufficient amount of the year's corn crop for making 100 gallons of whiskey daily or to build a more efficient still was near impossible, especially since Lynchburg didn't even have its own bank. Here in the backwoods, money was kept under mattresses, with the more wealthy citizens acting as lending institutions. Also, the drinking public had less money to squander on liquor; consequently, in the 1870s, the consumption of distilled spirits fell by over 20 percent nationwide.[21] Squeezed from multiple directions, Jack and Dan had to rely on their own resources and prudence.

The depression, which would persist into the late 1870s, was capped off in Lynchburg rather fittingly by a vicious storm that ripped through the area in April 1878. Rain and high winds blew down trees and ripped roofs off houses or flattened them entirely. Many people fell ill afterward, which was blamed on the fallen timber.[22] A more poignant storm that Jack Daniel faced—a gathering hurricane that would render Mother Nature's April storm meaningless—was the strengthening temperance movement, a drinking man's worst enemy. As with the financial panic, this development threatened Jack and Dan's partnership before it even had a chance to succeed.

THE *FAYETTEVILLE OBSERVER* NOTED that not many drunken men were being seen on the streets, speculating that the tight money market had something to do with it.[23] Although undoubtedly true, the rising ire of the temperance crusaders toward those displaying public drunkenness was also something to contend with—the thunderous words of the pious tended to have a searing effect. After losing momentum during the Civil War, leaders of the temperance movement rekindled the flame in the early 1870s, when a righteous wave swept the country. They organized camp meetings and revivals, intent on saving drunkards by the bushel. Women were at the forefront, marching under a number of banners over the years: Sober Societies, Aquatic Societies, Sons of Temperance, the Cold Water Brigade, and Children of Drunkards, among others. A favorite slogan: "The man takes the drink, then the drink takes the man."

Many a woman was all too content to sit in a saloon and tally the drinks consumed by each patron to embarrass him or to gather outside of the saloons to pray loudly for the fallen. Other activists preferred more violent means; beginning in 1877, attacking saloons and smashing up the interiors were all the rage for these reformers—nothing like a series of illegal actions to improve morality. They broke windows, glasses, and sundry smashable objects, the preferred weapons of choice being canes, hammers, hatchets, hatpins, pipes, rocks, sticks, and, of course, umbrellas, which remained stashed under cloak and cape until their leader exhorted, "Smash, sister, smash! Hallelujah! Glory to God!"

Pandering politicians, fearful of losing their cushy privileges, picked up the mantle of reform. In 1872, the Alabama legislature passed thirty-two local acts prohibiting the sale of liquor within certain distances of towns, churches, schools, and factories. The bourbon heartland was hit hard when Kentucky adopted a local option law, resulting in 207 of 259 towns voting against issuing liquor licenses. In Nashville, the United Friends of Temperance organized and pressured the state's legislature, which subsequently passed a local option law similar to Kentucky's. Thankfully, the governor vetoed it. Even closer to Jack's home turf, in June 1876, a temperance picnic near Fayetteville was a success, and in late November and early December, the United Friends of Temperance was holding meetings in Fayetteville, a foreboding development. It was reminiscent of the Civil War, when Union troops slowly formed a noose around out-of-the-way Lynchburg, only this time it was the dry forces. Sure enough, the prominent Reverend A. A. Allison lectured on temperance in Lynchburg, and a local temperance society quickly took root and flourished; the officers included Reverend B. J. Gaston, and Dr. S. E. H. Dance, once the Daniel's family doctor, now branded a traitor.[24] As pressure for reform increased, like a distillery boiler about to explode, Tennessee distillers and liquor salesmen suffered their first serious legal blow in 1877, the year the state's legislature passed the Four-Mile Law. This law made it illegal to sell alcoholic beverages within four miles of schools and other educational institutions in any unincorporated town that had a population of less than two thousand—fortunately, Lynchburg was incorporated. The fact that the prudish Mrs. Rutherford B. Hayes, the wife of the U.S. president and nicknamed Lemonade Lucy, banished liquor from the executive mansion didn't help matters for Jack and his comrades.

Striking close to the heart of Dan Call, the General Synod of the Lutheran Church adopted resolutions favoring a hands-on approach to temperance education. It was determined to use the pulpit and the press to spread its virtuous message and to influence politicians to enact virtuous laws. In some areas, southern Lutherans pleaded ardently with their congregations to forsake still houses, where "life-cherishing food" was converted into "life-destroying drink." Lutheran periodicals railed against church members "who engage in this business of the devil's because it promises them fast pay."[25] Like a typical rural Lutheran, for Dan it was indeed a matter of weighing ethics against economics, ideology against profits. For a religious man, it was a running warfare with hypocrisy. In this particular conflict, money won. Fortunately for Jack, his mentor was still relatively young and ambitious and not quite prepared to hand his entire life over to the church. However, Jack and Dan's partnership would come under increasing pressure, as Dan became ever more involved at the Lutheran Church.

Despite the renewed temperance movement, Lynchburg locals remained focused on alcohol, both on making it and on consuming it. There were letters to the editor on how to make home-brewed beer with molasses or sorghum, flour, hops, and water. There was a newspaper article on the cider brandy manufacture and trade in Connecticut, demonstrating the locals' interest in alcohol consumption in other areas. As for local watering holes, Fayetteville had six flourishing liquor shops and Lynchburg had three saloons, a plethora of options for a farmer seeking variation in his bartenders.[26] Despite a strong contingent of those with a thirst for the water of life, Jack would have to fight temperance forces his entire career—the battles to become more intense in the 1880s.

* * *

THE REVENUE MAN—or "revenooer," as some sneeringly called the government men in charge of collecting the tax on whiskey—was another challenge Jack personally had to face now that he was a distillery owner. The stillers' relationship with the revenue men—who were worse than boll weevils descending on a cotton field—was contentious at its best, murderous at its worst. The current chief of the oppressive Internal Revenue Service, General Green B. Raum, had really crawled under the skin of the Moore County distillers and, in fact, of any sour mash distiller in the region using the Lincoln County Process. Raum and his lieutenants, assuming themselves to be experts on whiskey making, were dictating terms of production that distillers using the Lincoln County Process simply couldn't meet. For one thing, Raum—a large man, balding but with a full, neatly trimmed beard—demanded that each bushel of corn yield 3 gallons of whiskey, whereas the Lincoln County Process yielded only 2.5 gallons. Well, as far as Jack and his fellow stillers were concerned, such a foolish stipulation would seriously compromise quality, if it even could be met. Some men in the Lynchburg area were already quitting the business as a result of Raum's heavy-handed dictums, while the more bellicose and resolute, including Jack, prepared for a serious fight over this disagreement and other issues.

It was not going to be easy to dissuade Raum from his ill-conceived rules and wayward management practices. Although he had a mild air about him, Raum was extremely shrewd—a dangerous mix that caused many a man to underestimate him.[27] He was a courageous fighter, too. An Illinois native born in 1829, he became a lawyer and an active opponent of slavery. When the Civil War broke out, Raum volunteered and was appointed a major, eventually rising to the rank of brigadier-general. In 1862, he led a bayonet charge at the Battle of Corinth and that year was severely wounded at Missionary Ridge. Unwilling to retire, he participated in the capture of Atlanta and in Sherman's march to the sea. After the war, he was elected to the House of Representatives, and then he voted to impeach President Andrew Johnson—about the only good thing Tennesseans could say of him. President Ulysses S. Grant tapped Raum for the commissioner of the Internal Revenue Service in August 1876.

The grim determination that Grant and Sherman brought to the war, Raum now brought to tax collecting. Although the value and the validity of the regulations Raum was instituting were up for debate, there was certainly no point in fighting the excise tax itself. In considering such a battle (or in placing trust in the government's wisdom, for that matter), all a distiller had to do was reflect on what had happened during the bloody Whiskey Rebellion of 1794 or the scandal involving the avaricious Whiskey Ring that had just rocked President Grant's administration.

THE WHISKEY REBELLION set the tone for what would always be a distrustful, downright nasty relationship between the distillers and the federal government. By 1790, there were 2,500 known distilleries in thirteen states—one estimate suggested there were actually as many as 5,000 log still houses, with 570 of them in four counties around Pittsburgh, courtesy of the strong Scots, Irish, and Scotch-Irish populations making rye whiskey.[28] During the nation's toddler years, these distillers had little reason to throw a tantrum. But then, at the urging of Alexander Hamilton, secretary of the Treasury, on March 3, 1791, Congress passed an excise tax on distilled spirits to pay off Revolutionary War debts. It now appeared that the virgin U.S. government was no different than the sullied oppressive British crown. The law was considered tyrannical by the freedom-loving farmers, particularly in Western Pennsylvania, who relied on whiskey to pay their debts. A typical farmer wouldn't see $20 in a whole year, but a gallon of whiskey was worth 25 cents in bartering with a local store.[29]

The stillers immediately revolted. They set about capturing excise revenuers—social lepers, for sure—then tarred and feathered the poor buggers. If a law-abiding farmer did pay the tax, his brother distillers would shoot up his still. The rapidly spreading violence in Western Pennsylvania came to a climax when General John Neville, a prominent citizen whose very name exuded aristocracy, attempted to aid a U.S. marshall from Philadelphia who was serving arrest warrants to rebellious distillers. One unruly whiskey-drinking band under a certain John Holcroft pinned Neville in his mansion, trading volleys of fire with the general, as well as with his slaves and servants. Results from the initial skirmish: one distiller killed and four wounded.[30] The rebels eventually seized the mansion, pillaged it, drank the whiskey in Neville's basement, and then set fire to the beautiful home.

That was enough for newly elected President George Washington, who happened to own a five-pot still for making rye whiskey at his Mount Vernon homestead—his farm manager also distilled brandy from peaches, persimmons, and apples. Regardless of his affinity for alcohol, Washington ordered more than 10,000 militia into Western Pennsylvania to suppress the rebellion led by Captain Whiskey. It was the theater of the absurd: such a large army against a band of farmers. The militia went on the march in October 1894; the distillers scattered; and by the end of November, the rebellion fizzled. Amnesty was offered to most, but Washington had shown who was boss.

The excise tax was eventually repealed in 1802, except for a brief period during and after the War of 1812, and the popularity of whiskey soared. The faithful imbiber Ebenezer Hiram Stedman, a Kentucky papermaker, recounted in a letter to his daughter: "Every Boddy took it [whiskey]. It ondly Cost Twenty Five Cents pr. Gallon. Evry Boddy was not Drunkhards. . . . It Brot out kind feelings of the Heart, Made men sociable, And in them days Evry Boddy invited Evry Boddy That Come to their house to partake of this hosesome Beverage."[31] It was indeed *wholesome*.

THE DISTRUST THAT DISTILLERS HAD for the meddling federal government was confirmed and acerbated not long after President Ulysses S. Grant took office in 1869. To begin, his administration not only cracked down on moonshiners, but the regulation of legitimate operations became more oppressive. With the passage of the Force Act of 1871, federal officials now had the power to summon troops to aid in law enforcement, which the revenuers immediately took advantage of. However, army officers opposed the idea of using military posses to enforce civilian laws; they complained that revenue agents used soldiers to avoid danger themselves.[32] It was true; the job had its hazards. As for the safety of revenue agents in Tennessee, a collector there wrote to the revenue commissioner that moonshiners "would be glad to kill for pure gratification and others to get what money he might have."[33] While unafraid to shoot down a revenuer, the moonshiners were hesitant to fight the army. As another revenuer observed, "[O]ne soldier is worth half a dozen armed men in citizens clothes."[34] When soldiers were sighted, the foxy moonshiners preferred to scamper into the woods to build a still another day. Yet there were a number of deaths on both sides, as a result of ambushes, pitched battles, and carbines accidentally discharging, due to edgy trigger fingers.

As revenues from the excise tax began to rise under Grant, the insidious seed of corruption soon took hold among the government men. At a local level, distillers bribed both the gauger and the storekeeper. On the national level, something more sinister was occurring. In the middle of it was John McDonald, the supervisor of Internal Revenue—the position originally created to prevent corruption—for Missouri, Arkansas, and Tennessee. A Civil War veteran and a Grant loyalist, McDonald was using his position, as well as physical force, to skim thousands of dollars in tax revenue. McDonald was just one of the leaders of what became known as the Whiskey Ring. Grant's personal secretary, Orville E. Babcock, profited, as did a number of revenue collectors, other federal officials, and compliant distillers. They used St. Louis as their base, and the plan was simple: both sides filed fraudulent revenue reports, and they all took a cut on the untaxed whiskey. All told, it was estimated that in the early 1870s, tax went uncollected on between 12 and 15 million gallons of whiskey, due to moonshining and corruption.[35]

Their conspiracy almost unraveled when McDonald was transferred to Philadelphia, but he convinced Grant to rescind the order. Invariably and predictably, it was the extravagant lifestyle of the crooked government men that was their undoing. According to Matthew Josephson, the author of the 1938 *The Politicos,* Babcock's "immoderate appetites for clothing, drink and fornication—all to be satisfied at the cost of the public Treasury—led him to ever more brazen adventures and needless risks." When Babcock visited St. Louis, for example, his boys presented him with a diamond shirt stud, weighing in at almost four carats and costing $2,400.[36] He was not the only Grant appointee who lived the gluttonous life, with his posh home, luxurious hotel suites, women of questionable character, and rich feasts. Eventually, there were enough raised eyebrows and jealous bystanders that informers stepped forward.

The informers wisely approached Secretary of the Treasury Benjamin H. Bristow, an honest man hailing from Kentucky, rather than Commissioner of Internal Revenue J. W. Douglass, with the news of a massive tax evasion scheme hatched in St. Louis. In March 1875, Bristow sent investigators into the field and positioned round-the-clock spies to observe how much grain went into targeted distilleries and how much whiskey the firms reported making. Any discrepancies were recorded for evidence. It was dangerous work, and there were instances of Bristow's stakeouts being exposed, then beaten to a pulp by goons or even local police on the distillers' payrolls. By May 1875, Bristow had evidence that only one-third of the taxes due on whiskey made it into the government coffer. The range of illicit activity was outlandish: distilleries were running illegally at night; 150 proof whiskey was being labeled 135; some whiskey was labeled as vinegar; federal stamps that certified that taxes had been paid were later being removed from barrels and reused; and on and on. As a result of Bristow's prowess, an astounding 230 indictments were handed down. The news splashed across newspaper front pages, even upstaging the juicy trial of Henry Ward Beecher, the prominent clergyman who had been accused of adultery.

Amazingly, there were no convictions except one—McDonald. He was convicted on November 23, 1875, and solicitously handed a three-year jail sentence and a $5,000 fine.[37] For a while he remained silent about the whole affair, hoping his belated discreetness would win him a quick release or a pardon. It did not. So, employing a ghostwriter, McDonald penned the *Secrets of the Great Whiskey Ring and Eighteen Months in the Penitentiary,* published in 1880. In his tome, he implied that Grant knew of the corruption. Perhaps he did. During his deposition, Grant had conveniently failed to remember many facts and conversations, which made for a skeptical public. Suspicions were further aroused when his personal secretary, Babcock, was acquitted on February 24, 1876—after Grant vouched for his character. Down South, anger and cynicism were extreme; after all, Grant was the Yankee general who had pounded them into submission—need more be said?

Although the *Lynchburg Sentinel* noted in November 1875 that "The war on the whisky ring goes bravely on," the distillers there were never directly affected until after the scandal broke.[38] It was when Commissioner of Internal Revenue J. W. Douglass resigned—having been labeled a coward—that the heat was put on Jack Daniel and the other Moore County distillers. The source: Douglass's replacement, General Green B. Raum. The general was determined to clean house and to use unprecedented force in doing so. Before Raum had been in office a year, his overbearing policies sparked a small but determined rebellion in Moore County, Tennessee.

6

A REBELLION AGAINST THE GOVERNMENT

۶۰۶

Come out and tell me who ye be. Fer if ye be one of them damned revenuers,
I'll mince yer shivering slats with the contents of my barker.

—Anonymous moonshiner

The Whiskey Rebellion was the stuff of legend; the Whiskey Ring seemed distant and of little concern, but now it got personal. The hardheaded commissioner of the Internal Revenue Service, General Raum, was attempting to exact too much from the men who made whiskey the Lincoln County way. To ensure that the Lynchburg area distillers toed the line, in January 1877, Raum ordered Deputy Revenue Collector Colonel J. W. C. Bryant to relocate his office from Shelbyville to Lynchburg.[1] Although there was already a bi-monthly change of revenue department officials at the various distilleries to protect against bribery, this latest move was a slap in the face.[2] On March 16, 1877, the *Lynchburg Sentinel* announced a "Meeting of Distillers"—it was time to fight back.

"There will be a meeting of the distillers of this and adjoining counties in this place to-morrow," the paper decreed. "It is expected that all will be present, as business, material to the interest of all will be transacted. We understand they are led to take this step by late

92

rulings of the Commissioner."[3] How great an impact had these "late rulings" had on the area? Only six distilleries were now operational, less than half of just a few years ago. Tolley & Eaton, the largest firm in the district, had even put its distillery up for sale. It included a brick malting house; a warehouse with an 800-barrel capacity; a second warehouse located adjacent to the town square, measuring 80 by 30 feet, with an elevator running from the basement to the second floor; a blacksmith shop; a wood shop; a stable and a barn; a framed building fitted up for a saloon; and a 4-acre lot.[4] This shuttering and sale of a sizable distillery did not bode well for the local economy.

Reflecting on the status of the local distillers, the *Sentinel* correspondent incisively pointed out: "It therefore becomes a matter in which we all are more or less interested. They [the distillers] furnish a home demand for the surplus corn crop at railroad prices–thus benefiting the farmer. They give employment to a considerable working force of laborers–thus furnishing employment to the idle. They have built up a large business in barrel making which not only supports a number of families, but creates a demand for a large amount of material out of which barrels are manufactured. The hundreds of cords of wood which are consumed is another considerable item in the aggregate." There was indeed a good deal of whiskey and money at stake here. As of January 1, 1877, the Lynchburg district had 373,203 gallons of whiskey in bond–that is, in the warehouse under government supervision. (In 1868, Congress passed a law creating the "bonded period," which allowed distillers to withhold payment on their excise tax up to 1 year for whiskey in storage. In 1879, it was extended to 3 years; in 1894, to 8 years; and in 1958, to 20 years–which encouraged aging and therefore better whiskey.) Another 30,068 gallons were made that month and 45,765 gallons taken out of bond to be sold–amounting to almost $100,000 in total sales revenue for the month, after backing out the 90 cent per gallon tax–a tremendous influx of capital for the Lynchburg area that the cummunity could ill afford to lose.[5] In a dramatic flourish, the reporter concluded, every individual in the entire county was impacted. "When we take into consideration the large amount of revenue paid the government annually in this section, it seems to us bad policy if the government continues a ruling which will crush them out entirely." So, what were these rulings exactly? And why might they obliterate Jack and his fellow distillers in what was known as Tennessee's fifth tax district? At their heralded meeting, the distillers intended to deal with these very questions.

IN MID-MARCH 1877, as a large crowd of Lynchburg citizens gathered to enjoy the spectacle of a balloon launch and the farmers were busy preparing for spring crops, the distillers—angry and seething—convened at Tolley & Eaton's Hall to air their grievances against the government and to plot strategy.[6] It was early morning, the air crisp and cold, the steamy breath of man and horse mingling. Also on hand was the reporter from the *Sentinel,* who listed out those distilleries represented and their capacity, based on bushels of corn consumed a day, with each bushel producing about 2.5 gallons of whiskey:

	Bush's	Gal's
Tolley & Eaton	51	128
Hughes & Co.	51	128
Hiles and Berry	44	110
Daniel & Call	39	98
Pitts, Parks & Brady	32	80
J. T. Motlow	28	70

and 14 more from Moore and adjacent counties, whose capacity ranged from 8 to 24 bushels, or 20 to 60 gallons of whiskey per day. On average these distillers had operated six days a week, about nine months of the year—until now.[7]

The tone in Tolley & Eaton's Hall was apprehensive and the men very businesslike—any proposals for action would be made by motion and then voted on, and committees organized. The meeting was called to order, and, on the motion of Mr. J. M. Stone, a modest but respected stiller, Captain C. H. Bean took the chair. Subsequently, a Jasper C. Avdelott was elected as secretary to record the minutes; he was also charged with drafting a letter that would address their concerns and be submitted to their enemy, General Raum. Now, the men, fearing for their survival, aired their grievances. The trouble with Raum first started in October 1876 when, in his desire to achieve greater management efficiencies, he unilaterally decided to combine the fourth and the fifth tax districts of Tennessee into one—the fifth district. Jack and his Lincoln County Process peers were of the fourth, while the fifth encompassed Nashville and surrounding counties. For a number of reasons, this move didn't sit well with the fourth district.

One primary concern was a marketing issue. In the 1870s, most distillers had just started selling their whiskey under their own name, carving out their own market niche, as opposed to merely shipping out barrels and jugs and allowing retail shops to brand it as they pleased; therefore, the current environment was becoming more competitive. This branding or labeling included their registered distillery number and tax district, which the customers were trained to look for. For the Lincoln County Process distillers, who took pride in the charcoal filtering of their sour mash, that meant being known to the public—and to the government—as Tennessee District Four. They didn't want to be associated with District Five, which had a number of sweet mash stillers who used a cheaper, faster method for making whiskey— an odious group to be linked with.

More ominous, in District Five there stood some of the country's largest sour mash distillers, concentrated in Robertson County, just to the north of Nashville, an area settled largely by Scots and Scotch-Irish, who had the capacity to squash any competition. The two reigning Robertson County chieftains were Charles Nelson and John Woodard. Bucking the Anglo hold on whiskey, Nelson happened to have emigrated from Mecklenburg, Germany, to Nashville, where he had started a grocery business. In 1870, he bought the Greenbrier distillery to supply his grocery store, selling the whiskey under the Greenbrier label, as well as distributing it from a warehouse on Second Avenue North, a very strategic location in the city. He would soon be the largest firm in Robertson County, with a capacity of 380,000 gallons a year. In contrast, Tolley & Eaton had a capacity of just 30,000 gallons a year, while Jack was at 23,000 gallons.[8]

The other Robertson County power, the Woodard clan, had been distilling since the 1830s. The patriarch was Wiley Woodard, born in 1810 but still a frenetically energetic man who was balding across his scalp and, lacking stylistic sensibilities, allowed his remaining hair to come straight down over his ears. He sported eternally pursed lips and a determined scowl. A relative of his, John Woodard, fifteen years his junior and the real power, presided over Woodard & Moore, which, like Greenbrier, had its own warehouse in Nashville. Both Wiley and John were elected to the state's legislature; therefore, these men had political connections, as well as a strategic location in Nashville, which greatly strengthened their grip on the market. They were formidable competitors.[9]

The Robertson County sour mash men also had an excellent reputation for producing fine bourbon whiskey, which prior to the war fetched 40 cents a gallon and immediately after commanded $3.75 a gallon. Lately, the Robertson and the Lincoln County Process men had been going head to head on both quality and price–$3.00 a gallon.[10] The latter contingent, however, was burdened with a major handicap: when it came to distribution, it was much farther away from the lucrative Nashville market, so it suffered higher costs and tighter margins than did the Robertson County boys. The higher profits enjoyed by the Robertson County distillers would greatly aid them when it came time to invest in the latest technology, a major factor in meeting one of Raum's other decrees.

THE DAGGER TO THE HEART–the proverbial straw that broke the camel's back–was Raum's demands that each bushel of corn yield 3 gallons of whiskey, not 2.5, the latter being the norm for Lincoln County Process men, and that distillers make their mash in three days, not a moment longer. Both commandments were designed to allow his field flunkies to more efficiently monitor the distilleries and detect any illicit activity. Courtesy of the former commandment, the storekeeper and the gauger could easily measure what went in and what came out and quickly flag any monkey business. But at the time, it was simply not possible for the Jack Daniel crowd to comply with this demand–it would compromise quality, if it could even be achieved. The only way these distillers could raise production efficiency would be to invest in sophisticated equipment–equipment beyond their means but affordable to the large Robertson County firms. Raum's decree rendered "resumption impossible" for many of Jack's compatriots who had shut down and threatened to shutter those who were struggling to remain open.

Compounding their troubles, Raum had decided that all distillers would be given three days for making the mash, no longer, or they would be in violation of the law. Designed to make the monitoring process not only dummy-proof but more efficient, the ruling permitted Raum's flunkies to check this stage in production at definitive time intervals, therefore allowing them to better plan their inspections of the respective distilleries. Well, that was fine and good for the sweet mash men, who could more easily control the process because they used fresh yeast each time. But for the sour mash men, they used an all-natural process, subject to the weather and the temperature—no two days were alike—so being constrained to such a fixed time was an impossibility. They required as many as five days to give themselves some leeway. The bottom line: Jack and the fourth district men didn't want to be compared against the larger distillers; they didn't want their wealthier brothers to be the ones who were able to either meet or set the standards.

Besides the fact that Jack and the Lynchburg area men were thrown into the same district as their archrivals—and, to be certain, pride was a factor here—how else did the consolidation affect the fourth district men? For one, a red-tape monster squelched their motivation. Even though Raum may have wanted greater efficiencies, the district was now so large and cumbersome to manage that it took two to six weeks, instead of only twelve to forty-eight hours to receive Tax Paid stamps when the distiller paid his tax to take his whiskey out of bond for selling. There were times when Jack had customers who couldn't wait that long for their barrels, so they took their business elsewhere. On other occasions, when the distillers requested these all-important stamps, they received letters from the commissioner's office granting the sale without the necessary stamps—a serious breach of protocol that could lead to criminal indictments. Another paperwork logjam involved the issuance of the annual permit to distill, which was sometimes delayed a month; meanwhile, the still sat idle, costing everyone money. Due to paperwork blunders alone, the Lynchburg area distillers calculated that since October 1876 the government had lost anywhere from $50,000 to $150,000 in tax revenue from their respective stills alone.

AT THE AFTERNOON SESSION of their pivotal meeting, the ornery distillers crafted and adopted a letter that explained their grievances in detail. Wasting no ink, their opening was blunt: "We earnestly protest against the longer continuance of said consolidation, as injurious to the best interests of the Government and *fatal* to our interests. . . ." Their lives in the balance, the men reviewed the various issues and concluded dramatically, "These and other similar established facts which have come into our possession, compel us to conclude that it is the intention to *crush out entirely the Sour Mash business,* and we now earnestly protest against this, and appeal to you as Commissioner of the Internal Revenue Service *not to permit this discrimination in favor of capital* and against us, who have not the capital to build costly Distilleries. We sincerely think it a manifest breach of faith as between us and the Government, though it may be to the interest of the Sweet Mash Distillers in the Fifth District of Tennessee, *who are thus enriched at our expense.*" Jack and his cohorts pointed out that "we are proprietors of small Distilleries operated entirely by hand."[11] Due to the unique techniques employed by the Lincoln County Process men, they had to be treated differently and requested to once again be separated from the fifth district.

Once satisfied with their literary masterpiece of protest, the men voted to hand deliver it to the commissioner himself in Washington, electing John T. Motlow and Jack Eaton to be their emissaries. Mr. Stone motioned that they should leave posthaste, within three days. To raise money to defray the trip's cost, the men formed a finance committee, which quickly determined that $200 was needed, with each distiller to be assessed a percentage of the expense based on his production capacity. Before the meeting adjourned, the men decided to create a formal organization to be called the Sour Mash Distillers' Association of the Old Fourth District. They elected Walten Hiles as president, J. D. Tolley as vice president, Eaton as secretary, and Motlow as treasurer. While Jack and Dan Call had a large stake in the outcome of these efforts, they were not drawn too deeply into the activism—the *Sentinel* reporter didn't even mention Jack in his article, even though Jack had the fourth-largest distillery. Jack, at age twenty-seven, was not yet a community leader. Also undermining his desire to become more entangled in their newly formed association, he distrusted anything smacking of politics.

The Tuesday after the meeting, Motlow and Eaton, with letter in hand, departed for Washington to lobby on the behalf of the distillers. While there, they were also to look into hiring a Washington-based attorney to represent their interests. The association would meet again on March 31, at which time Motlow and Eaton were expected to debrief everyone on their quest. How successful they would be in showing the commissioner the error of his ways was certainly in question, and the men were well aware of this. The Democratic Tennesseans eyed Raum with great suspicion. Rightly so, considering that the Yankee general was an ardent Republican; that Raum had been hired by Grant, whose alleged nonparticipation in the Whiskey Ring was suspect; and that Raum had congratulated Orville Babcock when he escaped conviction. And just how upright was Raum? He would eventually resign his position in the mid-1880s to lobby on behalf of what would be known as the Whiskey Trust, a monopoly that would find itself in federal court. Still later, in 1889, as commissioner of pensions under President Benjamin Harrison, Raum would be accused of using his public office to further his private business dealings. It appeared that his integrity had its issues. Meanwhile, the success or the failure of Jack Daniel and his comrades hung in the balance.

THE JOURNEY DEMANDED a day's carriage ride to Tullahoma, a train trip to Nashville, and then a second train to Washington, arriving via the Long Bridge, which spanned the Potomac River. Eaton and Motlow hadn't ventured so far afield since the Civil War and were uncomfortable when they alighted in their enemy's capital. Because it was centrally located among the original thirteen states, George Washington himself had handpicked the city in 1790 to be the seat of the new government. It became the most carefully planned city in the country, with the government's graying stone buildings nestled along the expansive parklike mall. From the train depot, the two Tennesseans passed by the majestic Capitol Building, the dome towering almost three hundred feet above them. In the distance, they could see the Washington Monument under construction, which, modeled after an Egyptian obelisk, would not be completed until 1884. A tour of the Executive Mansion would have to wait.

When Motlow and Eaton were ushered into Raum's office, he was in no mood to cater to legitimate distillers, due to the broadening war he was waging against illicit distillers. The illicit manufacture and sale of spirits—good ol' moonshining, bootlegging, and blockading, the latter term otherwise known as driving off the revenue men with blazing guns—remained extensive in certain districts of Alabama, Arkansas, Georgia, Kentucky, Maryland, Missouri, Pennsylvania, North Carolina, Texas, Virginia, West Virginia, and Tennessee, including in Jack's home district. While big-time moonshining was largely confined to the mountainous region of the Appalachians, including eastern Tennessee, counties adjacent to Moore—Coffee and Franklin—were considered part of the moonshining belt. And, in fact, there were plenty of small-time operators scattered throughout Jack's neck of the woods. Wildcat distilling was simply a means of survival for many families who, a dozen years after the Civil War, were still suffering economic indignities.

Raum had his hands full, especially after the prodigious 1876–1877 corn crop in northern Georgia resulted in a huge surplus and further fueled illicit stills; in his 1877 annual report, he wrote, "The extent of these frauds would startle belief."[12] He estimated that there were at least 3,000 illegal stills, each manufacturing anywhere from 10 to 50 gallons a day. "They are usually located at inaccessible points in the mountains, away from the ordinary lines of travel, and are generally owned by unlettered men of desperate character, armed and ready to resist the officers of the law. When occasion requires, they come together in companies of from ten to fifty persons, gun in hand, to drive the officers out of the country. They resist as long as resistance is possible, and when their stills are seized and they themselves are arrested, they plead ignorance and poverty, and at once crave the pardon of the government." Sometimes the brazen moonshiners displayed a comedic element, too, typified by a Kentucky moonshiner with jug in hand, who was apprehended by a revenue man. The captured man insisted his jug was filled with but water. The revenue man snatched it away and took a long pull. Of course, he gagged on the fiery rotgut. Cursing, he made the moonshiner take a sip and tell him it wasn't whiskey. "What do you know!" the moonshiner said with feigned surprise. "The good Lord's gone and done it again!" A miracle. Well, the revenue man had heard such lies before and put the culprit in chains. The moonshiners, who continued to view federal tax laws as unduly oppressive, had the sympathy of their neighbors, making Raum's job all the more difficult. "In certain portions of the country many citizens," he noted, "not guilty of violating the law themselves, were in strong sympathy with those who did violate it, and the officers in many instances found themselves unsupported in the execution of the laws by a healthy state of public opinion."[13] The Yankee general was now taking extraordinary measures to break up the illicit distillers.

Raum was spurred on by President Hayes, who took office in March 1877 and was in turn inspired by his dear wife, Lemonade Lucy. Characterized by some historians as courageous and honest as an administrator, Hayes was determined to reform civil service after Grant's somewhat lax leadership. Incidentally, to garner support from the largely Democratic South, the Republican president appointed a Tennessean postmaster general–the position of war secretary would have been more notable, but perhaps Lynchburg would finally be blessed with daily mail delivery. As for supporting Raum's aggressive initiatives, the president was influenced somewhat by the fact that excise taxes on distilled spirits raked in over one-half of the revenue the government collected.[14] Hayes permitted Raum to spend hundreds of thousands of dollars on enforcing revenue laws, which included hiring hundreds of revenue agents, who persevered with courage and cowardice and even drunkenness. Yes, drunkenness. When a revenue agent visited the distillery of an R. W. Drake, he discovered evidence that suggested someone was siphoning off whiskey. He informed the storekeeper and gauger, Charles Stokes, but found him "too stupefied with whisky to have any very correct knowledge of what he was there for." Continuing his report to Raum, the agent wrote, "From his appearances I think he is addicted to excessive use of alcohol. He has his gun with him and I think he spends much of his time in hunting, and that too during the hours the distillery is on operation." Mr. Stokes was relieved of duty.[15] Between drunkenness, corruption, and, most deadly of all, overwhelming paperwork, reforming the Internal Revenue Service wasn't going to be easy.

To bolster his troops, Raum called on U.S. marshals and federal soldiers. He quickly realized, however, that the soldiers' presence made for an indignant and irritated public, turning his still-bustin' operations into guerrilla warfare. Fast-moving civilian posses proved to be the most effective force, as Raum allowed these posses fairly wide discretion to punish evaders and delinquents, often resulting in charges of arbitrary conduct. In Jack's home state, deputies were "generally the roughest sort of illiterate men," according to Revenue Agent Olney, "who are unnecessarily severe." They were described as having no brains, no education, and no polish, as wayward cowards looking to establish reputations as tough hombres.[16] As General Raum ratcheted up the pressure, outwitting the revenuer became more of a game than ever before and the stuff of local legend.

ONE OF THE MORE CELEBRATED revenue men—or a raider, as he was called—was James M. Davis, a native of Tennessee who was determined to clean up his state. Muscular and standing over six feet tall, he had tracked escaped convicts before joining Raum's army. Like an Indian guide, he hunted his quarry; he was a deadly shot with his pistol; and a fellow deputy said that blockaders "quake at the bare mention of his name"—no surprise, considering that he ultimately captured over 3,000 blockaders and destroyed over 600 stills. But then, in 1882, while escorting a prisoner to court, he was ambushed by moonshiners hiding behind a log-and-brush barricade. The first bullet knocked Davis from his saddle. He stood and attempted to reach safety, only to fall in a hail of bullets, some twenty pieces of lead riddling his body—clearly, he had his enemies.[17]

A living legend on the other side of the law was moonshiner Bill Berong of Tennessee, who had eluded the revenue man for years. The termination of his career was not quite as ignoble as that of Mr.

Davis. His downfall began when Berong discovered that a posse was moving on his still in Towns County, forcing him to recruit seventy-five kind neighborly men, who took up strategic positions in the formidable landscape. "A revenuer described the road to Berong's house as 'hemmed in for the greatest part of the way by mountain slopes and laurel thickets, running through narrow defiles, and as crooked as the Ganges,'" wrote the historian Wilbur Miller. "As the posse approached a church, 'a yell ascended from a knoll on our right, taken up from one on the left, and thence was echoed along the defiles of this road.' They realized that a man waited in ambush at every bend of the road. Appalled at the thought of inevitably losing some good men if they engaged the desperadoes, the tax collector, a certain Deputy Hendrix, called for a retreat."

A few months later, Hendrix returned with a bit more stealth and captured Berong's two sons. Two days later Berong, the inflated legend and most intimidating man, surrendered. Imagine Hendrix's surprise to find his archenemy to be "a diminutive, dried up old man." "Arms to arrest this man!" he said sarcastically. "Why, I could pick him up, and carry him out of the mountains on my shoulders."

At his hearing, Berong was asked how he pleaded. "Guilty, if I am hung for it," was the surprise answer. "I am through with this blockading business. It has given me a fame that I don't deserve."[18]

Moonshining was indeed hardly glamorous. The men set up their stills in caves, under rock overhangs, behind large boulders—any place that was inconspicuous and inaccessible. Their homes, crude log cabins, weren't much better than the average still house, with its dirt floor, one door, and no windows, located in narrow, deep valleys where the sun doesn't shine and the mood could be equally dark. They lived a hundred miles or more from any telegraph or railroad, their own roads no more than bridle paths that were barely passable with buckboard or ox cart. A good meal included wild hog, hot cornbread, young onions, honey, and coffee. There was no butter for the bread and no sugar for the coffee. Utensils were a luxury—most moonshiners used their jackknives to eat, then wiped them clean on their trouser legs. A smoke or a chew followed, the women using tobacco as incessantly as the men. This lifestyle was in complete contrast to that of up-and-coming Jack Daniel, who had his 140-acre spread on the outskirts of Lynchburg and was determined to live a southern gentleman's life.[19]

While Berong may have been lionized, most moonshiners were vilified and slandered in the press. "Indeed," wrote a correspondent for the *Southern Bivouac,* "the gaunt and taciturn mountaineer who comes into the United States Court in the pursuance of a systematic conspiracy to plead guilty to or defend the accusation of 'manufacturing and selling spirituous liquors, without license, against the peace and dignity of the United States,' is more of a genuine barbarian and closer related in instincts, habits, and morals to the Huns and Visigoths that hung on the girdle of Rome and drove arrows into the bosom of the Mother of the World, than would appear first thought." The arrogant writer continued his colorful depiction: "Rude in speech, figure, and habit; barely lettered, though rarely entirely unlettered; cunning, bold, determined, and reckless of life, he is apart from the men of any of the people who dwell on the plains of either side of his mountain range, and has a code of manners, customs, and morals that is unknown to the outer world."

Stories abounded about revenue men meeting their deaths at the hands of moonshiners or innocent strangers being shot because they were suspected revenue men; however, in reality these were rare circumstances. As a reporter for the *Atlantic Monthly* discovered, "the instances of captures and tales of fights tended rather to show the general harmlessness of the distiller save when in local troubles he fights his fellow mountaineer." Yet, the writer acknowledged, "The gospel of their people teaches them to hate the revenue man as their natural enemy."[20]

Having massacred the moonshiner's character, the harsh *Bivouac* correspondent was just a slight bit kinder in his physical description of them: "The type of mountain man is a rather tall and angular person of no superfluous flesh, square-jointed, raw-boned, stooping, from the task of climbing and descending, and slouching in his gait; keen of eye, slow and deliberate in his speech, but alert and quick in action, he is usually insignificant in appearance, but capable of immense exertion, and often living to great age. The women are usually gaunt and masculine, or wilted slatterns who show some traces and suggestiveness of beauty when young."[21] Ultimately, moonshiners were portrayed as barbarians; they were descendents of penal slaves and convicts; they were dwarfish people who intermarried and interbred; and so went the slander and half-truths.

The only truth that mattered: these people lived in hopeless poverty and were forever menaced by famine. For moonshiners gripped by destitution, there was a certain pathetic smallness to their offense and arrest. Many of these so-called barbarians were merely trying to feed their families—and family was very important to them, as indicated by Berong's surrender to save his boys from certain imprisonment. Callous to their plight, by 1880, General Raum could claim that "during the last four years and four months, 4,061 illicit distilleries have been seized, 7,339 persons have been arrested for illicit distilling, 26 officers and employes have been killed and 57 wounded, in the enforcement of the internal-revenue laws."[22] Clearly, Raum was not to be toyed with. On the bright side, Tennessee senators had a habit of arguing for suspended sentences for convicted moonshiners. In fact, between 1877 and 1880, some 2,500 sentences were suspended in Tennessee and other states, further provoking Raum's ire.[23]

BACK IN LYNCHBURG, the sour mash distillers eagerly awaited Motlow and Eaton's return from Washington on March 29. The two men immediately announced that they had accomplished what they set out to do: speak directly with Raum. Other than that, there was nothing else definite to report.[24] There was no fanfare, no victory party. The two districts were not split apart, and today 1 bushel of corn yields 3 gallons of whiskey—all indicative of how successful the two emissaries were. Not very. And to think they would be stuck with the hardnosed Raum for the next seven years, his term marked by relentless perseverance.

On the legal front, there was one positive development, which was called the "Carlisle Allowance." To date, distillers were taxed on the whiskey that went into the barrel; however, for years they had been arguing that they shouldn't pay tax on the portion of whiskey that subsequently evaporates during aging, called the angel's portion. As much as 10 percent of the alcohol volume would be lost in the first year alone—maybe 4 to 5 percent in each subsequent year.

Democratic congressmen from such states as Kentucky and Tennessee lobbied hard for changing the tax code to take into account the angels' portion. Vocal Republican opponents attempted to slander the Democrats by snidely declaring that whiskey was the Democrats' national beverage, that they coddled the industry. Representative Hiram Casey Young, a Democrat from Tennessee, sparred with humor, "Forming my opinion from frequent declarations of my Republican friends, I had concluded, before the commencement of the discussion which has been had upon this bill, that the subject of whiskey was peculiarly under the charge of the Democratic party. . . . But it must be admitted, I think, that Republican gentlemen have in the discussion evinced an acquaintance with the subject so thorough and intimate that it could hardly have been acquired otherwise than by closest relations and most frequent contact."[25] In 1880, Congress finally amended the excise tax, excusing that which evaporated, the just law nicknamed the "Carlisle Allowance" after its champion, the Kentucky representative John G. Carlisle. Because there was no longer what amounted to a penalty for aging whiskey, it also encouraged the distillers to let their whiskey age longer and thus elevated standards for quality. It would be one of the distillers' few notable victories.

Due to changing laws, increased competition, and the holy temperance movement, distilling had become a complex business. As the liquor market became ever more complicated in the ensuing years, Jack Daniel would witness a war of attrition. It would be survival of the fittest.

7

IDENTITY CRISIS

❧·❧

A good gulp of hot whiskey at bedtime—it's not very scientific, but it helps.
                    —Dr. Alexander Fleming, the renowned
                    bacteriologist who discovered penicillin

Survival of the fittest. The phrase was coined by Herbert Spencer, an English scientist and a philosopher who was briskly applying Charles Darwin's theories on evolution to society at large, in an effort to explain who would excel and why. This distortion of Darwin's work, which was winning attention in the 1870s and sparking the imagination, became otherwise known as Social Darwinism. In the business arena, the oversimplified notion of "survival of the fittest" justified brutal competition. And America's capitalists were embracing it with great enthusiasm. Meanwhile, in the United States, the Industrial Revolution—an unstoppable force—was now picking up steam. It was indeed becoming a fight for survival in urban America, as people migrated to the cities in search of factory work. While such industrialized cities as Chicago, Cleveland, and Pittsburgh were distant places, Jack Daniel was also embroiled in a race for survival. In addition to Raum's debilitating dictums, Jack had to continue to contend with a strengthening temperance movement. The pious teetotalers would put such pressure on the devout Lutheran Dan Call that he would begin to waver as a distiller, at the very moment Jack needed him most as a pillar. As a result, the Daniel and Call partnership would face a breakup, and Jack would be thrown into an identity crisis.

Before Jack faced these new hurtles, Dan and he did witness a measure of prosperity in the last years of the 1870s as the Lynchburg area's whiskey business actually improved, following the fruitless Eaton and Motlow meeting with General Raum. That very March of 1877, the area distillers—consuming all excess corn and thousands of cords of wood—made 51,450 gallons of whiskey, a substantial increase from the 30,068 in January, and sold 56,175 gallons stored in their warehouses, an increase from the 45,765 sold in January.[1] Over the next two years, production continued to increase dramatically: for the eleven months ending on May 31, 1878, all of Tennessee exported a little over $1 million in distilled spirits; for the same period ending May 31, 1879, the figure ballooned 250 percent to $2.5 million![2] Tennessee sour mash was making a name for itself.

Reputation wasn't everything; there were several reasons for the prodigious increase. Foremost, any sour mash distiller wanting to stay in business had to upgrade his plant so that a bushel of corn would yield the required 3 gallons. Then, there was Raum's encouragement of illicit distillers to go legit. A legal operation made sense for everyone: former moonshiners could enjoy a life absent of government raiders; and it was cheaper for the government to assign storekeepers and gaugers to one-time moonshiners, even if they had a capacity of only 10 gallons a day, than it was to crack down on the moonshiners. Legal distilleries more than tripled in some districts of the moonshine belt that Raum had targeted.[3] By 1880, there were 84 registered distilleries in Tennessee, while North Carolina entertained the most at 374 and Kentucky was second at 242. There were 1,050 total in the United States. In 1897, there would be over 1,600 registered distilleries and liquor warehouses in the United States, with 106 in Tennessee.[4] Considering that the population of the United States would increase from 40 million people in 1870 to over 76 million in 1900, there were a good many more thirsty people to satisfy.[5]

Another contributing factor to the rapidly expanding market was the improving relationship with the northern states and the flourishing trade that accompanied it. In the summer of 1879, the multitalented J. B. Killebrew, now acting as Tennessee's commissioner of immigration, made a trip through New England and, reflecting on his journey, wrote a letter that was reprinted in the *Nashville Banner:* "Not a day passes that I am not invited to some New England home to take a meal with the family. In this particular I have been agreeably disappointed in New Englanders. My idea was that they were cold and as inhospitable as their climate, but I find much warmheartedness and genuine hospitality." Killebrew had his set of prejudices and misconceptions—shared by many Tennesseans—that were now being overcome. He found the people intelligent and refined. "Their homes are perfect models of comfort and convenience," Killebrew noted. "I never realized before how far behind we are in this particular." He did find the diet lacking in variation, as little meat was served and baked beans and pies were standard fare. "New England is a land of pies. Pies are served for breakfast, dinner and supper." The same could be said for grits in the South.

More poignant to his southern brethren, Killebrew observed,

> People and stock live well here on a little; we, on the contrary, live poorly on an abundance. With the same habits of economy practiced in New England, our poorest people could live like lords.
>
> But I must confess that I like the freedom and independence of our people, their habits of self reliance, better than any I have seen North.[6]

Jack certainly embodied the habit of self-reliance, but he also practiced economy.

Despite the increased competition, Jack was prospering in 1880. Assuming that Dan and he were selling about the same number of gallons as they were making—which was at least 28,000 annually, at 3 gallons to a bushel—the two were generating almost $60,000 in total revenue net the federal excise tax. Add to that whatever income Jack, who had bought another 66 acres out toward Lois, was deriving from his produce and livestock sales. After backing out modest expenses and the more than $2,000 Jack paid in state and local taxes, he was pocketing at least $5,000.[7] (By comparison, in the mid-1880s, a highly skilled steel mill laborer might earn $600 a year, which made for a somewhat comfortable existence.[8]) Another measure of Jack's success during these years: in 1881, he would purchase an additional 28 acres in the Lynchburg area and throughout the 1880s and 1890s would continue to add to his landholdings.[9] He had a voracious appetite for land, fueled by the interminable need for corn and wood.

At the time, farmers who owned 100 to 200 acres tended to be the most successful because that amount of acreage was large enough to achieve economies of scale but was still manageable. While Jack certainly fell in this category, he had his agrarian challenges. There was the need for restraint in trying to cultivate too much land, in overextending oneself. There was the eternal need for capital, good labor, cheap transportation, and fencing. There were the packs of wild dogs running rampant in the area, pillaging the chicken coops and ripping up the gardens. And then there was the weather—one's fate was too often left in the hands of God. Just in April 1879, the weather had been too cool and wet the first half of the month, thus the wheat too thin. Some crops had been damaged by Hessian fly, too. Yes, farming required undivided attention, as Mr. Killebrew had repeatedly propounded. Yet Moore County farmers persevered, planting corn over vast amounts of acreage to satisfy the area's ravenous distillers, who were consuming about 150,000 bushels, or 9 million pounds annually.[10]

Jack had help. Now living with him in his two-story farmhouse was his older sister Bette, in her early forties, and her husband, James Serrel Conner, another Civil War veteran who was now in his early fifties.[11] Bette had given birth to two children, but both had died in infancy—so now Jack was their boy. While Jack remained a most eligible bachelor, sister Bette managed the household and played hostess for any social gatherings. Also boarding on Jack's farm was Lu Motlow, a sixteen-year-old black girl who was the housekeeper, and Nick Evans, a twenty-eight-year-old farm hand.[12] Farm hands were paid $8 a week plus board, or $12 to $15 without.[13] (This wage was on par with what unskilled workers in northern factories earned, but it could not support a family, regardless of the geographic location—dual-income households were standard fare but not because women were liberated.) Many farmers, however, preferred the "share system," in which they paid their laborers with part of the crop instead of with money. This method decreased the risk for the landowner, which was crucial now that slavery had been abolished.

Jack was recognized as the family pillar. When his brother-in-law Felix Motlow needed money in 1880 to keep his farm afloat, Felix came to Jack. Instead of demanding repayment in gold, Jack accepted Felix's offer to allow him to grow wheat on 20 acres of his land and on 30 acres belonging to his mother.[14] The next year, when Felix had to borrow more money, in return Jack accepted "48 heads of hogs" and the right to grow corn on 40 acres of Felix's land.[15] He was generous in loaning money and somewhat forgiving when it came to repayment. For his part, Jack couldn't seem to abandon his family; he had to be surrounded by them—a compulsion that revealed his insecurities, as well as his devout loyalty to them. In Jack's idyllic sphere of existence, however, there was trouble afoot. His partner and mentor Dan Call was wavering.

TEMPERANCE REMAINED IN THE SPOTLIGHT, debated with passion across the nation. In the good ol' days—the pioneering days—alcohol was considered a beneficial necessity. On the eve of the Industrial Revolution in the mid-1800s, factory workers with no chance of advancement demanded on-the-job drinking privileges—and were granted them. But now that the Industrial Revolution was in full swing, the ever-procreating dry forces considered imbibing on and off the job a hindrance to an advancing civilization. Men like Dan and Jack understood the word *moderation;* however, many a man didn't—the proverbial axiom of one bad apple can ruin the barrel came into play. Dan was particularly worried about how being in that barrel was affecting his standing in the community, particularly at his Lutheran church.

Whiskey was blamed when men couldn't keep their jobs; whiskey was blamed when men abandoned their families; whiskey was blamed for sexual transgressions; and whiskey was blamed when one man stabbed another. The most shocking statistics to the dry forces: in 1880, there were four times as many drinking establishments as churches, and there were nine times as many liquor dealers as ministers. The fact that barkeeps slipped free drinks to children, to acquaint them with the taste, didn't help either; nor did stories of the Wild West. In legendary Tombstone, for example, the local newspaper playfully lamented, "Bad men and bad whisky are said to be plentiful . . . and measures are being taken to stop the mingling of the two. In a climate where the mercury sports around 110 the whisky should be only of the best quality." Devious saloonkeepers from Denver, Colorado, to Taos, New Mexico, diluted their whiskey with "additives," the "inventive whiskey" bringing on the shakes so bad that it was said a man couldn't pour a drink back into an opened barrel. All of these hijinks made for bad publicity and provoked the dry forces.

The temperance movement had always had an ebb and flow to it, with specific events spurring waves of reform, which then receded; however, now it appeared to just flow over the land. In 1880, the temperance movement received a boost when its ally James Garfield won the presidential election. The next year he hosted Miss Willard, president of the Women's Christian Temperance Union, at the Executive Mansion; however, at the soiree Garfield proved to be lukewarm when it came to wholly endorsing nationwide prohibition. His noncommittal attitude only served to stir up a hornet's nest. A painfully assiduous Miss Willard immediately organized her own political party with a prohibition platform. In 1883, her Prohibition Party established a chapter in Tennessee, which, as a major exporter of whiskey, was a primary target for the righteous. One social critic, Anne Royall, who traveled widely and recorded her observations, wrote, "I'm afraid my brave Tennesseans indulge too great a fondness for whiskey."[16] Of course, much of their bravery probably resulted from the whiskey.

It was the April 1880 Nashville Centennial that proved to be a lightning rod for the temperance debate in Jack's home state. The centennial was supposed to be celebrating progress, yet a great quantity of alcohol, allegedly the primary hindrance to progress, was going to be doled out, a situation the teetotalers found unacceptable. A fiery group of evangelical Protestants, fearing that drunken louses would ruin the event for families, demanded that alcohol be banned from the exposition grounds. The Reverend John B. McFerrin decried Nashville—a primary distribution point for Jack and his comrades—for being filled with "too many drinking saloons; too many gambling halls; too much lasciviousness; too many open gates leading the young men to destruction." Little good their campaign would do, considering that the area's saloons were advertising 10-cent drinks to appease the city's thirsty visitors. Ultimately, only beer was served on the centennial grounds in a house adjacent to the ornate exposition building, which boasted soaring Victorian towers and Romanesque arches.[17]

WITH THE STILL'S COPPER COIL–the "serpent"–still the bete noir of preachers, churches remained a leading force in the prohibition movement, which strengthened as hypnotic clergy leaders emerged from their ranks. In the 1880s, a Methodist minister and reformed alcoholic from Georgia, Sam Jones, held revivals with roaring sermons across the South, including rousing events in Nashville, Memphis, and Knoxville. Fighting distillers and saloonkeepers with both scripture and fist, he reduced grown men to weeping like "whipped children." "Christian Rum is the king of crime," he preached, a "vampire which fans sanity to sleep while it sucks away the lifeblood."[18] To make their point, one trick that more pragmatic temperance leaders used was to drop a wriggling worm into a glass of whiskey. After a moment or two, it died. The preacher then said quietly to the audience, "Now my friends, what does this tell us?" He could only hope that some brazen buzzard didn't pipe up, "If you drink whiskey, you'll not be bothered by worms."

Sam Jones also supported the Women's Christian Temperance Union, which had been under attack by men for being too aggressive and full of "masculine women." Close to Jack's home turf–to the distillers' and all men's dismay–in the 1880s, these emboldened women produced a play, *New Woman,* which debuted in Fayetteville. The performance was held in a theater on the second floor of Bright Hall, situated on the south side of the town square. The actress in the lead role, the "new woman," was dressed in a suit jacket, a necktie, a frill-less skirt, and a hat that resembled a cowboy's sombrero, rather than a bonnet, the entire costume representing the savvy, modern woman. Other actresses, portraying the subservient mothers and grandmothers of yesteryear, were garbed in traditional dowdy gowns and bonnets, the only comforting image for the few men who ventured a peek. The message emanating from Fayetteville and elsewhere was clear: women wanted equal rights and a strong voice in society—a society rid of drunken louses who abused them. The times were clearly changing, and public opinion–sensitive politicians who were practiced at the art of playing weather vanes took note. The political success of temperance preachers like Jones and their female allies could be measured by such facts as this: in Alabama, fifty-four counties were dry as of 1881, due to local option enactments, up from thirty-two counties ten years earlier—an ominous sign of things to come.[19] In Tennessee, there was actually a movement to repeal the "Four-Mile Law," but it was squelched. Instead, a law prohibiting the sale of liquor to minors was passed—so began the children's game of raiding the parents' liquor cabinet.

DARKENING AN ALREADY-GLOOMY CLIMATE, Dan Call's Lutheran church became ever more vocal on temperance. In North Carolina, the Lutheran leadership endorsed prohibition laws, and in Newberry County, South Carolina, leaders endeavored to visit every family in the church to rally them for legal prohibition.[20] The same pressure was brought to bear on Tennessee Lutherans. This didn't bode well for Dan Call. In fact, his Lois Lutheran church held a religious revival, at which, like many rural churches in Tennessee, the emphasis was on individual repentance and salvation, which included forsaking drink. Still serving as a lay preacher, Dan was now under enormous pressure to make a clean break from the distilling business, to seek salvation. Meanwhile, in diametric opposition, Jack was laying plans for expansion, plans that included building a distillery in the same hollow where the legendary Alfred Eaton made whiskey—plans he intended to see through, regardless of temperance-crazed preachers.

Dan attempted to fend off the righteous, but it was no easy task. His wife, Mary Jane, who was increasingly concerned about their children being raised around a distillery, had joined the chorus singing to him. They now had 9 children, ranging from age 18 to 1; 4 were under the age of 7, the 5 oldest worked the farm.[21] For the children's sake, Mary Jane argued, Dan needed to be an upright, exemplary parent. The jig was up. Dan had to make a choice: Stay with Jack and expand, which meant joining the fight against the dry forces, including his own church; or relinquish his partnership. Beginning to succumb to the pressure as early as September 1877, Dan leased Jack the land on which they had their distillery and substantially removed himself from the business. Before 1882 was out, Dan Call made his choice: he broke completely with Jack.[22]

The forty-six-year-old Dan liked to say the Lord instructed him to either stop preaching or stop making whiskey, but the truth was, the congregation and his wife instructed him. (One Call ancestor wished he'd given up preaching instead because the Jack Daniel Distillery was eventually worth tens of millions of dollars.[23]) For the next twenty years, Dan worked his 280-acre farm, raised eighteen children, and preached. Becoming increasingly civic minded, he donated land for a school in Lois, on which the citizens built a two-room school.[24] Many years later his church burned, the schoolhouse rotted, and the family cemetery located on the Call farm was bulldozed, pieces of headstone lying shattered. (Fortunately, Dan and his wife, Mary, escaped the destructive progress; they were buried in the Mulberry Cemetery, located near the village of Lois.[25]) Despite such calamities that tend to erase history, this man who taught Jack the distilling business remains a local legend today.

The loss of Dan Call portended big changes for Jack. The boy distiller would have to make a choice himself: come out from the shadows and make his mark on the distilling industry or succumb to a now-acute identity crisis and slip into obscurity.

FROM THE DAY JACK VENTURED FORTH to sinful Huntsville, he had proven himself the prodigal salesman, yet the marketplace was rapidly becoming ever more sophisticated and discerning. No longer did consumers purchase their goods from barrels, crates, and hogsheads; now looking for specific brand names, they asked for Borden's Eagle Brand Condensed Milk (1866), Campbell's Soup (1869), Levi Strauss's Overalls (1873), Quaker Oats (1878), and Ivory Soap (1879). The same specific requests were being made for bourbons and whiskies, from Old Forester to Greenbrier. Did Jack have the capacity to adapt—or evolve, as Darwin would say—to the new marketplace?

As complicated as it was simple, all he had to do was approach his whiskey about the same way he branded his cattle. The brand was the problem.

As Daniel and Call of District Four, their distillery had enjoyed a distinct identity, which, again, was why they were so loath to be consolidated with District Five. When Jack peddled their sour mash to saloons and grocers, to music halls and theaters, everyone knew of Daniel and Call—the government stamp with their distillery and district number was clearly visible on their barrels and jugs—and had confidence in the quality of their whiskey. But District Four no longer existed, and now Call was out of the picture. Instead, there was this Jack Daniel's Distillery from District Five. What had happened to the venerable Mr. Dan? How was the quality of this apparently new sour mash? There were many raised eyebrows. Jack's image was muddled in the minds of his customers. Something had to be done.

Jack perceived that he had to bring his own brand into focus, to give it a rebel yell of quality. In these first years of the 1880s, the earthenware jugs simply stenciled with

JACK DANIEL

WHISKEY

LYNCHBURG

TENN.

didn't cut it anymore. In his first marketing efforts, he labeled jugs "Jack Daniel's Old Time Distillery," to exude a sense of tradition and quality. That wasn't enough either. He needed something bolder. It was then that he struck on a brilliant idea that retains a mystic charm over a hundred years later: the brand name of Old No. 7. Over the years, it took several forms: Jack Daniel's Old No. 7; Jack Daniel's No. 7; Fine Old Jack Daniel No. 7; and Old Time Distillery No. 7, among others. It wasn't flashy by any means, but it caught the customer's eye and created a buzz among the public. What was this Old No. 7? What did it mean? What inspired the No. 7? Undoubtedly, something very special.

Several stories behind the legendary name have been promulgated through the years. The most popular was trumpeted by the Jack Daniel raconteur Ben Green, who wrote, "Almost no one knows how the famous Jack Daniel's Old Time No. 7 Brand whiskey truly got its name." He then divulged the supposed secret. One day Jack was visiting a merchant friend in Tullahoma. In the course of their discussion, his friend explained how he had started with one store but now had a chain of seven stores, thus cutting his costs through quantity buying and growing sales through coordinated marketing efforts. So, very impressed with his diligent friend, Jack rushed back to the distillery and retold the story to Bill Hughes, the son of Jack's old employer Colonel Hughes and his head distiller at the time. According to Green, their conversation went as follows:

> "Billy, I've got the name for our best whiskey," shouted Uncle Jack with his small feet dancing a jig.
>
> "It's Jack Daniel's Old Time No. 7. Now you guess how I got the idea," continued the gleeful man.
>
> "Gee wiz, how do you think I could figure out that?" answered Bill Hughes.

Jack went on to explain his merchant friend's success and how naming their whiskey Old No. 7 would pay tribute to him, including his hard work and attention to quality. It was Bill Hughes's daughter, Mrs. Frank Parker, who allegedly regaled Ben Green with the story.[26] The story was and remains false.

Another version—with a truer ring to it—was handed down by Jack's nephew, Lem Motlow. Lem once told a friend that the distillery's warehouse was overstocked, the reason being they had misplaced a batch of whiskey that should have been sold several years earlier. When Jack did sell the whiskey, he labeled it "Jack Daniel No. 7" because it was now seven years old. This smooth-tasting batch was so popular that he decided to keep the name, even though his whiskey generally didn't sit in barrels for more than four years or so. There was indeed a seven-year-old No. 7 brand, but that batch surfaced from the warehouse years after Jack had created the No. 7 brand.[27] Once again, the story was and remains false.

Ultimately, locals became resigned to the fact that "With Jack and his contemporaries long since gone, the meaning and significance of that number is now lost to the deep past. Though many have speculated, one guess is as good as another, or so it would seem."[28] Today, the Jack Daniel Distillery's official position on the source for No. 7 is, "We just don't know." "Ask seven different distillery tour guides," claims the company, "and you'll get seven different stories. We don't know why Mr. Jack named his whiskey Old No. 7, but he must have had a good reason."[29] Lost to the deep past? Not quite.

Here's the undeniable truth: when Jack and Dan first registered with the government back in the 1870s, they were given a unique distillery number in their designated tax district by which the Internal Revenue Service identified their operation, placing the numbers on all of their barrels, jugs, stamps, documents, and other sundry paperwork. Then, in 1876, the tax district Jack and Dan were in, the fourth district of Tennessee, was consolidated with the fifth of Tennessee. In this newly designated district, the Daniel & Call distillery was given a new number, 16, for identification purposes. Incidentally, for whatever reasons, no one else from the old fourth required a new number.[30] Now to the great secret of where the Old No. 7 name of Jack's flagship black label brand came from. Yes, No. 7 was his old number in District Four, thus Old No. 7.

By adopting what appeared to be a bland, even boring label name, Jack was actually indulging in civil disobedience. He was effectively rebelling against the federal government by reminding everyone of the despised consolidation of the two districts. He was reminding everyone of the competition between the sour mash and the sweet mash distillers. More poignant, he, along with Dan, had built a reputation among saloons, grocers, and wholesalers who looked for that No. 7 government stamp, so by reproducing it on his jugs and barrels, he jogged their potentially booze-addled memories. It was marketing genius. Ingenious, yet so simple that for decades no one knew the real tale behind the label Old No. 7. Indeed, it was an unanticipated marketing coup for Jack, as it created mystique.

Why else was Jack so enamored with Old No. 7? It represented yesteryear's old way of doing things. He was steeped in the importance of maintaining traditions—namely, the Lincoln County Process—and he wanted to convey that to his customers. Handcrafted quality was paramount for Jack. He also desired the return of many things from his innocent childhood, which extended to his family. He wanted to be surrounded by his mother, his father, and his family, as well as by Dan Call; he dreamed of happier times before the Civil War. Nostalgia permeated every fiber of his being. While commendable, his nostalgia and desire for excellence would both drive Jack forward and restrain him as he grasped for the mantle of leadership.

8

SEIZING THE
LEGENDARY HOLLOW

'Y God, every day we make it, we're going to make it the best we can.

–Jack Daniel

In evaluating whether to expand his operations, Jack had to consider the repressive power being wielded by both the Internal Revenue Service and the temperance movement, the latter desiring nothing less than prohibition. He had to ruminate over how these forces would affect the whiskey market. Would there be continued growth? Would there even be a market in five or ten years? On the revenue front, distillers and moonshiners across the nation breathed a collective sigh of relief when the fanatically dedicated bureaucrat General Raum elected to resign in 1883.[1] Surely, his replacement, Walter Evans, would be more lenient. No such luck.

Keeping the pressure on, in Evans's first year his men made over nine hundred arrests and seized almost four hundred stills—an admirable accomplishment among the killjoy crowd. As for the legitimate operators, there was some hope for relief when rumors spread that President Chester Arthur, who succeeded the murdered James A. Garfield in 1881, was going to abolish all internal taxes. With the government rapidly paying off its Civil War debt, it was thought that duties levied against imports would provide sufficient revenue. But then Arthur announced that there would still be a tax on one American industry: distilled spirits. He believed that the tax on whiskey and other sundry spirits was the "least objectionable to the people."[2] Yes, least objectionable to the dried-up prohibitionists. Compared to Jack's concerns with the revenuers, the battle with the dry forces remained far more onerous.

To combat the ultra-radical prohibitionists, Jack and his fellow distillers were forced to lobby more aggressively against the "ugly women, the henpecked husbands . . . and $3 preachers."[3] More to the point, they had to influence the politicians by any means necessary. To do so with greater effectiveness on a national level, brewers, distillers, and liquor dealers convened in Chicago, in May 1882, to plot a cohesive strategy. At the meeting, they formed the National Distillers and Spirits Dealers' Association. In September they met in Cincinnati, and, hoping to spur on their winemaking comrades, promptly renamed themselves the National Spirits and Wine Association of the United States. To protect their individual rights—the rights of all citizens, in fact—guaranteed by the Constitution, the wet forces also organized the National Protection Association. In October 1882, they convened their first meeting in Milwaukee, at which time they promptly renamed themselves, choosing the more noble-sounding Personal Liberty League of the United States. Branch chapters were subsequently organized in major cities and towns across the United States to lobby politicians at local and state levels.[4]

In Tennesee, Jack and his comrades formed the State Protective Association and elected a Nashville wholesale liquor dealer, George S. Kinney, president. Their obvious objective was "to safeguard and uphold the manufacture and sale of whiskies, brandies, wine, ale and beer as at present regulated by law against the aggressions of the prohibition movement in the state."[5] Employing aggressive tactics, the association bribed newspapers to control editorial policy on liquor, lobbied politicians with jugs of money, and even committed fraud during elections to swing the vote in their favor. The association's primary target was the state senator J. H. McDowell, who, hailing from Obion County, had usurped General Raum as its most imminent enemy. A fervent reformer and the leader of the Tennessee Temperance Alliance, McDowell proposed an amendment to the state's Constitution that amounted to prohibition: "No person shall sell, or keep for sale as a beverage any intoxicating liquors whatever." Short and sweet. There was an immediate outcry that such a law would violate the rights of the individual, but McDowell argued that "individual liberty" becomes "unrestrained license" when it interferes with social order and the happiness of others; in other words, drunks were a social menace that had to be eradicated.[6]

The distillers would win a round in 1887 when McDowell's temperance amendment failed to pass, the vote 145,237 against and 117,504 for. In terms of financing its cause and deviousness, the association's strategy had proved effective: the ladies and the preachers in the temperance movement were no match. But the black vote was also considered decisive, which served to harden the prohibitionists' negative view of blacks (the "Negro problem"), whom they considered to be serious abusers of alcohol. Wet forces would breathe another sigh of relief when the Republican Benjamin Harrison was elected president in 1888. He drank wine openly at public functions; his vice president, Levi Morton, owned a hotel that sold liquor; and his secretary of state, James Blaine, a great friend of the country's capitalists and of dubious reputation, lobbied on behalf of the beer industry.

Ultimately, the charismatic temperance leadership of the early 1880s did take its toll on Moore County distillers. Dan Call wasn't the only one to quit the business; by 1886, the number of registered distilleries fell from twenty-three to fifteen.[7] Tolley & Eaton, located at County Line, remained the largest—much of the operation now run by machinery—with a capacity of 300 gallons per day. Jack Daniel's was second in capacity at 150 gallons per day. The thirteen other distillers averaged 70 gallons daily, for a grand total of 1,360 gallons daily. Assuaging their battle wounds, they enjoyed a national reputation for making some of the finest bourbon whiskey in the United States; bourbon was now the nation's favorite. As evidence, in 1885, corn displaced rye as the top grain used in whiskey making. Regardless of their reputation and the fact that distilling was the largest manufacturing industry in Tennessee, by the end of 1887, there would be only three fully operational Moore County whiskey manufacturers left standing: Tolley Brothers in Lynchburg, John Eaton in County Line, and Jack Daniel.[8]

AS JACK WATCHED the more timorous men shutter their distilleries, he realized that the downturn provided an opportunity for the bold. The time was ripe for expansion, and he was determined to fill the void by building a distillery that could compete with the likes of Tolley & Eaton and the Robertson County boys. As for the location, he knew exactly where he wanted to be: in the heart of Lynchburg, both the center of the county's attention and strategically located to access distribution points in all four directions on the compass. The precise location: the hallowed Cave Spring, where the legendary Alfred Eaton had established the area's first distillery and allegedly discovered that leaching whiskey through charcoal mellowed and purified it of verdi gris and fusil oils.[9] It was a magical place.

Just on the outskirts of Lynchburg proper, separated from the town square by a swath of trees, was a hollow with a rugged ravine running several hundred yards before abruptly meeting a limestone cliff. At the base was a cave, from which a cool draft of air blew and a stream of sparkling water bubbled forth like the mythic fountain of youth. With dense foliage veiling the cave's mouth, moss clinging to the rocks, and humidity hanging in the air, it was a Garden of Eden. It was a fairyland where the Scottish little people and Irish leprechauns played in the underbrush. The same mystical qualities that enshrouded what would become known as the Hollow, Jack wanted for his whiskey. He had to have it—only it belonged to the firm of Hiles & Berry, whose still on this property sat dormant.

The two partners were reluctant to part with the historic property, but they were moving along in years, the leading partner Walten Hiles now in his early fifties, and were scaling back their activities. Finally, they decided to hold a trustees sale, with Hiles acting as trustee for the two men. On June 16, 1884, those interested in bidding on the 142-acre property gathered to survey the Hollow, the pivotal landmark in the deed being "a small stump in the valley below Cave Spring near the old still house." After the preview, the bidding was opened. Not to be outbid or outclassed, Jack offered the winning figure of $2,180.40–

a far more modest price than if the market had been booming.[10] It would become a priceless piece of property. If there was any doubt about the value of the 56-degree, iron-free Cave Spring water, it was erased when Tolley & Eaton approached Jack about piping the water to their own nearby distillery. While Jack may have harbored a desire to sweep his competition from the field, a spirit of cooperation still pervaded among the whiskey men, and he agreed to their proposal. In October 1884, he gave the Tolley & Eaton company rights to pipe water from the legendary Cave Spring for $100 a year to be paid in four installments.[11]

Never one to twiddle his thumbs, Jack immediately erected a brick distillery and a one-room office building with a creaky front porch, which was easily mistaken for a shack. Fearful of compromising quality and of overextending himself in an uncertain market, he prudently kept his capacity at 150 gallons a day. Shortly after he was operational, a reporter working for Goodspeed Brothers, a Nashville publishing house hell-bent on producing a monumental county-by-county history of Tennessee, toured Moore County. When the book was published in 1886, Jack was featured, with the writer noting that the Jack Daniel Distillery "has the capacity of fifty bushels per day and turns out some of the finest brands of 'Lincoln County' whiskey. Mr. Daniel is the owner of a large and productive farm, which he manages in connection with his distillery, and on which he raises large numbers of livestock." The surrounding land was "teeming with thousands of horses, mules, cattle, sheep, and hogs," but Jack's prize livestock consisted of a herd of cattle—beneficiaries of the stillage—grazing in the undulating verdant pastures that graced each side of the Hollow.[12] One of the few Moore County men to receive a brief biographical sketch in the voluminous book, Jack had secured a preeminent status in a few short years.

LYNCHBURG WASN'T EXACTLY BOOMING, unlike many American cities that were experiencing an influx of country folk and immigrants during the Industrial Revolution. Hindering local progress, the year before Jack bought the Hollow, the town was consumed by fire; this

At the Hollow, Jack's office was no more than a shack with a porch.

Jack's office, including a photo of the legend and his nephew Lem, is now part of the distillery tour.

included the Christian Church, which was then being used as a court-house. During the conflagration, many important records went up in smoke. The town was rebuilt, of course, and as of June 1886, Lynch-burg had four general stores, one drugstore, two hotels, five churches, a pork packer, the Parks and Evans Saloon, Tolley & Eaton Whole-sale Liquors, and the Jack Daniel Distillery, among just a few other businesses. Also, the townspeople erected a commanding Italianate-style brick courthouse in the center of the village square. Despite the makeover, the *metropolitan downtown* had stagnated since its initial growth spurt after becoming the Moore County seat, and the popu-lation was a mere 350.[13] It was as if the square were a preserved stage set and would remain so more than a hundred years later. Moore County also continued to embody a fierce frontier soul, with many men still packing pistols.[14]

Now a man about town, Jack, who rode with a light hand and savored speed, cut a sharp figure astride his horse. "He loved fine horses," recalled his grandnephew Felix W. Motlow, "and other fine things, and he kept two thoroughbred Kentucky horses, and drove one of these spirited horses daily from his home to his place of busi-ness."[15] Habitually, at midday he would come trotting through town and take lunch, fried catfish and okra a favorite, at the Salmon House, a traveler's hotel built in 1867 in the Greek Revival tradition. Later, the hotel became famous as Miss Mary Bobo's Boarding House, purchased in 1908 by the venerable Mary Bobo, who lived to the fine vintage of 101 years. The locals catered to Jack, who was their reigning king but the king of a village—the proverbial big fish in a little pond. National adulation was not yet his.

Jack's grandnephew Jess Motlow, a superb whiskey taster and raconteur, recalled that Uncle Jack "was a tidy little man, vain, exactin', but generous."[16] At times quick tempered, Jack had to have that elu-sive quality of "exactin'" to succeed—especially with the revenuers looking over his shoulder. As for his vanity, who else was going to boost his ego? Not his mother and father, both long dead. Vanity was a prerequisite for every great capitalist and industrialist, especially when making a product constantly judged by the consumer. Jack was fond not only of himself and of his own liquor but of the ladies. He enjoyed female companionship and always had an eye on an eligible young woman; he loved to dance and was a favorite partner among the ladies for his quickness of foot. A romantic interest eluded him, however; for now he remained a preening bachelor, his matrimonial fate up for grabs.

THE TRUTH IS, the apple of Jack's eye was the Hollow, where he enjoyed the camaraderie of man and beast and had no time for female entanglements. Even though his distillery's capacity had increased 50 percent from 1877 to 1884, he remained a jack-of-all-trades at the Hollow. He was very hands-on–"exactin'"–and still insisted on tasting every barrel of whiskey, relishing the musky flavor and the tingling in the nasal passages. He did so with good form–that is, using the tip of the tongue. He never let the whiskey reach the rear of his mouth and absolutely never swallowed, as that would numb his tastebuds, and he kept water close at hand to rinse the palate between tastes. Maximum sensitivity to every nuance of his whiskey was paramount. While Jack vigilantly monitored the quality personally, he knew he needed help managing the operation, especially since he was planning to double his capacity.

To delegate some of his responsibilities, Jack turned to the son of his one-time mentor Colonel John Mason Hughes: William "Bill" Hughes, whom he hired circa 1885. Jack's hiring of Bill, whom he'd first met fifteen years earlier, signaled how much respect he held for the colonel. Bill was a strapping young man, standing 5 foot, 10 inches and weighing in at 175 pounds, with black hair and brown eyes. Now age twenty-four, he had been around stills almost his entire life and, both physically intimidating and mentally quick, was perfect management material.[17] Bill was very bright, even attending a military academy for a time, and he'd learned Latin, which was quite unique, considering that the language was reserved for those planning to attend an elite university or join the priesthood. Because Bill was also nimble with numbers, Jack initially charged him with handling the bookkeeping. Within two years, however, Hughes would become the head distiller. Now his physical presence came into play, as he easily discouraged the workers from taking it upon themselves to taste the whiskey–whiskey they wouldn't spit out.

Jack Daniel, who loved fast horses, was the big man about town. In 1886 he posed for a professional photographer in Nashville.

It was Hughes who would groom Jack's other pivotal hire: Lem Motlow, his sister Nettie's boy and Jack's eventual heir apparent. Lem, who enjoyed the luxury of a few years of schooling at the Lynchburg Normal Academy, first came to work for Jack in 1880 when he was about ten years old.[18] He had no choice: as the oldest of ten children, he had to help support the family. Lemmie, as Jack called him, was big and husky and enjoyed portraying himself as the mountaineer type. Yet contradicting that image, his voice was high-pitched, which resulted in the other boys teasing him mercilessly. Fortunately, Lemmie wasn't afraid to mix it up; he was always fixin' to fight.[19] Like Uncle Jack, he had his idiosyncrasies of dress: in later years he wore a fine black broadcloth suit, with a white shirt unbuttoned at the collar, and sported a wide-brimmed black hat but never a tie, regardless of the occasion. He was fond of saying, "I think wearing a necktie is a hypocritical display."[20] Perhaps he knew that men were base creatures, ultimately interested in only carnal pleasures, like whiskey.

Lem's first jobs were restricted to the farm and included slopping the hogs, tending the cattle, and chopping cordwood—just as his rising uncle had done for Dan Call. When one of Jack's friends, the Civil War veteran Scott Davis, swung by for a visit, he encountered Lem up to his knees in mud and unspeakables, slopping the hogs. Davis turned to Jack, "What in the Hell do you mean letting your sister's boy do this? You could give him somethin' else to do."

"I'm just tryin' him out," replied Jack. "If he sticks, I'll give him this place." Yes, Lem was going to have to climb the ladder from the bottom rung in the dung.

Jack didn't bring Lem into the distillery until his nephew was almost eighteen years old; it was August 1887. He put Lem in charge of making the charcoal, an important job because the quality of the charcoal affected the whiskey during the pivotal stage of filtration. When the sap was down in the winter, Lem would trudge into the tree groves, along with a team of mules, to cut the hard sugar maple trees. The wood was sawed into narrow, square lengths—like over-sized matchsticks—then stacked in racks six feet high and burned but extinguished before it turned to ash. To grind up the charcoal to the proper size, Lem, who was paid $9 a month, used the same machine that ground up cattle bones for fertilizer.[21]

About the time that Lem was brought into the still operations, he moved in with Bill Hughes, who was living in a little house on the distillery's property. Adopting the mentor role, Bill taught Lem book-keeping and prepared him to eventually take over the distillery. In appreciation of Bill's value, Jack rewarded him well. When Bill married Mary Emaline Merrill of Winchester, Tennessee, Uncle Jack, as he was now known to all his employees, hosted a fine reception for them when they returned to Lynchburg, presenting the newlyweds with a full set of Iron china and a bounty of twenty $20 gold pieces at the reception.[22] Lem continued to board with the couple until the arrival of their first child, Joe Daniel Hughes, yet another Jack Daniel namesake. Also in Jack's honor, Wiley Daniel, who remained close to his little brother, had named a son Jasper Newton, born in 1876, and

Sister Nettie christened her youngest, born in 1889, Jack Daniel Mot-low.[23] Clearly, family, friends, and employees adored Uncle Jack.

A savvy manager of men, Jack hired both Bill and Lem because they were young and enthusiastic, they could be molded in his image, and, of most import, he knew that they were completely loyal to him. Loyalty was paramount to a man who had learned to be distrustful of everyone since the days of the Civil War. Intent on extending his nepotistic empire—and once again demonstrating how important family was to him—Jack brought in another nephew, Wiley's eldest of six children, Felix Calaway "Dick" Daniel, who was born in 1868 and named in honor of his grandfathers. The reason behind the nickname Dick remains elusive. Though Jack assumed a patriarchal role, his quick temper—and he did have one—brought him into conflict with his nephews, especially with Lem, who was also strong-willed. To keep Lem sharp, as well as to show him who was boss, Jack staged arguments with his nephew over everything from predicting the corn crop to the importance of quality. One acrimonious and recurring dis-agreement was over production capacity. No matter how wildly pop-ular No. 7 became, Jack capped off daily production at 300 gallons of whiskey; he preferred to focus on maintaining high standards. Even though this amount was twice what Jack had been distilling and had the potential annual sales revenue net the excise tax of over $150,000, Lem wasn't satisfied; he was always pushing to expand, to extend the No. 7 franchise.

DESPITE THE ARGUMENTS, whether staged or real, Jack and Lem's relationship endured, and the mood at the distillery was upbeat and playful. As a testimony to Jack's endearing persona, among the work-ers were Uncle Nearis's rather brawny boys George, now in his late twenties, and Eli, in his early twenties. The two young men saw the same dignified qualities in Jack that their father saw in Dan Call. To create an esprit de corps, Jack encouraged tests of manhood between still hands, who numbered between six and ten, which became a most entertaining daily affair. The greatest test was to lift a 50-gallon barrel of whiskey (more than 400 pounds, considering that a gallon weighed in at 8.3 pounds), set it on a knee, and then drink from the bunghole.

Chief Alton was one of Lem's prized Tennessee walking horses. The Nearis boys relished lifting his horses, to the delight of distillery visitors.

Only Eli, nicknamed Samson, succeeded, to rousing cheers of the crowd. Even more delightful to onlookers, but to Lem's dismay, the Nearis boys would lift his 1,200-pound Tennessee walking horse, named Sport—one boy with a shoulder under the front legs, the other with a shoulder under the less-desirable end.[24] At such festive times, Old No. 7 was poured liberally—for favored customers.

The boisterous Jack Daniel Distillery was the antithesis of a gloomy northern factory. Just consider the steel mills in the Pittsburgh area, ruled over by another man with Scottish blood in his veins—Andrew Carnegie. Death by accident occurred indiscriminately in mills, with such fatalities accounting for as much as an astounding 20 percent of the area's total male mortality—the list of dead in a given year equivalent to that of a minor battle in the Civil War.[25] In such places as Pittsburgh, according to an investigation by the Senate Committee on Labor and Education, the average working man couldn't afford a "decent maintenance" for his family. In the dank, drafty, and generally dilapidated rowhouses that dominated industrial centers, there was no indoor plumbing (privys were often built over any small streams) and much of the water was polluted; therefore, typhoid was rampant. This putrid situation was in stark contrast with Moore County, where the spring water was pure and the air clean. Also, the poor factory town housewives had little or no room for a garden to supplement their husband's meager earnings, while men like Eli and George Green enjoyed a bounty of their own fresh produce and even a modest tobacco patch to supplement their income. A strained back from shifting a cask of whiskey was about the worst the Green boys faced.

The destitute conditions of northern factory workers sparked such labor strikes and violence as the Haymarket Riot of 1886. This nasty episode transpired in Chicago, where men working at the McCormick Reaper Company (the reaper was a godsend for southern farmers) went on strike for better wages. The company brought in nonunion strikebreakers, sparking a pitched battle between labor and police on May 3. The next day a protest against police brutality was held in Haymarket Square, at which time enterprising anarchists elected to throw a bomb into the police ranks. Rioting ensued, with seven policemen and eleven protesters losing their lives. It was a tumultuous and desperate time for America's factory workers, as their flesh and blood built the country into a powerhouse. To soothe their pain, they turned to the comfort of the tavern and whiskey. Whiskey invigorated them, made them feel alive, and it was, they believed, medicinal in keeping the throat cleared of dust and smoke spewing from the factories' brick chimneys.

Contrary to the avaricious capitalists who drove their laborers like mules, Jack was not only a paternal employer, but he was fast becoming a patriarch of the community. His pivotal role in bringing a bank—the town's first—to Lynchburg epitomized the leadership position he had now assumed.

THE JUPITER OF WALL STREET and the Napoleon of American banking was J. Pierpont Morgan, who financed many an industrial enterprise, as well as many an Episcopal church, to cleanse his philanderer's soul.[26] In the 1880s, Morgan, when not romancing the ladies, and his firm, Drexel, Morgan & Co., were busy spending tens of millions of dollars consolidating and controlling railroads–to achieve marketplace stability, naturally. In 1889, they also handled the initial public offering for Edison General Electric, a company of some repute over a hundred years later. While men like Morgan and the nation's big cities, which were wired with electricity and telegraph and phone service, marched bravely toward the twentieth century, in Lynchburg, key elements for modernizing the town's infrastructure were nonexistent. There wasn't even a bank. Like an old man reliving his youth through twice-told stories, Lynchburg, it appeared, was stuck in the past.

For those seeking the speediest escape route from the quaint but primitive Lynchburg, there were only two major routes: the pike to Fayetteville or the pike to Tullahoma. The road was narrow, graveled, but rough, and travelers had to pay a toll; therefore, you ventured to the larger towns only if it was absolutely necessary. Now, as for banking, there was a hack that made a daily run up to Shelbyville for those who wanted to deposit their money in an institution, but most merchants simply kept large sums in their own safes, and citizens employed the old mattress method. However, by the late 1880s, the inconvenience of not having a bank had become overly burdensome.

Finally, one day in 1887, the cashier of the First National Bank of Tullahoma, L. D. Hickerson, got to talking with Jack Daniel and some other prominent citizens about building a bank in Lynchburg. He proposed that if the men in Moore County raised half the needed capital to start a bank–to be called Farmers Bank–he and his associates would contribute the other half. It was agreed, with capital set at $50,000 and the charter granted in April 1888. (In comparison, Pierpont Morgan and his father, Junius, were together worth about $30 million in 1889.)[27] Farmers Bank boasted twenty-five original subscribers, including Jack, who bought ten shares for $1,000, and one fellow who went so far as to buy twenty-five shares. All told, a total of two hundred shares were issued initially, or $20,000 of the authorized $50,000. While Jack certainly could have invested more, he remained haunted by the poverty of yesteryear, refusing to overextend himself even by such a modest amount. Besides, his priority was to conserve his capital for buying large quantities of corn for his distillery and for paying taxes when he took whiskey out of bond.

Jack and the other investors purchased a building on the north side of the town square from the distiller John Eaton for what is still the bank's home today. An ideal six-ton safe for locking up the deposits was located and bought; however, carting it to Lynchburg would prove considerably more difficult than raising the money. It had to be shipped over from Tullahoma, a daunting prospect, considering that the twelve-mile stretch of graveled road was in rotten shape from spring rains. Relishing the challenge, Jack took charge of this semi-herculean task. He sent his most reliable driver, Lee Waggoner, and a team of six mules to Tullahoma. Under normal conditions, it was an eight-hour journey between Lynchburg and Tullahoma, but with the roads wet and soft, Lee didn't get more than a few miles on the return trip before his wagon was sunk up to its hubs. The bedeviled man sent for help.

On arriving at the scene and unloading the safe, the Lynchburg men scratched their heads as they looked from the safe to the wagon, to the mules, to one another, and then back to the safe. Presumably, the mules, for their part, simply stared blankly into the distance. The men decided to lay parallel tracks in front of the safe and pull it along, but the process proved far too slow. At this point, Mr. Monroe Green, a Lynchburg timber man, volunteered to assume the task. He had the strongest mules, accustomed to pulling heavy loads of cut trees via sled. Even so, it took him almost two months to transport the safe to the bank. For the townspeople, it must have seemed that the pyramids of Egypt had been built quicker, and the daily progress of the six-ton safe became the town's running joke. Despite the debacle, these men were heroes for finally bringing banking to Lynchburg.

Due to strong leadership, Farmers Bank would become one of the richest "country" banks in the country. For its president, Jack and company elected Captain W. H. Holt, a thick, serious man in his late thirties. Holt, who would remain president until 1901, had proven his business acumen; he had the largest farm in the county, with many hundreds of acres, and lived in a palatial brick mansion in Lynchburg. For the cashier, the man who would actually handle the money, they hired J. W. Motlow, a studious yet whimsical-looking fellow with a receding hairline, long but trim sideburns, and a walrus mustache. By putting one of the Motlow clan in this key position, Jack had an inside ally, which was always a savvy strategy. After the first year of operation, in April 1890, the bank's board declared a 6 percent dividend—in subsequent years it would increase to 10 percent—and for the next fifty years a dividend would be paid every year except one, an astounding record for any institution. Also, in April, Jack Daniel, already a director, was elected vice president, a position he would hold for some twenty years.[28] It was a major personal triumph; the boy who once had but a few dollars to his name was now a banker. It signified that Jack had ascended to community leader, a dozen years after the 1877 distillers' meeting—a meeting that the *Lynchburg Sentinel* reporter had not even mentioned Jack's attending.

IT WAS A PROSPEROUS TIME for Lynchburg and for America at large. The post–Civil War period was marked by rapid industrialization, with U.S. national wealth eventually ballooning from $30 billion in 1870 to almost $127 billion in 1900, achieved, in part, by the ruthless pursuit of profit.[29] In 1889, the protectionist, procapitalist Republicans, led by U.S. president Benjamin Harrison, were back in the Executive Mansion, promising an ever fervent worship of mammon. It was now the heart of the Gilded Age, a nickname bestowed by Mark Twain in 1873, when he and Charles Dudley Warner coauthored *The Gilded Age,* a satire of get-rich-quick schemes and political shenanigans. It was the eve of the Gay Nineties, a decade in which Caligula-like excess and conspicuous consumption would achieve new heights. Not confined to Fifth Avenue, New York, the gilded life was also on parade in Nashville. The flashy Nashville saloons in what was known as the Men's Quarter, where upstanding patrons could lead double lives with impunity, would become favored destination points for Jack Daniel. This man on the rise—now entering his forties and still without wife—would have to withstand the enticing indulgences offered by the Gay Nineties.

9

TAKING ON NASHVILLE

✶·✶

The cheapest and easiest way to become an influential man and be looked up to by the community at large, was to stand behind a bar, wear a cluster-diamond pin, and sell whiskey.

—Mark Twain

Touted as the "Minneapolis of the South," Nashville boomed economically, as railroads and steamboats vied for business at this major river port. Where cotton had been the dominant crop in the antebellum days, now corn, oats, wheat, and hay were the leading crops to be found along the wharves and at the grain elevators used by the railroad. In addition, sweat-stained farmers drove their livestock to market here; slimy speculators shipped barges of oil; and gritty hill men floated massive 200-foot-long timber rafts down the Cumberland River. Although steamboats still lined the wharves, many of them nothing more than a muddy bank with wooden planks extending to the ship, railroads—being faster and more dependable—were increasingly the dominant mode of transportation. The growing network of tracks opened up relatively cheap access to markets well beyond the reach of the meandering rivers. Consequently, if you didn't have a presence in Nashville, now the thirty-eighth largest city in the country, you were nothing. This included Jack and his fellow distillers.

No longer was it adequate to merely ship a few barrels to the city. To compete with the much larger and more flourishing distilleries to the north, Jack had to securely establish himself in Nashville; he had to make his mark on this thriving metropolis and distribution center; and he had to avoid the pitfalls of the Gilded Age, including the conspicuous spending, the gambling, and the greed. If he allowed sin to envelop his soul or if he became stagnant as a businessman, he would be squashed. In 1890, Jack had reached another pivotal point in his career.

Though he was no Vanderbilt living a gluttonous life on Manhattan's Fifth Avenue, Jack, who had taken to sporting a diamond ring and a matching pin, was certainly prosperous by Lynchburg standards. Except for a moderately receding hairline and a few flecks of gray, he still exuded a youthful energy with his sporty goatee and soft, boyish face. By 1890, he owned over three hundred acres and would soon be paying over $17,000—a substantial sum—in local and state taxes.[1] In addition to the accolades he garnered for his strong, yet smooth whiskey, he was recognized as a prominent farmer and was referred to as Captain, out of respect for his social position. When he sold livestock, it made the papers; on one occasion the *Lynchburg Daily Falcon* noted, "Cap. Jack Daniel has sold a hundred head of fine beef cattle."[2] Unlike in his youth, luck now seemed to follow him, even to rub off on his hired hands, including the one-time petty thief Ned Waggoner, who, the paper reported, "dug up an old copper cent piece on the farm of Jack Daniel a few days ago which was made in 1808."[3] Luck tended to make men soft.

It would have been easy for Jack to become complacent, but one man was determined to prevent that from happening: Lemuel Motlow. Now in his mid-twenties, Jack's nephew was more headstrong than ever and had assumed most of the managerial duties at the distillery. His mentor Bill Hughes, along with his wife, Emma, and two young boys, would soon move on to a Winchester, Tennessee, distillery, and the Green brothers would disappear to places unknown.[4] One driving force behind Lem was the unfortunate fact that his mother—Jack's sister Finetta—died in 1891, leaving behind six children in need of support. Lem accepted much of the financial responsibility for his siblings. Not wanting to emulate Jack's bachelorhood, four years after his mother's death he married Miss Clara Reagor, a fine girl from Flat Creek in Bedford County. He then bought the family farm that once belonged to John T. Motlow, where matriarch Agnes was buried.[5] Taking on these paternal and spousal roles made Lem more controlling at work; specifically, he pushed Jack to expand, which became a bone of contention between the two.

Jack still refused to make more than 300 gallons of whiskey a day, however; he cared too deeply for quality, desiring to make whiskey a gentleman's drink. He was content with establishing a niche for himself in the high-end market. His adopted motto: "'Y God, everyday we make it, we're going to make it the best we can." In addition, while Jack was charismatic, when it came to whiskey making, he preferred to keep a relatively low profile to avoid undue attention from the extremist temperance soldiers; in the 1890–1891 *Tennessee State Gazeteer,* a business directory, the only distiller listed in Lynchburg was John Eaton. Besides, why expand further when he now owned the Hollow and held the dominant position in the local market? Heck, he was even buying whiskey from quality Lincoln County Process distillers for resale through his warehouses. On May 21, 1890, under the careful watch of a government agent, he bought and transferred 1,880 gallons of whiskey from J. E. Spencer & Co. He purchased additional barrels from Spencer later in the year and again in 1891.[6] Jack also bought 100 barrels from Tolley & Eaton, stored in their Kelso warehouse, and 52 barrels from Tolley & Cannon, paying 65 cents per proof gallon and 60 cents, respectively–a nifty bargain.[7] What Jack had to recognize was that he had gained his elevated status, in part, through attrition.

Many of the leading old timers were finished. Although Jack was only in his early forties–entering the prime of his business career–John T. Motlow and Walten Hiles were in their sixties and John D. Tolley was in his fifties. While a decade earlier there had been eighty-four distilleries in Tennessee, as of January 1, 1891, only forty-seven had survived. Tennessee had a collective daily capacity of 2,608 gallons, bested by ten states, with Illinois in the lead at over 180,000 gallons, followed by Kentucky at over 140,000 gallons.[8] Thankfully, the federal government's high tariff on imported spirits resulted in virtually no

The Motlow clan included the Civil War veteran Felix, center, and Lem, lower left (the only one without a tie and with his son Reagor). His wife, Clara, sits respectfully a step behind.

imports—only top-shelf straight whiskies made it across the border— which aided the American distiller's cause. On the other hand, for many of the modest Tennessee distillers like Jack, who handcrafted their whiskey, the top-shelf straight whiskies were their primary competition.

Ultimately, Jack Daniel's survival—whether he had a niche in the high-end market or mass produced his whiskey as Lem wanted to— remained contingent on establishing a significant presence in Nashville, particularly as the railroad made the country ever smaller. But as he encountered competitors more fervent than his local Lincoln County Process comrades, would he have the stomach for the ensuing battles over market share?

AS THE RAILROADS and the markets expanded—the Tennessee sour mash men pushing north, while the Kentucky bourbon boys pushed south—Jack became better acquainted with his northern brothers.

There was no love lost here. Having declared itself neutral during the Civil War, Kentucky was considered gutless, in the eyes of some southerners. And while it leaned toward the Confederacy early on, it gravitated toward Lincoln later. But like Tennessee, Kentucky had rich soil and clean, cool water percolating through limestone rock. The horse folk who were raising champions were convinced that the mineral-rich, limestone-filtered spring water made for strong bones in their thoroughbreds; the distillers credited the water for a superior bourbon. They were proud, almost arrogant, about their whiskey. A barrel with a Kentucky bourbon label, according to them, was unequaled. It was due time for Jack to change that perception.

The Beam family distillery, in particular, had the tradition and the name recognition Jack wanted for himself. It's been said that what this family didn't know about whiskey making wasn't worth spit. It began with Jacob Beam. In 1788, Jacob had breached the Cumberland Gap and settled in the blue hills of Kentucky. An enterprising farmer and a miller, he used his excess grain to distill bourbon and sold his first barrel of whiskey in 1795. Now Jack never knew Jacob, but the founder's great-grandson, James "Jim" Beauregard Beam, was another matter. Affectionately known as "Big B," charismatic Jim kept his prematurely gray hair close-cropped and his mustache neatly trimmed; his defining feature was the bowler hat he tended to perch on his head at precarious angles. Once he and his brother-in-law Albert J. Hart took the reins of the family business in 1894, Big B would guide the distillery for sixty-seven years, which included waiting out prohibition. He also cultured their famous strain of yeast—a guarded family secret—which is still used today, and he relocated their plant to Clermont, just south of Louisville, where he could look out over verdant Bernheim Forest.[9] Prior to Big B's ascension, D. M. Beam and Son were distilling just over 360 gallons a day in 1890; within two years of taking charge, Big B boosted production to 450 gallons a day and had built three warehouses capable of holding 10,000 barrels. Beam and Hart "are known as being among the best practical distillers in the county," the *Nelson County Record* extolled, noting that "the product is not to be excelled by anyone." At the time they had one brand: Old Tub. Not exactly an alluring name, but the distillery did indeed excel and Big B enjoyed "the comfort of life at his country residence, where he entertains with lavish hands."[10] Big B sounded very much like J. D.

There were other formidable competitors on Jack's horizon in Kentucky, such as Captain George T. Stagg, who was aggressively creating a national name for the Old Fashioned Copper Distillery brands of Leestown, Kentucky, one of the state's oldest settlements. A hundred years later, Stagg's Ancient Age and Blanton's Single Barrel would still be rolling out of Leestown warehouses. There was the Labrot & Graham distillery, established in 1838 near Frankfort, whose impressive plant with its limestone walls stood out starkly against surrounding blue waters and green pastures. There was the Louisville native George G. Brown, a descendent of William Brown, who had been a scout for Daniel Boone. In 1870, George G. started distilling what he would soon label as Old Forester and founded the company that would become Brown-Forman, a powerhouse over a hundred years later. In addition, what would become the venerable Maker's Mark, another enduring label, was founded in the 1840s by T. W. Samuels, a *college-educated* man. Located in Deatsville (now in Loretto), Samuels's distillery had a daily capacity of 645 gallons and storage for 14,000 barrels. The *Nelson County Record* described Samuels as "one of the most solid business men in the county, and personally is quite an interesting and companiable gentleman, being well posted upon historical and industrial subjects." His plant was "well constructed, and equipped with all the modern improvements known in the distiller business. . . . The warehouses are well arranged and perfectly ventilated and are iron-clad."[11] Most of these bourbon operations were managed so effectively that they would survive the ages, an indication of who Jack was up against.

ANOTHER POTENTIAL THREAT Jack faced was the despicable Whiskey Trust, an amalgamation of distilleries and distributors that had been organized in Peoria, Illinois, to control the region's whiskey trade by either absorbing or destroying competitors. While Jack didn't compete with the blended whiskies of Illinois, there was a possibility that other distillers might follow suit in organizing a powerful amalgamation. (In fact, in the late 1890s, a group in Kentucky would do just that.) A prominent name attached to the Whiskey Trust was none other than General B. Raum, who had quit the Internal Revenue Service to lobby in Washington on behalf of the trust, to protect it from any politicians who refused to turn a blind eye to monopolies. Raum was all the more reason for Jack and the sour mash men to despise this gargantuan that was cursed in the same breath as John D. Rockefeller's Standard Oil, the model trust of the day, if there can be such a thing. It was a matter of economics and greed.

The Whiskey Trust had been sown in Peoria because the region, extremely rich in corn and cold spring water, was a natural breeding ground for distilleries. The result was overproduction, one catalyst for firms to merge. Another contributing factor to the glut was that the stillers in this area concentrated on making blended or rectified whiskey that didn't require aging; therefore, they could make huge volumes cheaply. Debilitating price wars broke out as they attempted to unload their whiskey. Eventually, a few of the more powerful distilleries recognized the need to control the market, to sustain prices, if they were to make a profit. As the Illinois distiller Charles C. Clarke said, "We thought we could make better profits and create a more stable business by organizing into a trust. A trust agreement was drawn up, which was a copy of the Standard Oil trust agreement, but changed to suit our business."[12]

In 1887, desperate and avaricious blended-whiskey producers like Clarke turned their stock over to nine trustees, essentially a board of directors that was charged with making policy and managing the business. In this early incarnation, it was known as the Distillers' and Cattle Feeders' Trust, or the "Octopus," with its headquarters in Peoria. The trust soon controlled more than eighty plants in Illinois, Indiana, and Pennsylvania. A number of tactics were used to force independents to join up or to drive them out of business: the trust lowered prices (and would then later raise prices to reap profits); it bribed distributors not to carry competing brands by offering substantial rebates, which were illegal, if the distributor didn't handle competitive brands for six months; and it paid men to stay out of the business. For those distilleries that refused to join the trust, more nefarious consequences awaited. When the Chicago distiller H. H. Shufeldt & Co. refused to join up in 1888, dynamite was thrown onto the distillery's roof, causing much damage but resulting in no convictions. Shufeldt joined the trust within three years. In 1891, the secretary of the trust, George Gibson, offered an undercover agent for the Internal Revenue Service $25,000 to blow up another Chicago distillery.[13] Mysterious fires hit other uncooperative distillers. Of the eighty-six distilleries that joined—mostly in Illinois and Indiana—only about a dozen were kept in operation, as any inefficient or geographically undesirable plants were shut down; even so, during the early 1890s, the trust produced 95 percent of the alcohol consumed in the United States.[14] The fact that the trust was clearly in violation of the 1890 Sherman Anti-Trust Act was apparently inconsequential; the government rarely enforced the associated laws.

Not until 1893 did a congressional committee investigate the trust, and shortly thereafter, the Supreme Court ordered the trust dissolved. Yet it was promptly resurrected under the awfully similar-sounding Distilling and Cattle Feeding Company. Every time the amalgamation ran into trouble, it simply renamed itself, changing to the American Spirits Manufacturing Company, then to the Standard Distilling and Distributing Company, and next to the Distillers' Securities Corporation. Even in 1899, it was still reaching out with its tentacles, grabbing up rye whiskey operations in Pennsylvania, and it rivaled Standard Oil in notoriety.[15] Like the Whiskey Ring had been, the Whiskey Trust was a distant evil that didn't directly affect Jack Daniel—for the moment. However, it did present a formidable challenge to those bourbon men who desired to penetrate the lucrative midwestern and northern markets. By obstructing the northern migration of bourbon whiskey, the trust created heightened competition in southern markets.

THOUGH HE WAS VEXED BY the arrogant Kentucky bourbon boys and the "Octopus" to the north, it was the appearance of a worthy rival not far from Tullahoma, in adjacent Coffee County, that threatened Jack Daniel's status as the region's preeminent distiller. This rival was Emmanuel "Manny" Schwab, a German Jew with big aspirations. When one took into consideration Schwab's family background, he was clearly a man to be reckoned with and a man of questionable ethics who might not play fair. During the Civil War, his father, Abram Schwab, a merchant based in Knoxville and Nashville, had pocketed a tidy profit smuggling goods through Union lines. Once Union troops occupied Tennessee in 1862, he and a partner, Meier Salzkotter, contracted a Nashville carpenter to build a light spring wagon with a false bottom, providing about three inches between the two floors. Schwab smuggled everything from much-needed medicine to gray caps for the Confederate soldiers, making $20,000 in blood money off the latter. Salzkotter, who smuggled quinine and other medicines from Louisville to Nashville, was eventually caught and imprisoned. His wife, who happened to be Abram Schwab's daughter Cecelia, turned to prostitution while he was in jail—that and the fervent pursuit of blood money were telling commentaries on the Schwab family's morals.

After the war, Abram's son Emmanuel went to work as a bookkeeper for the George A. Dickel Company. Dickel, an immigrant from Frankfurt-am-Main, Germany, and a former cobbler, had founded a liquor wholesale company in Nashville.[16] Like many distributors, he bought whiskey from a variety of distilleries and blended it at his discretion for resale. But then he discovered the modest Cascade Distillery in Normandy, Coffee County, which was making exceptional whiskey, and started selling the Cascade brand, rather than blending it. Meanwhile, Emmanuel Schwab married Dickel's sister-in-law and slowly took on more responsibility at the firm. To better assimilate and promote himself in Baptist country, he dropped the "c" from his name and added Victor as a first name, an indication of the ambition he harbored. As one of the company's secretaries observed, "Mr. Victor was the shrewdest, smartest fellow around this part of the country."

In 1886, Dickel suffered a riding accident and had to remove himself from the company's daily affairs. Finally realizing his opportunity, Shwab took charge, bought two-thirds' interest in Cascade—he would attain complete control by the late 1890s—and made Dickel its sole distributor. Aggressively pushing Cascade as the finest sour mash, Shwab marketed it as "Mellow as Moonlight." As the story goes, McLin Davis, a partner at Cascade, had hypothesized that cooling the mash under the light of the moon delivered a smoother taste. And that's what they did. The distillery started bottling some of its product in 1891, transporting the whiskey in unfinished wooden boxes with a picture of a still burned into the side.

What really piqued Jack's interest was Shwab's construction of two saloons in Nashville to extend his Cascade franchise. In 1887, Shwab, in partnership with Dickel, built the Climax Saloon at Church and Union Streets, and in 1893, he built the Silver Dollar Saloon at Broad Street and Second Avenue. The Climax advertised itself as the headquarters for "Old Cascade Tennessee Whiskey"–the use of "Old" taking a page out of Jack's marketing book. However, it offered a wee bit more than just the headquarters for Old Cascade. Of all the saloons in Nashville, the Climax was the most famous, or infamous, sporting house in the city.

With four sculpted angels greeting guests outside and marble floors inside, the Climax was the most ornate and debauched, fashionable and rakish saloon. It epitomized the Gay Nineties. On the first floor and the basement level were the saloon and a theater, where cancan dancers and other acts paraded across the stage. The second floor featured another bar and pool tables. Above that . . . a brothel–and it wasn't a noble tribute to Shwab's fallen sister. The rooms were decorated with embossed wood or papier maché wallpaper and offered false interior walls for hiding, in case of a police raid. Now Jack– though not a churchgoer, he was from a good Primitive Baptist family–wasn't about to open a saloon with a brothel upstairs. However, the notion of becoming a saloonkeeper to extend the No. 7 franchise was appealing. As Mark Twain said, "The cheapest and easiest way to become an influential man and be looked up to by the community at large, was to stand behind a bar, wear a cluster-diamond pin, and sell whiskey."[17] Jack already had the pin and the whiskey.

IN THE SPRING OF 1892, Jack was in the midst of planning to open two saloons in Lynchburg–the Red Dog and the White Rabbit–to satisfy his local patrons. The White Rabbit had a bar running the entire length of the room, spittoons at intervals that were conducive to convenient spitting, a brass rail to rest a weary foot, impressive mirrors for keeping an eye out, and a fancy palmetto fan. The saloonkeepers were clean-shaven except for a waxed mustache, had neatly oiled hair parted in the middle, and sported suspenders and ties tucked into their white dress shirts, sleeves rolled up to the elbows. But then, in November 1892, Lynchburg suffered a devastating blow.

It was a typical Friday morning–about 5 A.M.–when Harry Dance, trusted proprietor of the Dance Drug Company, arrived at his pharmacy. As was his habit, he swept up any loose trash and then burned it in the street in front of his store. He failed to notice, however, that some sparks had clung to his broom, which he stored away. Within minutes, his pharmacy was burning. Shortly after 5:30, he sounded the alarm. Men, women, and children came on the run and did everything in their power to check the fire, passing buckets of water and beating back the flames. Despite their efforts, the east side and most of the south side of the square burned to the ground in a flash. Frantically, merchants dragged their wares from their stores, only to witness the goods burn in the street as the fire continued to spread. Lem Motlow lost two vacant buildings, as well as two others, one occupied by the Moore County Theatre, the other by a grocer. All four were only partially covered by insurance. Rising from the smoldering ruins, wisps of smoke snaked through the air–the smell of this smoke far more acrid than the gentle odor of sugar maple burning at the distillery. "Lynchburg presents a scene of desolation that beggars description with most of her business houses in ashes," the *Lynchburg Falcon* correspondent reported, "her business men burned out, and leavings of the wreckage scattered here and there about the square."[18] Once again, Jack escaped unscathed. The saloons would do a brisk business as the town was rebuilt.

Another Jack Daniel addition to the town was a Silver Cornet Band. To promote his No. 7 throughout the countryside, as well as to cultivate a festive atmosphere conducive to drinking whiskey, he established a ten-member cornet band in 1892. The instruments included a cornet, a helicon bass, alto horns, a snare drum, and a bass drum, the latter with Jack Daniel's Old No. 7 painted on each drum head. As the current master distiller Jimmy Bedford said, "Mr. Jack had a philosophy that good music and good whiskey make a great combination."[19] Jack bought a wagon especially designed to carry the band, and he ordered uniforms for the musicians from a Sears & Roebuck

The White Rabbit Saloon, with its fancy palmetto fan, was a favored Lynchburg watering hole.

catalog, spending $227.70—even so, they were a bit motley looking, with their crooked ties and a mix of bowlers, felt hats, and caps.[20]

In the 1890s, the cornet band became a social hub all across rural America. On hot, lazy summer evenings, Lynchburg townsfolk came down off their verandas and gathered around an octagonal bandstand near the courthouse to listen to the music. Those farther out arrived by surrey and buggy. Kids flocked to barrels filled with ice, grabbed a handful, and sucked on the refreshing coldness. Outside of Dance's drugstore, reputedly the first establishment with electricity, a peanut roaster was set up. In addition to the local concerts, the Jack Daniel's Silver Cornet Band played at saloon grand openings, July Fourth celebrations, political rallies—in 1896, it played at rallies supporting Democratic presidential candidate William Jennings Bryan—and even funerals.[21] "Amazing Grace," "Tennessee Waltz," and "Dixie" were favorites.

* * *

In 1892, Jack organized the Silver Cornet Band to promote his whiskey and create a festive atmosphere for drinking whiskey.

HOWEVER INSPIRING the cornet band was, it lacked sex appeal. Sex, even in the Victorian Age, sold. And, in his drive to become more competitive, that's the direction Jack now took. Sex. To appeal to a younger generation of drinkers, as well as to the female customer, Jack realized that he had to offer another brand to complement his Old No. 7. For this new brand, he settled on the Belle of Lincoln, a name suggesting that whiskey and women went hand in hand. Considering Jack's status as a bachelor, there was great speculation as to who this belle was. Was he secretly courting a lady from Lincoln County? Was he in love? In addition to this romantic vein, there was the possibility that he had named it after his half-sister Belle. In spite of his ill feeling toward his stepmother, he showed favor toward Belle, who, when she died prematurely in 1902, he had buried in the Daniel family plot. Closest to the truth, however, was the fact that many a distiller had a Belle label. There were, at varying times, the Belle of Nelson and the Belle of Anderson, among others. Just the name softened the throat-burning drink and enticed customers, who naturally felt more refined swigging a Belle than a less appetizing-sounding Yellow Spring or Old Crow. In a side note, these brands had yet to be sealed in bottles with fancy labels, but when distillers did do so, Jack opted to put an actual bell on his Belle label, rather than a beautiful woman—indicative of his relatively wholesome ways. By the mid-1890s, Jack's Belle would be as popular as his Old No. 7 and would have a strong presence in Tennessee, Louisiana, Alabama, and Texas. He had now taken several steps to bolster his franchise; however, there was still the need to establish a physical presence in Nashville.

JACK ELECTED TO leapfrog Nashville. Instead, in his most incisive move to buck the Kentucky boys, in 1892 he opened a large wholesale warehouse in Hopkinsville, Kentucky, at the corner of 7th and Virginia Streets. That's right, *Kentucky.* North of Nashville and not far across the state line, Hopkinsville was the county seat for Christian County—a mighty fine county for peddling sinful liquor—and, with a sizable railroad depot, it was a major center of commerce. More so than liquor, the citizens of Christian County took their tobacco very seriously, as was made evident during a 1907 riot. That year, members of the Dark Tobacco District Planters' Protective Association, which, like the distillers' trust, had been formed to control the sale of tobacco, became outraged when tobacco men bought cheap tobacco from farmers who weren't members of the association. In retaliation, about 250 masked "Night Riders"—that is, members of the association—attacked and captured police posts and cut telephone and telegraph wires. They proceeded to hunt down city officials and tobacco men to punish them. Even after the violence, Hopkinsville remained a crucial marketplace, and Shwab would open shop there, too. In Jack's warehouse, he had 10-gallon jugs, half-barrels, and barrels, which, in the *Lynchburg Sentinel* and other newspapers, he offered "for sale at reasonable prices. For further particulars, write us."[22] Simple and honest. Yet it appeared that he had foolishly neglected Nashville. Not so.

In his first serious foray into Nashville, Jack contracted with a liquor distributor there, W. T. & C. D. Gunter, a well-established firm located at 205 Broad Street, to handle his whiskey. At the same time, with the enthusiasm of a police raid on the Climax, Jack personally invaded the city's saloons. Jack's idea of marketing was not flashy ads in the newspapers or billboards plastered across buildings; no, he preferred to mingle with the people, the patrons of the Nashville saloons, and build a grassroots movement. With 158 saloons listed in the *1895 Nashville City Directory,* there were plenty of roots to cultivate. One reason for the proliferation of saloons was the introduction of mechanical refrigeration, which resulted in breweries doubling their capacity since they could better keep their beer from spoiling. More beer meant more saloons. Also, as pathetic a commentary as it was, in Nashville booze was safer to imbibe than the water. So much of the water was polluted that typhoid raged through the city. Consider that by 1898, the Nashville population was over 80,000 human beings, but the entire city, including private residences and public houses, hosted a mere 682 toilets and 52 urinals. Most people used outdoor privies indiscriminately–and death rates increased throughout the 1890s.[23]

When Jack ventured to Nashville, he didn't just avoid the water, he also steered clear of the ring of slums encircling the business district–slums filled with ramshackle houses, brothels, gambling dens, pawnshops, and, of course, saloons serving watered-down whiskey. Black Bottom was the most sordid of neighborhoods–the nickname alone requiring no further explanation. Racial tension remained acute, especially in these slums where blacks had been effectively herded, with violence often fueled by whiskey. One particularly grisly incident in April 1892 originated outside of Nashville but culminated in a bloody climax in the city. In a small town to the north, two black men were accused of raping two white girls. One of the men was hung without delay by a mob; the other, Eph Grizzard, was thrown in a Nashville jail. When evidence allegedly linking him to the crime was made public, a bloodthirsty crowd of several thousand gathered in Nashville's public square. After attempting to disperse the crowd–an act of futility–the police stepped aside. The crazed people busted Grizzard out of jail, put a rope around his neck, and then threw him off the Cumberland River Bridge. There he hung, as gun toting vigilantes pumped more than fifty bullets into his semi-naked body; others enjoyed jerking the rope to see his limp body dance.[24]

The wharves were also a rough-and-tumble neighborhood that Jack now avoided. Even though the shipmates and the dockworkers guzzled whiskey while playing cards, shooting craps, and doing their utmost to out-curse each other, and the steamships, Jack knew from his Huntsville days, were an excellent place to peddle whiskey, in Nashville the market had all but dried up. This reversal of a once-lucrative market was courtesy of a certain Captain Ryman, who held a virtual monopoly on Nashville steamboats and who had gotten religion. Ryman had lips as narrow and stiff as his collar and sported no facial hair, the latter trait most uncharacteristic and suspect for the time. He founded a packet steamboat company that controlled trade on the Nashville section of the Cumberland River. For years, he served patrons whiskey in his floating saloons. But then, in 1885, the Methodist evangelist Sam Jones converted him. Out went the whiskey and in came the Union Gospel Tabernacle, funded by Ryman.

JACK'S TARGET WAS NOT the sordid slums or the wharves but the Men's Quarter, which was located on Cherry Street (now Fourth Avenue), between Church and Union Streets. This strip—about a hundred yards long—was the city's social center from 1895 to 1909. Bankers, lawyers, politicians, and newspapermen congregated here; the respectable and the wealthy, including judges, indulged their appetites on Cherry Street. They could smoke, drink, spit, and curse at will. Their more base instincts—not so far removed from the habits of their brethren in the slums and down at the wharves—could run wild. Needless to say, the only women found in the quarter were ladies of the evening, who rode carriages up and down Cherry Street soliciting business. As for women who stayed in surrounding hotels, they were not permitted in the lobbies and they always used a side entrance to access their room. Segregation of the sexes here typified the Victorian period: the men ruled the outside world, and the women were expected to remain at home, part of a secluded community. In a society governed by stringent etiquette, women kept house and entertained.

Three establishments served as the center of the action: Shwab's Climax Saloon at 210 Cherry Street, with its Italianate style and a façade of impressive stone detailing; the six-story, sixty-room Utopia

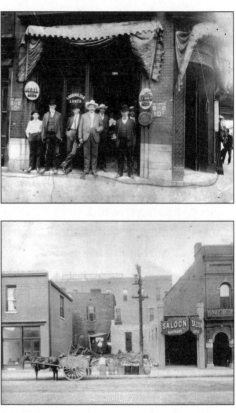

The Men's Quarter in Nashville included, clockwise, the Climax, the Silver Dollar, Hartman's, and the Maxwell House Hotel, among other raucous joints.

Hotel at 206 Cherry Street, completed in 1891 and also with a beautiful stone façade; and the most ornate saloon in Nashville at 222 Cherry Street, the Southern Turf. Built in 1895 by Marcus Cartwright, it boasted mahogany woodwork, gilded walls, large mirrors, tropical plants, bronze statuary, paintings, and racing prints. In addition to flowing whiskey and beer, a decent meal could also be purchased. A local businessman recalled that some of the saloons, like the Utopia and Southern Turf, served lunch "for thirty-five cents but the $40 a month telephone company clerk, of course, could not afford such costly gourmet food." The main establishments also offered gambling—craps, faro, and poker, among other games—for the gentlemen. Any such gambling was as illegal as selling liquor on Sunday, but the police tended to ignore the indiscretions, for fear of discovering a judge with cards in his hand or a prostitute on his lap.

A more respectable locale on the fringe of the quarter was the Maxwell House, one of the most prestigious hotels in the city. Across the street from the Climax, it offered a side door for respectable ladies, to protect them from any unseemly Cherry Street sights. Just off Cherry, there were also tailors, plenty of pawnshops for those who literally lost their shirts gambling, fine cigar shops, and Bryer's Russian and Turkish Baths. "The relationship between Bryer's Russian and Turkish baths and the saloons on Cherry Street need not be elaborated," a local historian said—no doubt with a sardonic smile.[25]

Jack made a day of it when he visited Nashville. He relished touring the Nashville saloons—with their ornate wooden bars, chandeliers, mirrors, and rows of scintillating decanters and flasks—where he set everyone up with drinks. It was quite a scene, the energetic 5-foot, 2-inch distiller pushing through a crowd of men who averaged a good 5 inches taller than him, slapping them on the back and shaking hands. An adept social creature, he could recall most anyone's name, a feat that always impressed. When he couldn't, he used a standard trick: rarely did Jack go into a saloon where he didn't have at least one friend, so, if he didn't know someone or had forgotten that person's name, he'd have his friend introduce him and then Jack would say the individual's name without missing a beat and with a tone of great familiarity. Few saloongoers who met Jack ever forgot him, thanks to his signature outfit and his eternally youthful looks. As for his youthful appearance, here again, Jack used a little deception. The day finally came when he looked in the mirror and detected gray hair in his goatee, so he started dying his hair black. After all, he had to sustain his legendary boy-distiller image. Ten years later, at fifty, Jack would look thirty. While his well-groomed appearance exposed his vanity, he had yet to fall prey to any crippling excesses of the Gay Nineties.

Jack remained focused on his distilling business; he had undertaken some colorful and prudent initiatives to attempt to keep pace with his competition. There were the saloons, the cornet band, the Belle brand, the warehouse in Hopkinsville, and the distributor in Nashville. But had the diminutive man made a lasting impression up North? In the bourbon heartland, was anyone going to seek out whiskey made by a small outfit in sleepy Lynchburg? Had he done enough? To put it all in perspective, the White Rabbit Saloon in Lynchburg was no Climax saloon in Nashville.

10

BIG MAN, LONELY MAN

No married man is genuinely happy if he has to drink worse whisky than he used to drink when he was single.

–H. L. Mencken

The news spread like the 1892 fire that scorched the town: a reporter and a sketch artist from the prominent *Nashville American* newspaper were coming to town to write a feature on Jack Daniel. The town was abuzz with excitement. Yes, Jack had made the right kind of impression in the powerful Nashville business circles.

Before visiting the distillery, in early March 1896, a certain Mr. R. Christopher made a tour of the surrounding countryside. The *Nashville American* correspondent was duly impressed with what he witnessed: there were signs of progress; and the people were thrifty, awake, active, and cheerful. In his March 8 article, he extolled Lynchburg as "one of the most prosperous and promising towns in Tennessee" and surrounding Mulberry Valley as one of the richest regions in the state, with its prodigious corn crop, and he hailed Moore as the "banner corn county." Just as impressive were the meaty cattle herds grazing in the fields.

At the time, Jack, who bought cattle and hogs from other farmers in the county, owned two hundred head of cattle and as many hogs.

He sold beef to buyers from across the country, some of his meat even finding its way overseas.[1] Not all was a glowing success on his farm, however; the pigs and the poultry had their conflicts. All was peaceful until Jack bought a sow from fellow farmer Jim Neal that, unbeknownst to him, ate chickens. A pig that thought itself a fox would not do. But then, redeeming itself, the pig subsequently attacked the geese on Jack's farm—garden-rampaging geese that he wanted exterminated. When Jack ran into his friend, he quipped, "Well, Jim, I'd given you $5 more for that sow if I'd known she'd eat geese!"[2] The *Nashville American* reporter, however, was not there to interview a goose-slaying pig.

The reporter praised the reason he was in Lynchburg: "This county has also gained fame from its large and superior output of fine whiskey." Despite the fame, what had once been thirteen active distilleries in the county was reduced to but three: Jack Daniel, John Eaton, and Tolley Brothers. Incidentally, in two years' time, there would be a new name on the government's list: W. B. Daniel & Co., located at County Line.[3] After all these years, Wiley, also a prominent citizen, whose home was a landmark, had entered the business in partnership with Felix "Plumb" Motlow, first cousin of Lem's dad, Felix Motlow.[4] Big brother would never be a threat. The acknowledged reigning lord was Jack Daniel, now the largest sour mash producer in Tennessee. His whiskey, the reporter declared, was in every state that sells whiskey and

> was known in almost every country where this liquid is used. . . . His widely known "No. 7" has attained more popularity than any brand of whiskey that has been put on the market in many years. His other popular brand, "Belle of Lincoln," is found on nearly every sideboard and in every retail establishment in the South. He has the most enviable distillery trade in the South and will always retain it because of the extra fine quality of his products. They are growing more popular every day and his trade is constantly increasing.[5]

Four years after his 1892 assault was launched in earnest—using everything from the Silver Cornet Band, to a Nashville distributor, to the Hopkinsville warehouse—Jack had realized his wildest dreams of success.

To meet the increasing demand, preparations were under way for constructing a new distillery with the latest technology. Like all great manufacturers, Jack comprehended the importance of having the most efficient facilities and advanced machinery. Currently, he used four fermenters to achieve the purest sour mash, with each fermentation tank holding 60 gallons—a long cry from the old single batch days, but he had yet to break his commitment to distilling more than 300 gallons a day. To store his barrels, Jack had just finished building a mammoth warehouse—longer than a football field and sixty-five feet in width—able to hold 6,000 barrels. Made of metal and painted a terra cotta color to look like brick, it was three stories high with a central elevator. As of 1896, the distillery had never suspended operations, except for nights and Sundays—a remarkable achievement. In fact, according to the *Nashville American* reporter, it had been "in continuous operation longer than any distillery in the United States"—a record Jack would not relinquish.[6]

IN HIS BUSINESS DEALINGS around Lynchburg, Jack became more aggressive as he further expanded his operations. To supplement the 300-gallon daily capacity at the Hollow, in August 1895, he bought one of the old Tolley & Eaton distilleries near County Line, just north of Lynchburg, for $3,900. It included 65 acres of land, the distillery, some machinery, a wooden warehouse, a sheet-iron house, and a tenant house. Although it hadn't been used in a while and was rundown, the warehouse rotting, Jack wanted to take possession of the property immediately, making that a condition of the sale. He was so anxious, in fact, that he paid more than the property was worth.[7] There was demand to meet. Jack was equally aggressive in buying land and protecting the land he already owned.

Land disputes were common—whether for grazing, wood, or crops, land was invaluable. Even a squabble over a small amount of corn would end up in court. Such was the case in 1893, when Jack was named a codefendant in a lawsuit involving two bushels of corn.[8] One of Jack's corn suppliers, W. W. Holt, owed another man, J. H. Frame, $200. In lieu of cash, Frame agreed to take two bushels of corn, but then Holt sold $45 worth of that corn to Jack. Frame took them both to court. Yet more often, Jack, who owned almost 450 acres in multiple counties by 1895, was on the offensive.[9] He brought suit against a Mrs. Elizabeth White and others of Giles County, accusing them of timbering land that belonged to him. He demanded whatever profits they had made.[10] In 1902, he brought suit against another Giles County couple, John and Etta Word, and in a separate case, against a T. O. Dougherty, accusing them all of attempting to take possession of land he had purchased.[11] Jack didn't lose.

LAWSUITS ASIDE, Jack's popularity in Moore County soared. As the *Nashville American* reported, "Jack Daniel, who is deservedly the most popular man in his section of the country, enjoys life to its fullest extent. He lives like a prince in one of the finest residences in Moore County. . . . It is fitted up with all the appurtenance for perfect home comfort. The furniture is the richest and finest to be found, and everything from the front entrance to the kitchen and from the cellar to the garret is suggestive of good taste, comfort and luxury." Jack's farmhouse had been transformed into a breathtaking mansion that rivaled those of antebellum plantations.

The parlor, or drawing room, was 50 by 30 feet, the ceiling close to 15 feet high. It featured polished wood floors, windows that ran almost the height of the room, and rich red velvet drapes. Jack's sideboard was always filled with both foreign and domestic vintages, to be tasted before an enormous fireplace with a marble mantel. "On each side were cupids," recalled a distant relative, "nearly life-sized, hovering like welcoming angels to the warm glows of a fire. Above and across the mantel were cherubs with wings approaching from each side to the center." The marble mantel, which Jack had special ordered from Italy, had its own story to tell. When the mantel was en route to New Orleans, the story goes, pirates attacked the cargo vessel in the Caribbean, looted it, and then sunk it. On inspecting their booty, when they saw that the mantel was addressed to Jack Daniel, they crated it back up and sent it on its way—out of deference to Captain Jack. For these particular swashbuckling pirates, whiskey was obviously preferred to rum.

Another foreign prize that Jack took great pride in was his piano, an inlaid grand piano from France that the *Nashville American* reporter described as "incomparable." One of Jack's neighbors, Fannie Blythe, who studied music and taught the piano, considered his piano one of the most beautiful she'd ever seen. She often played classical and non-classical music on it when Jack was entertaining. Before extending an invitation to Fannie, who had yet to reach her teenage years, Jack respectfully asked her father's permission first. Only after receiving his consent did Jack send his finest carriage, with fringe trimming the interior and drawn by matching gray mares, for Fannie and her mother.[12] In addition to her musical talent, another motivational factor lay behind Jack's invitations: he was smitten with little Fannie.

A FREQUENT ENTERTAINER, Jack hosted an annual Christmas feast, to which he invited hundreds of guests—every name in all of Moore County was apparently in his address book.[13] The next week was Lynchburg's New Year's Ball, a gala affair that began with another dinner feast at Jack's home. Afterward, the carousing guests would parade into town for a night of foot-stompin' round and square dancing. On a more spiritual note, Jack always played host to the touring preachers whose words resounded in the Mount Moriah Primitive Baptist church; he arranged feasts for the other Baptist churches; and, most notable, he hosted the annual May Day dinner, held after the foot washing on the second Sunday in May and lasting from noon until evening. Originally, the May Day dinner was for members of the Mount Moriah church, but in the coming years it came to include some three hundred guests. Preparations took a full week, and horses and carriages from surrounding liveries were booked up solid well in advance. As the bewitching hour neared, Jack would ride up to the church with great flourish and shout in, "Hey, Elder Webster, you've talked long enough. Turn loose your congregation and come with me for dinner." One year, he arrived at the church to find several members fast asleep in the pews, so he shouted, "Your congregation has all gone to sleep. Finish your sermon in a hurry and come with me for dinner."[14] Tables were set up inside his home and outside on the lawn.

The food included a half-dozen young shoats, fat lambs, a veal calf barbecued over pits filled with charcoal, baked turkey and chicken, pies, cakes, and preserves. In his parlor, Jack kept a collection of fine whiskies and brandies in decorative decanters and flasks for Baptists practiced in the art of discretion.

While Jack could be cynical about church, he did respect it. He understood how important the church was to the community and he so desperately wanted to be a part of the community. Although he did not attend services, he never prevented his employees from going, regardless of responsibilities at the distillery. On one particular Sunday when he needed some repair work done, he sought out his mechanic, only to find the man on his way to church, "with a Bible as big as a bale of cotton under his arm." Jack didn't have the heart to call him away.[15] As for his monetary benevolence, legend has it he donated money to every church in Moore County. This generosity begs the question: Was he atoning for his sins? Those sins having to do with whiskey making or debauched activities in Nashville? Or was he an agnostic simply hedging his bets? Certainly, Jack's liberal support of the local churches kept the more pious from attacking his distillery operation.

It's been said that he also donated money to every school project carried out in Moore County, whether it be the construction of a new building or the buying of books. The *Lynchburg Falcon* recalled that Jack "was always ready with a helping hand for the distressed widows and orphans. He was ever ready to help build schoolhouses and churches, and there are but a few that have been built in this county but that have been built with the aid of this man, and they stand as monuments to his memory."[16]

Now known as a "donation man," Jack loaned money to individuals, family members, farmers, and businessmen—he felt obliged to share his good fortune even in small ways. On one occasion, his niece Dora Enochs Stephens and her four-year-old daughter, Carmine—or "Carmie," as she was known—met Jack in Lynchburg. "It was then that Uncle Jack gave the child her first piece of silver!" Dora recalled. "How proud she was of this money."[17] When a farmer who'd suffered a fire at his home brought his corn in for weighing—$1,000 worth— Jack slipped him an extra $100. Displaying his wit and generosity,

Jack told one friend he loaned money to, "Now I'll give you money this time, but if I ever hear of your spending your money for that moonshine rot-gut whiskey instead of my good whiskey I'll never give you another cent."[18] In recognition of his benevolence, one election year Lynchburg made Jack the honored guest at the President's Inaugural Ball.

Of course, Jack's philanthropy could never measure up, in terms of monetary value, to that of industrialists and capitalists like Carnegie, Morgan, Rockefeller, and Vanderbilt, who made headlines by building palatial mansions on Fifth Avenue, buying million-dollar yachts, and spending lavishly on philanthropy to alleviate their respective consciences, while they oppressed thousands of the laboring class. Both Rockefeller, a Baptist, and Morgan, an Episcopalian, gave millions to their respective churches to pay for their entry through the pearly gates. They were all too familiar with the words of Jesus, "For it is easier for a camel to go through a needle's eye, than for a rich man to enter into the kingdom of God." Regardless of what they gave to church or community, these titans were never loved by their neighbors as Jack was.

ALTHOUGH A SOCIAL BUTTERFLY, Jack continued to shun one realm of society: politics. Considering that Jack, by his calculations, had forked over close to $1.5 million to the government in excise taxes on more than 1.6 million gallons of whiskey, which generated approximately $5 million in total revenue in the twenty-two years he'd been in business (1875 to 1896), one would think he'd take some interest in politics.[19] Even more consequential, there was the continuing battle against the dry forces, in which local and state politicos played crucial roles. No, he lumped politicians with the clergy: of no use when it came to the pragmatism required for everyday life. It was the hard-headed politicians, after all, who were easily blamed for starting the Civil War that ripped apart his family. The only politico he took a liking to was Robert Love Taylor, who was the same age as Jack and hailed from Happy Valley in Washington County, Tennessee. In 1896, Taylor was running for governor of Tennessee on the Democrat's ticket. At the time, the country was mired in a depression, largely blamed on the quack monetary policies of the Democrats, currently led by President Grover Cleveland.

Fondly called "Our Bob," Taylor aroused the common people with his folksy ways, which made him Jack's kind of man—folksy, even though he had studied law and been admitted to the Bar in 1878. He knew the game: his father had been a congressman and his uncle a Confederate senator. Under normal circumstances, a Democrat would have been a shoo-in; the problem was that he was up against his brother Alfred "Alf" A. Taylor, the Republican nominee. Tennessee's "War of the Roses" commenced, aptly described by brother Bob: "We had dreamed together in the same trundle-bed, and often kicked each other out. . . . seen visions of pumpkin pie . . . pulled hair . . . But now the dreams of our manhood clashed. . . . With flushed cheeks and throbbing hearts, we eagerly entered the field, his shield bearing the red rose, mine the white."

Both men were skilled fiddle players and storytellers, so it made for a colorful campaign that turned into a battle of entertainment, not issues. One of Bob's favorite yarns was about preacher Billy Patterson. The story goes that one Sunday, after moving to a mill town and sizing up the situation, Patterson went on a tirade against Satan and sin, against whiskey and the town bully, Bert Lynch. Well, Bert didn't take to the minister and the next week challenged him to a fight, threatening to "suck the marrow out'n them old bones o' yourn." Preacher Patterson asked if he could pray first, which Lynch granted. Bowing his head, Patterson spoke to God, "O Lord, Thou knowest that when I killed Bill Cummins and John Brown and Jerry Smith and Levi Bottles, that I did it in self defense. Thou knowest, O Lord, that when I cut the heart out of young Slinger and strewed the brains of Paddy Miles, that it was forced upon me." And on went the list. When the preacher looked up, the hoodwinked Bert Lynch had disappeared in a cloud of dust.[20]

On his campaign tour, Bob came to Lynchburg to speak on behalf of himself, the Democratic Party, and William Jennings Bryan, who was running for U.S. president against the Republican William McKinley. McKinley, the governor of Ohio and a laissez-faire tariff man, was in the Yankee capitalists' back pocket, while Bryan supported free trade and the free coinage of silver for several confounded

For Tennessee's own War of the Roses, the people gathered at the Lincoln County Courthouse in Fayetteville to hear the Taylor brothers duel verbally.

reasons that never added up. Jack Daniel and his Silver Cornet Band—each band member fitted with a free silver hat, representing the Democrats' monetary position—met "Our Bob" in Mulberry and paraded down the pike to Lynchburg. Sitting on the driver's seat of the bandwagon, beloved old-timer Uncle Jep Austin carried the American flag. Trailing was "a long string of ladies and gents on horseback," including Tom Holt, a merchant, standing in his buggy and singing "Away Over Yonder in the Promised Land." Also in the crowd was Miss Mary Bobo, who was smartly dressed in a riding habit of brown domestic, adorned with pearl buttons.[21]

The parade arrived in Lynchburg at dusk, the town aglow with hundreds of candles. "Our Bob" spent the night at the Salmon House, and the next day the Silver Cornet Band carried him off to Shelbyville. There, they saluted good-bye with "God Be with You Till We Meet Again."[22] Come election day, Bob's marginally better fiddle playing and coarser rhetoric upstaged his brother, and he won. His genial personality brought an evenhandedness to Tennessee politics, but his stumping for Bryan was of little help; McKinley trounced

Bryan. The fact that corporations donated an astounding $7 million to McKinley coffers aided the cause a wee bit.[23] The Republicans buying the Executive Mansion signaled an economic boom time and a full-scale resumption of the Gay Nineties that would carry into the next century and that included a pervasive party atmosphere in Lynchburg.

QUICKLY CLOSING IN on fifty years of age, Jack was now thinning across the scalp but sported a tremendous, flowing mustache that cascaded all the way down to his collar, complemented by a trim goatee. Rich food and drink were beginning to catch up with him; he had the makings of a potbelly. As of 1900, he still lived with sister Bette and her husband, James Conner. Not quite prepared for a half century of life, he bought himself two years by listing his birthday as August 1851.[24] And he still wore the same distinctive garb. "He was a dapper little fellow," recalled Lant Wood, who would become the distillery's taster after Lem. "He always wore a Prince Albert Coat—wore about a number 5 shoe, I guess. He was always on dress parade wherever he went."[25] No matter where Jack was or when, he and his business were indeed always on parade, which greatly contributed to his success. According to grandnephew Felix W. Motlow, who was well acquainted with the latter years of this legend, "Jack Daniel was a unique character, noted for his wit, his good humor, a jovial spirit, and general good fellowship. He would greet his friends with a flattering remark or kindly banter—especially the younger set, of whom he was very fond."[26] The young girls, in particular.

Although past his prime, Jack was still considered a lady's man. At the various balls and dances, they enjoyed him as a partner—his feet remained quick, as he glided across the floor and they saw each other eye to eye. In fact, Jack would go out of his way to eye the girls, even to relatively distant churches. On the first Sunday in May, he would ride out to the Chestnut Ridge Baptist Church on Big Hurricane Creek for their annual foot washing. Jack was always expected—not as a participant but as an observer. Arriving in a sporty black surrey drawn by two black horses, he attracted a crowd of eager-faced boys. But his gaze rested beyond them, to the "fair damsels," to the young girls in calico, gingham, or woolen dresses, with hoods or fascinators on their heads. In the winter, the ladies habitually wore blue veils over their faces to ward off the harsh cold, so May was a time for flowers and women to bloom. Jack tended to let his eye fall on ladies young enough to be his daughter or even granddaughter. According to a Mr. Hall, he would then inquire of the boys about "this pretty girl and that pretty girl and who their families were." For information, he doled out nickels and dimes.[27]

Jack was particularly taken with Fannie Blythe, his lovely neighbor and a soulful piano player, and he asked for her hand in marriage. Her father denied him, telling Jack, who was unwilling to recognize his own age, that he was "a little too old for such a young girl." Born in July 1884, she was thirty-five years his junior—a stretch, even for those days.[28] Not one to hold a grudge, Jack later attended Fannie's wedding ceremony in the Christian Church in Lynchburg—she married Lee Andrew Enochs in 1906.[29] The church was small, the crowd large, so Jack remained on the porch with other guests during the ceremony. As Fannie passed by, Jack slipped her a $10 gold piece as a wedding present.[30]

According to Lant Wood, Jack also took a paternalistic view of Lynchburg's young ladies; he would be hurt when a "fine damsel" didn't marry well. After the daughter of one family friend eloped, he hung his head and muttered, "Constant association will cause some folks to fall in love with a damned alligator."[31] Extremely self-conscious of his bachelor status, Jack advised his nephews and other young men not to follow in his lonely footsteps. "Damned to hell! You can't compete with the boys in town," he warned them with a smile. "They always use town oil on their hair. No, you can't do any good until you can use town oil." Rumored to have had several serious courtships, perhaps he didn't marry because he was so particular, so "exactin'," and couldn't find a companion up to snuff. Complicating any wooing, his work was demanding, with Jack often on the road in the company of men, and, when at home, life with sister Bette was very orderly. Why disrupt his habits and rituals? It appeared that he was condemned to a solitary life. Fortunately, whiskey drinkers the world over benefited from his ongoing love affair with distilling. Harnessing his creative energies, Jack's greatest triumphs were yet to come.

11

BRAND MAGIC

❧·❧

Always carry a flagon of whiskey in case of snakebite and furthermore always carry a small snake.

—W. C. Fields

The U.S. government was the distiller's nemesis—it was also his friend. Legislation, always deemed oppressive, sometimes, just sometimes, aided the whiskey business and actually resulted in a better product. In 1894, for example, the bonding period was increased to eight years, which meant that distilleries could warehouse their liquor longer without tax consequences and thus pour a much finer whiskey from the barrel. It was an opportunity to pursue honey-silk perfection for those who preferred an allegedly more civilized drink. Another major development occurred three years later: the Bottled-in-Bond Act of 1897, which would lead to a new era of higher quality and flamboyant advertising. Jack Daniel would take advantage of both developments.

To date, the bottling of whiskey was a limited affair; it was costly, with the technology needed for cheap mass production of glass bottles still a few years away. One of the few who bottled his whiskey in notable quantities prior to the 1890s was George Garvin Brown, who wanted to prevent the adulteration of his brand. (A future incarnation of Brown's company would buy the Jack Daniel Distillery.) Based in

Louisville, his flagship whiskey was Old Forester, named in honor of either Nathan Bedford Forrest or his personal physician, Dr. Forrester, depending on which story you bought into. The fact that the second *r* was lost somewhere between the distillery and the printer was negligible, as the real key to his success was the motto on his bottle's label, which exuded excellence: "This whiskey is distilled by us only, and we are responsible for its richness and fine quality. Its elegant flavor is soley due to original fineness developed with care. *There is nothing better in the market.* George Garvin Brown."[1] Whiskey in a sealed bottle instilled confidence in the consumer; it couldn't be tampered with by underhanded resellers.

Other early experimenters with bottling included Quarter Century, Old Guckenheimer, Old Crow, and Hunter's Baltimore Rye. However, the use of glass remained largely limited to making fancy bottles, decanters, and hand-blown flasks to celebrate special occasions or to give as gifts to bartenders and grocers to induce them to promote that particular whiskey. The flasks, which became known as commemoratives, were particularly interesting and came in all shapes, from crude commentaries on the drinking life to unique works of art. One artist designed a pint-size flask that sat in a clay model boot to commemorate "Bootleggers," the name inspired by stagecoach travelers who carried their flasks discreetly in their boots and refilled them at taverns situated along the grueling roads. Fancier flasks were modeled on George Washington's bust or had the likeness of Benjamin Franklin molded into one side—even though the very first of Ben's "Thirteen Virtues" listed in his autobiography was "Temperance: Eat not to dullness; drink not to elevation." Frankly, most flask-toting drinkers were bent on becoming elevated. E. G. Booz, a prominent Philadelphia grocer and *booze*'s namesake, had one designed to look like a log cabin and inscribed with "E. G. BOOZ'S OLD CABIN WHISKEY." And another had the frightening image of the hatchet-wielding temperance crusader Carry Nation imbedded in it—one can only imagine the wry smile on the face of its creator.

Meanwhile, most whiskey continued to be distributed via barrel and jug, with the respective distilleries' names and numbers stamped on them. Once these left the warehouse, there was no more government supervision, thus allowing unscrupulous bartenders and storekeepers to cut the drink and save themselves money. Oblivious consumers were often unaware of the deceit, but then the Committee on the Judiciary of the House of Representatives decided to investigate this side of the liquor business. The outcome: to protect the consumer against adulteration and counterfeiting, they recommended a new law that would allow distillers to fill bottles at their place of operation—the bottled whiskey had to be 100 proof, a minimum of four years old, and made at one location—and have those bottles sealed with a green government stamp, signifying that it met with regulations. Before leaving office in early 1897, President Cleveland signed off on the legislation. Not only was the consumer assured of a certain quality, but the distillers were given an opportunity to pursue a whole new field of marketing.

JACK DANIEL HAD USED GLASS on a very limited basis; however, he would soon introduce a radical bottle that would further secure his eminent position in whiskey history. First, in 1897, he issued a limited-edition glass bottle to commemorate the Tennessee Centennial Exposition, which celebrated the state's one-hundredth year in the Union. It was hosted by Nashville, the city now calling itself the Athens of the South, instead of the apparently downgraded Minneapolis of the South. When Jack arrived by train from Tullahoma, he was not disappointed—no hyperbole could serve the colossal scale of the event.

On opening day, May 1, 1897, President William McKinley inaugurated the celebration by flipping a switch in Washington, D.C.— over seven hundred miles away—that sent an electrical impulse to Nashville, igniting a cannon and an electric dynamo. The dynamo, a generator that brought light where there was darkness, was the most exalted symbol of progress. The dynamo was the symbol of infinity and was even godlike, according to Henry Adams, who wrote in *The Education of Henry Adams,* "As he grew accustomed to the great gallery of machines, he began to feel the forty-foot dynamos as a moral force, much as the early Christians felt the cross." He felt compelled to pray to it.[2] Ah, progress! There were forward-looking industrial and educational exhibits, but many displays reflected on glorious history. There was a Little Egypt; a Chinese village; a Colorado gold mine; a full-scale replica of the Parthenon, a Greek temple dedicated to the goddess Athena, which housed an art exhibit; and a reproduction of the Acropolis, which housed historic relics, these latter two tying in nicely to Nashville's promotion of itself as the Athens of the South. The day was filled with parades and brass bands, including a Centennial Orchestra and a Prohibition Band that played everything from works by Verdi to songs by Stephen Foster. And there were, of course, endless speeches.

Governor "Our Bob" Taylor's opening-day speech was most noteworthy; he predicted what life would be like in one hundred years:

> I see the sun darkened by clouds of men and women flying in the air. I see throngs of passengers entering electric tubes on New York and emerging in San Francisco two hours before they started. I see the gloved and umbrellaed leaders of the Populist party sitting in their horseless carriages and singing the harvest song, while the self-adjusting automatic reapers sweep unattended through the fields, cutting and binding and shocking the golden grain. I see swarms of foreign pauper dukes and counts kissing American millionaire girls across the ocean, through the kissophone. I see the women marching in bloomers to the ballot box and the men at home singing lullabies to the squalling babies. I see every Republican in America drawing a pension, every Democrat holding an office, and every "cullad pusson" riding on a free pass; and then I think the millennium will be near at hand.[3]

The speech was part H. G. Wells science fiction but was quite accurate in some respects, particularly the women marching in bloomers and men singing lullabies, which drew a raucous laugh—if they only knew.

At the time, expositions were all the rage, and this one would carry on for six months. Always captivated by history and nostalgia, an inspired Jack Daniel designed an eleven-inch round bottle made of clear, hand-blown glass that spiraled downward like a gently pleated drapery. On the side was Jack Daniel's Tennessee Centennial Whiskey in black enamel lettering. He presented the heartfelt commemoration and advertising gimmick to select friends and customers.

* * *

DESPITE THE BOTTLE-IN-BOND ACT, mass production of glass bottles didn't begin in earnest until 1904, when bottle making was perfected with automatic machines—the bottles capped first with corks and then later fitted with screw tops. Still, in the late 1890s, the existing plate mold inserts in mold-blown bottles and glued-on labels immediately permitted personalization, as distillers began to take advantage of the act to further establish their brands. The very same phenomenon was occurring in the food industry, as canned food became a diet staple. Having been duped over the years by bogus patent medicines and poisoned foods, the public welcomed the safety and the improved quality offered by particular companies' sealed containers. Consequently, advertising and the fight to win market share were kicked up a notch in intensity, as companies fought for the more sophisticated consumer's attention. Adding to the frenzy, the further proliferation of magazines continued to offer unlimited advertising opportunities targeted at specific demographics; in the 1880s, *Cosmopolitan, Ladies Home Journal, McClure's,* and *Munsey's,* among others, were founded. End consumers, including whiskey imbibers, received far greater attention, as not only their palates, but their imaginations, now had to be captured like never before. To win over customers, in addition to the green government stamp and emerging brand names like Old Tub, Rebel Yell, Mountain Dew, and Chimney Corner Bourbon, distillers started plastering every slogan imaginable on their bottles and in their ads.

To invoke quality, some slogans played directly and deceitfully on the new laws to suggest that certain distillers' whiskey was endorsed by the government: "Uncle Sam says its all right. . . . We dare not take a gallon of our own whiskey from our warehouse unless it is all right." Others claimed, "Uncle Sam is Our Partner."[4] Of course, cheap whiskey wouldn't taste any better even if aged for all eternity and put directly in a bottle, but it sounded good. The same declarations of government approval would be echoed when the 1906 Pure Food and Drug Bill was signed into law by Teddy Roosevelt to further protect consumers. Distillers would have to fess up whether they were selling straight whiskey or blended, but they could then incorporate the tantalizing word *pure* into their marketing. Pureness by Uncle Sam's standards couldn't get any better, right? One particularly brazen jingle promised such perfection in its pureness that it was "The whiskey without a headache." Of course, any distiller with that sort of whiskey was a wizard who should have been able to make millions with the wave of a wand. Another promised, "Every Swallow makes a Friend." Certainly, if you're buying. And too many swallows makes an enemy, but that wasn't in the fine print. There was an "anti-trust" whiskey, its distiller's ads designed to win over the customer who despised the monopoly, and closer to Jack's marketing pitch was, "The Whiskies of Our Daddies."[5]

Wholesalers got into the act, too; the St. Louis firm George Buente referred to itself as the "The Miner's Friend" and in 1896 offered Old Kentucky bourbon for 50 cents a bottle. George Buente, no doubt, did make the miner's life more tolerable and could be considered friendly, since the generous company didn't impose a shipping charge on kegs or jugs.[6] Further intensifying the branding battle, in the late 1890s, customers could indeed mail order quart bottles and cases; for example, Hayner's of Dayton, Ohio, advertised four quarts of seven-year-old pure rye whiskey for $3.20, prepaid.[7] Less so than ever, it didn't matter where you were, as the country was becoming smaller and smaller, thus the market larger and larger.

Then, at the turn of the century, came a burst of sex. Sex in advertising. The days of the Victorian woman depicted in tailored shirtwaists with leg-o'-mutton sleeves and floor-length skirts was fast disappearing. A little more risqué than Jack's Belle of Lincoln label, Mountain Dew made up posters with three fine young ladies–two of them showing ankle!–gently cradling bottles of whiskey. These ladies in white dresses suggested more than pureness of product. A Kentucky Dew ad displayed a young lady fishing, who had caught her dress with a poor cast and inadvertently lifted it. Meanwhile, a bug-eyed boy catches a rather compromising reflection of her in the water. It had nothing to do with whiskey. In another ad, Harvard Pure Rye depicted two couples, the boys having apparently just graduated college and the women scantily clad, whooping it up. And in another for Royal Velvet: Kentucky Straight Whiskey, a young woman places her foot on a man's knee and her hand on his hand while he ties her shoe, all very suggestive of matters other than whiskey–although the whiskey might lead to such matters. Taking top prize for shameless bawdiness was the Louisville-based Belle of Nelson: Old Fashion Hand Made Sour Mash Whiskey. There was nothing old fashioned about its advertising, which included voluptuous women bearing breast and buttock in a harem-like setting.[8]

Jack's ads were anything but risqué, and his slogans were hardly catchy jingles. In fact, it didn't matter whether his paper labels, which first appeared in 1895, were black, green, purple, or brown; whether it be flask or bottle, Jack's Old No. 7 and Belle of Lincoln brands had the same basic slogans: "Pure Lincoln County Corn Whiskey," "Old Time Sour Mash," and "Old Time Distillery." His style and tone echoed Royal Baking Powder's simple slogan of "Absolutely Pure" and the nostalgic advertising used by Chase & Sanborn Company, a coffee company that associated its product with the down-home comfort of a country store. Jack's message was also simple: tradition counted most and that was what he built his business on. He stood behind his whiskey, personally guaranteeing every drop.[9] He did have his cornet band, his occasional fancy commemorative bottle, and once in a while he ordered up colorful, decorative metal boxes to hold his special bottles, but it was all very tame. Rumor has it that Jack sponsored hot air balloons to garner attention, more in the tradition of the flamboyant P. T. Barnum. And to really create a stir, he shipped a barrel of No. 7 to Queen Victoria, who would die in 1901. He did not, however, pop out of his bottle at expositions à la Aunt Jemima, who popped out of a flour barrel at the 1893 Chicago World's Columbian Exposition. One of Jack's most defining and lasting branding endeavors had nothing to do with jingles or stunts, yet it would capture the drinking man's imagination as much as a naked woman did.

JUST AS BOTTLING on a large scale was about to be realized, Jack became acquainted with a salesman from the Illinois Alton Glass Company, who happened to be promoting a square bottle with a fluted neck. While Jack mulled over the square bottle, Lem argued that round bottles would be cheaper, easier to handle, and easier to pack. All true. But knowing a good idea when he saw one, Jack begged to differ; he realized that this was an opportunity for a major marketing coup. Square bottles stood out from the crowd, and he wanted his whiskey to stand out. "Well, Lemmie, being as how my whiskey is different from anybody else's whiskey and is the best there is, we'll have square bottles and the bottles will be different, too." The square bottle, he insisted, would also symbolize that he was a square dealer—it would indeed complement his reputation for quality.[10]

To box his square bottles, Jack hired Lem's younger brother Tom, who was on vacation from school. It was a perfect opportunity for the young man, who was planning to go to Vanderbilt University and could use the money. For their initial shipment, Tom filled two hundred cases with twenty-four bottles of No. 7. When the square bottle started appearing on grocery and liquor store shelves, it had a major impact on the discerning customer: not only was the whiskey good, but when brought along for a ride in the countryside, the bottle didn't roll around on the floor of the buggy and smash. For future generations, that would be the floor of a pickup truck. How successful was the square bottle? In over a hundred years, the Jack Daniel Distillery has never reversed that decision and remains one of the few to use a square bottle. The square bottle, the black label, *no* powdered damsels—all of this appealed to the men among men, those looking for a belt of robust whiskey.

EVEN THOUGH Jack's marketing strategy of keeping his message simple and direct throughout the Gilded Age and the Gay Nineties appeared to succeed and Jack was content to peddle his reputation among saloon patrons, nephew Lem pushed hard for greater glory on the public stage. Lem craved the spotlight. He wanted influence. A fast-approaching opportunity to climb on the public stage was the 1904 Louisiana Purchase Exposition, also known as the St. Louis World's Fair, which would entertain about 19 million people. It was to celebrate the centennial of the Louisiana Purchase, the visionary acquisition of the territory of Louisiana—almost a million-square-mile tract of land between the Mississippi River and the Rocky Mountains that doubled the size of the United States—from France for a mere $15 million. The formal transfer took place on March 10, 1804, in St. Louis.

The Louisiana Purchase Exposition was yet another celebration of progress, providing American industry and inventors with a center stage for their machines and creations. In addition to the numerous exhibits, there were a series of competitions, from dairy shows to whiskey tasting. Whiskey was included in what was called "Group 93: syrups and liqueurs, and distilled spirits; commercial alcohol." Rumor had it that Group 93 would include top-shelf brands from Kentucky, Canada, and Scotland—it was a chance to see how No. 7 measured up. So, as the exposition approached, a number of people, from state politicians to still hands to Lem, encouraged Jack to enter his whiskey into the competition. But Jack demurred, simply shrugging off the suggestion, apparently uninterested in garnering glory for himself.

Unbeknownst to everyone, Jack was in fact laying plans to enter the competition and travel to St. Louis—he simply didn't publicize it because if he failed, he preferred to keep the whole incident under wraps. Finally, one June morning in the summer of 1904, Jack broke the news to Lem: he was going to the World's Fair. Lem's first question was whether Jack had entered their whiskey in the competition. With a grin, Jack glibly replied that he'd already sent in their entry, which included two cases of whiskey.

Then tragedy struck. Jack lost a dear friend before the St. Louis adventure could begin. On August 30, his mentor Dan Call, who had built a prosperous farm and owned over 450 prime acres, "passed over the border." Thankfully, Call was at home surrounded by family, but the sixty-eight-year-old legend did leave behind his beloved wife, Mary Jane, who had given birth to eighteen children, only four dying in childhood. The funeral was held at the Union Lutheran Church in Lois. From there, a long procession of surreys, buggies, and wagons followed the horsedrawn hearse to the Mulberry Cemetery, where Dan was interred. The *Fayetteville Observer* eulogized him as "One of Moore County's most prominent and leading citizens."[11]

With a heavy heart, Jack pushed on. To get to the exposition, he booked passage on a Pullman run by the Louisville & Nashville Railroad that would take him north to Louisville and then directly west to St. Louis. Aboard the Pullman, he discovered a plush interior that epitomized Victorian décor, with its inlaid woods and marquetry, plate-glass mirrors, ornate light fixtures, and velvet drapes. The leather-and-cloth chairs converted into beds and additional bunks pulled out from the walls. While sleep may have been difficult on the swaying train, Jack's diet hardly suffered. A typical menu in the elite dining car in-cluded Saddle Rock oysters on the half-shell, baked bluefish with Madeira sauce, leg of mutton with caper sauce, beef tongue, and English plum pudding with brandy sauce, among many other selec-tions. Imported wines, liquors, and cigars were always on hand.

On arrival in St. Louis, Jack hired a hack, then picked up his whiskey from the shipping company and went directly to the George Washington Hotel, one of the more posh destinations for the exposi-tion visitors. Diminutive Jack, in his swallowtail suit and fancy vest, blended right in with the mostly flamboyant foreign legions—visitors arriving from all over the United States and overseas—who poured into the hotel. It was a circus show, and the freaks were arriving en force. At the hotel, an exposition representative took charge of Jack's whiskey, storing it in a secret warehouse, not to be touched until the competition. Jack, who was immediately labeled as the "Little Guy from Tennessee," wondered if he would ever see it again.

That first evening Jack strolled through the milling crowds for a while, then retired to his room. It was not a night for socializing, for swapping stories, and for setting the house up—then again, it was also not a night for sleeping, thanks to nerves. There was too much to worry about: scoundrels tampering with his whiskey, the bribing of judges, and even the rules governing the event. The "Rules and Reg-ulations Governing the System of Awards" was a daunting pamphlet, eight pages long, with thirty points that detailed how the judging would be handled. A Group Jury was in charge of examining each exhibit in the respective group and recommending the awards. Its recommendations were then certified by the chief of the department to which the group belonged and a Superior Jury determined "finally and fully the awards to be made." To add some science to the com-petition, there was a points-based scoring system: if the judges awarded a total of 95–100 points, that entry was the Grand Prize win-ner; 85–94 was Gold; 75–84 was Silver; and 60–74 was Bronze.[12]

Jack wouldn't have long to wait to see how he measured up—the whiskey competition was to begin at 1 P.M. the following day.

THE NEXT MORNING Jack couldn't suppress his natural curiosity; he was compelled to tour the exposition. After entering the main gate, he strode along the Plaza of St. Louis, his eyes on the 100-foot high Louisiana Purchase Monument, a column topped with a sculpture of peace alighting on the globe. Across from the monument could be found one of the focal points of the fair, the Festival Hall. It housed a 3,500-seat auditorium for hosting musical and theatrical entertainment and was crowned by a gold-leafed dome larger than the dome of St. Peter's Basilica in Rome. Also in the hall was the world's largest organ, boasting 10,159 pipes. The exposition's organizers were determined to awe the visitors.

On the fairgrounds were a series of ornate palaces, their arched entrances graced with colonnades of great Doric columns and crowned with elaborate sculptures, which covered anywhere from 7 to 14 acres and housed various exhibits. Among them was the Palace of Minerals & Metallurgy, home to working models of an ore mine, a coal mine, and an oil well; the Palace of Manufacturers, home to a shopping arcade where merchants hawked thousands of goods; the Palace of Machinery, which burned five hundred tons of coal daily to fuel generators and boilers; and the Palace of Electricity, where Thomas Edison himself directed the setup of the exhibits, including an electric broiler that could cook steak in only six minutes. As for food, there were the expansive East and West Pavilions situated on either side of a magnificent fountain, offering German and Italian food, respectively, with each able to accommodate two thousand patrons. An additional forty-three full-service restaurants and eighty food vendors were on site. Here Jack and America were first introduced to such American "delicacies" as hotdogs, peanut butter, ice cream cones, and cotton candy. Despite the displays of ingenuity and power, Jack was drawn to the Agricultural Palace, the largest structure, where Group 93 would hold its competition. He lost himself among these more familiar exhibits, analyzing the cattle with a trained eye and taking careful note of the educational programs. Finally, it was the anointed hour for No. 7 to take the stage.

At 1 P.M., Jack and his fellow whiskey competitors were escorted to the appropriate hall, where their whiskey was arrayed on twenty-four tables, surrounded by a head-high fence of chickenwire to impede the more devious. The nine judges were dressed formally and were quite somber, including the chairman, Henry Hoctor, a British citizen who was running for the House of Commons. For the next four hours, the judges tasted the more than twenty entries, sometimes whispering comments to one another, sometimes not. How this should be interpreted was impossible to know. Tension built. At day's end, Mr. Hoctor stood before the competitors and announced: "Gentlemen, the Gold Medal for the world's finest whiskey goes to Jack Daniel Distillery, Lynchburg, not Virginia, but Lynchburg, Tennessee." The crowd was stunned. Who the heck was Jack Daniel? Jack was the little man with the stovepipe hat, the little guy from Tennessee.[13] His victory threw the spotlight on the modest distiller, on those pursuing an excellent, handcrafted whiskey, and, in the process, Jack greatly aided the creation of a more exclusive, high-end market.

Hoctor and Jack subsequently became friends, with Hoctor encouraging him to export his whiskey in large quantities and to enter other competitions. Jack heeded the advice, and, in fact, the next year he would win the gold medal at the world competition in Liege, Belgium. His return from the World's Fair was not exactly triumphant, however. While he set everyone up at the Lynchburg saloons with the best whiskey in the world and ordered a special decanter to commemorate the event, the once most-admired man in this part of the country received but scant notice in the newspapers. "Jack Daniel's 'No. 7' was awarded the gold medal at the St. Louis World's Fair," was all the December 8 edition of the *Fayetteville Observer* had to report on such a glorious moment. More coverage went to a Chicago man who filed a petition in court, asking for an injunction to stop his wife from talking.[14] The pathetic reason for the subdued press: the temperance movement had sunk its fangs into society's conscience more deeply than ever. One of the more pugnacious leaders was Carry Nation, a bulldog-faced woman who brandished a hatchet more adroitly than Geronimo.

12

ENEMIES

✢·✢

Men are nicotine-soaked, beer-besmirched, whiskey-greased, red-eyed devils.

—Carry Nation

O f the Christian soldiers fighting against the heathen liquor industry, Carry A. Nation was the most outrageous and the most
inspirational. She was adamantly against all vices, from drinking to
chewing tobacco, from smoking to sex—although she must have indulged in the latter at least once because she gave birth to a child.
This desire for righteous living was, in part, to make amends for her
father, a failure of a farmer who moved the family a dozen times, across
Kentucky, Missouri, and Texas. Another force in shaping Carry's radi-
calism was her first husband, Dr. Charles Gloyd, a physician and a
Civil War veteran, who was drunk when they exchanged vows and
never did stop drinking. Not long into their marriage, he died and
was buried in a drunkard's grave.

While living in Kansas and not yet a temperance agitator, Carry
met her second husband, David Nation, a lawyer, a minister, and also
a war veteran. Despite his credentials, he struggled to make a living,
and they barely fended off destitution. During these hard years, Mrs.
Nation came to consider herself a confidante of God; she spoke with
Jesus in the dead of the night; and she experienced an epiphany, dur-

ing which she concluded that her calling was "to destroy saloons wherever they exist."[1] Now in her early fifties, Mrs. Nation, who stood almost six feet tall, had a large oval face with heavy jowls and deep creases from persistent scowling. Her round wire-rimmed glasses and black alpaca dress with a high collar and a white bib—no doubt, she was in mourning over the sinners' souls—served to harden her pious image.

Mrs. Nation selected a pleasant summer day in 1899 to make her first attack. In her hometown of Medicine Lodge, Kansas, she marched up the street, announcing to anyone who would listen that she was going to attack Mort Strong's saloon. When she entered, Mort promptly threw her out. But within a few weeks, her tirades closed four of the six saloons in town. In February 1900, she hefted her first sledgehammer, and, with friends in the Women's Christian Temperance Union (WCTU), smashed up a pharmacy that sold brandy. Mrs. Nation then ignited the liquor as it was poured into the gutter. After taking care of her hometown, a voice told her to move on to Kiowa, Oklahoma, home to a dozen illegal saloons. From there, it was on to Wichita, Kansas, where she wielded her first hatchet in 1901. These radical anti-liquor ladies took great pleasure in shattering the large mirrors behind the bars, shredding posters and paintings with suggestive sexual content, and smashing barrels of liquor and anything else within reach that was breakable. When destroying a saloon, Mrs. Nation enjoyed singing her favorite hymns, her preferred being "Who hath sorrow? Who hath woe?" Having moved on to Topeka, Kansas, she was good enough to warn the saloonkeepers with a letter:

> I came to rescue you as well as those you are murdering. Do not delay, for he that being often reproved hardeneth his neck shall suddenly be destroyed and that without remedy.
>
> We invite you to join us in the destruction of the machinery hell has set up here on earth to literally devour humanity.[2]

As she made her way west to California and east to New York and on to London, her exploits were splashed across the front pages.

Invariably, wherever she ventured, Mrs. Nation was insulted, pelted with rotten eggs, beaten, and jailed—it once took four police officers to wrestle her to the ground. Her growing legion of supporters made and sold little souvenir hatchets to pay her fines. Once she was released, a mob of women greeted her with exaltations. Saloon owners and distillers, on the other hand, made Carry Nation bottles and flasks—she herself was conveniently bottle-shaped—to poke fun at her. To further humiliate her, a few drinking houses even changed their name to the Carry Nation Saloon. Such acts certainly wounded her husband, who hung on bravely for twenty-four years before divorcing her. As for members of her family, she so embarrassed them that they "considered her a blot on the family Bible."[3] Still, she rallied thousands of supporters with her ardent lectures. Mrs. Nation's last saloon-smashing escapade was in 1910, and then, while lecturing in 1911, she suffered a stroke. Five months later, on June 2, 1911, she died. By then, the damage was done, and Jack Daniel and his comrades would be on the run.

IN THE GOOD OLD DAYS, the Women's Christian Temperance Union, among others, had found local option laws on prohibiting the manufacture and sale of liquor acceptable, but not now. In the first years of the twentieth century, nothing less than national prohibition would satisfy the dry forces, who were more potent than ever before. The Anti-Saloon League, for example, had expanded into almost every state and wielded great power in the ten years since its founding in 1893, in Oberlin, Ohio. Its goal: a saloon-less nation by 1920 to celebrate the 300th anniversary of the pilgrims landing at Plymouth. Saloons were slandered as "tools of the devil"; "the home breaker"; "the road to the poorhouse"; "the enslaver of men"; and the "drunkard's bank."[4] Hundreds of heartbreaking songs that played on guilt were sung in homes, in schools, in churches, and in front of saloons. A popular 1900 tune included conscience-pricking lyrics:

> From the bar-room, drunken laughter
>   sounds on the night,
>   While across a little death bed, falls the
>   moonbeam cold and white.

Go search for father, where the wine is red
  Tell him our hearts are breaking, tell him
    little Lou is dead.[5]

To his chagrin, Jack Daniel noticed undesirable changes in Nashville. As early as 1891, a citizens reform movement organized, bent on expelling what they termed the "saloon-gambler machine" that ruled the city.[6] Strengthening the temperance hand, in 1899, the Local Option League in Tennessee became the state's chapter of the more compelling Anti-Saloon League. Then, in the early 1900s, a wave of serious reform swept through Nashville. Local ministers and the Anti-Saloon League led the charge to sweep Cherry Street clean. The *Nashville American*—only several years removed from lauding Captain Jack lavishly—was running editorials denouncing the debauchery in the Men's Quarter. By 1903, unannounced police raids made life difficult for the saloons selling more than just liquor. Gambling tables were trashed, fines levied, and ladies of the night were reduced to being just ladies.

On the legal front the distillers were dealt a setback when, in 1899, Tennessee's Four-Mile Law, which had previously impacted unincorporated towns only, was extended to include towns of two thousand people or less that elected to incorporate *thereafter*. In other words, if a town elected to incorporate itself, which towns often did for legal reasons, all saloons within four miles of their schools had to be shuttered. Once again Jack dodged the bullet—Lynchburg had been incorporated in the 1840s. Two years later, a new bill proposing the extension of the Four-Mile Law to include towns of four thousand, called the Peeler bill, was introduced in the Tennessee state's legislature. It passed in the House of Representatives, so now it was up to the state Senate. Liquor lobbyists worked feverishly to block it, and their allies in the Senate cleverly revised the bill so that it would encompass towns of up to 104,000 people, thus including every city in the state, which was tantamount to prohibition. Because it was too radical, this sly maneuver guaranteed defeat. Indeed, the Senate shot it down with an eighteen-to-fifteen vote. In the aftermath, charges were levied that the liquor lobbyists had bribed several senators. The House and the Senate investigated and discovered that there had been a covert meeting of liquor men, including Victor Shwab, which allegedly resulted in raising $2,400 to be used to defeat the Peeler bill. Only $400 went toward legal fees. The rest? Well, Shwab's son George admitted that his father treated legislators to certain favors and gifts and sent liquor to their homes. When it came to questioning Shwab himself, he couldn't testify because he just happened to be in Florida for an extended respite. Ultimately, the investigative committee concluded that the money was for devious purposes but had insufficient evidence to indict individuals.[7]

Such setbacks served only to inspire the Anti-Saloon League and its cohorts. In 1903, they succeeded in extending the Four-Mile Law to towns of five thousand, but it was applicable only to towns that reincorporated after the bill's passage. For a variety of reasons a town might elect to recharter, thus reincorporate, and, indeed, many chose to do so simply because the prohibitionists demanded it in order for the new law to take effect. The activists carried banners with slogans designed to play on the guilty conscience, including, "Vote for Purity, Manhood, and Prosperity" and "Will You Stab Virtue and Support Vice?" At some polling locations, preachers and temperance activists—railing against Satan's devices—would stand by the ballot box and call out the names of those who supported the saloons. So much for freedom of choice and democracy.

By 1903, the tide had turned radically in favor of the dry forces. With great dismay, Jack faced the fact that fifty-five of the ninety-six Tennessee counties did not have legal saloons.[8] Drinking problems plagued Moore County, thus making Lynchburg ripe for reform, too. For example, on February 4, 1904, the *Fayette Observer* reported, "Last Sunday morning, Jack Porter, a Negro, was found dead in a barn near Lois, just across the line in Moore County, with the top of his head shot off. It is supposed that a crowd was gambling the night before and the game ended in a row. Porter had the name of being a rough, dangerous fellow. Two or three of his brothers have been killed before him."[9] Drinking and gambling went hand in hand. Despite such violence, Lynchburg voted 76 to 0 against a recharter.[10]

Somehow, the liquor industry continued to flourish outside of the Bible Belt. In 1896, the American public consumed more than 70 million gallons of distilled spirits; in 1907, the amount doubled to slightly more than 140 million gallons. Meanwhile, the population had only increased from a bit more than 70 million in 1896 to 87 million in 1907.[11] Obviously, somebody somewhere was awfully thirsty. While this upward trend offered hope, it would also make the prohibitionists that much more fervent.

JACK FACED ANOTHER potential enemy—an enemy within his own ranks. It was that firebrand of a man Lem Motlow. Lemmie wanted to fight the dry forces more vigorously; he wanted to expand their operations to include other liquors; and he drew Jack into a few undesirable legal scuffles. All of this went against Jack's temperament and provoked vicious arguments between the two. There were sensitive, yet pertinent, questions of whether Lem was getting too big for his britches, of whether he sought too much power, and, on the flip side, of whether Jack was a bit jealous of his nephew's rise as a big man around town.

Lem, a solemn-faced man who wore a white shirt, brown ducking pants with suspenders, and a big western hat, made quite an impression when he rode through town on his imposing bay horse with a blaze face. And he always rode at a gallop. Perhaps he was often in a foul mood and always traveled at a fast pace because death haunted him—his wife, Clara, died in 1901, not yet thirty years of age, leaving behind Lem and their son John Reagor Motlow. While Jack was still in search of wife number one, on September 23, 1903, Lem married his second, Miss Ophelia Verna Evans, with whom he'd have four children: Robert Taylor, Daniel Evans, Clifford Connor, and Mary Avon.[12] He was also busy accumulating hundreds of acres of land, owned several saloons, and was a leading mule trader. Indicative of how important Lem was becoming, news of his wedding was as big in the local paper as that of the annual corn show, the Moore County stock show, and Mule Day.[13] Well, maybe not as big as Mule Day, which involved months of planning—namely, getting your mules fat so that they fetched good prices. However, the *Lynchburg Falcon* even noted that Spoon Motlow, Lem's cousin, came up from Gadsden, Alabama, for the wedding—further evidence that the Motlow clan was deeply rooted in the community and still on the rise. In fact, by all appearances, it looked like the Motlow family was taking control of Farmers Bank.

In April 1901, Lem Motlow and cousin Spoon bought out the Tullahoma men who were partners in Farmers Bank.[14] Another savvy Motlow, Spoon had moved from Lynchburg to Gadsden, Alabama, where he opened a saloon and then started a distillery in 1899.[15] Now a major partner at Farmers Bank, he was made president, serving until 1916, and the two cousins hired Lem's younger brother Tom to take over the cashier position. They simply wrote him a letter, stating, "You're the cashier now. Full authority." At the time, Tom Motlow still had two months before he graduated from Vanderbilt University, where he was studying classic literature—he envisioned himself becoming a college professor. As the top student in his class, he could have written his own ticket anywhere. Instead, he agreed to return to Lynchburg and, like Jack, was so attached to the town, he lived out his life there. For those two months before he graduated, Tom went to Dr. Alexander Fall, of Fall's Business College, for an hour of instruction on banking each day. Still, "horse sense" counted most to him. Tom also restrained Jack's ballooning spending habits and ensured that he had money tucked away for "retirement."

JACK'S RETIREMENT SEEMED TO BE approaching briskly, as the battle with the Carry Nations of the country became ever more heated and he fought more bitterly with Lem. Control of the bank wasn't enough. A dominant position in mule trading wasn't enough. Being the bookkeeper and the de facto manager of the Jack Daniel Distillery for almost a decade wasn't enough. Lemmie, intent on extending his burgeoning empire, wanted his own distillery, too. This suppressed desire was hidden from Uncle Jack, who, traveling less, was at his distillery "nine-tenths of the time," until an explosive argument in 1905.[16]

To help with tasting and with managing the distillery, Jack had hired Walter Dreaman, who hailed from Nashville. One day, Lem ordered Dreaman to select some prime whiskey to ship to his own saloons. Dreaman began working his way through the barrels, picking and choosing them regardless of age. It wasn't long before word reached Jack, who, when he found out, exploded. He berated Drea-man for not taking the barrels in an orderly manner by the serial num-ber and thus "messing up" his whiskey. One's as good as another, Jack argued, there's no need to be picky. He then sought out his nephew, and a war of words ensued. Towering over his Uncle Jack, Lem took a stab at him by threatening to build his own brandy dis-tillery—which he had been arguing in favor of for some time—and to heck with whiskey. Jack said to heck with it all and went into town to cool off.

Change—and a brandy distillery definitely meant change—was anath-ema to the legendary boy distiller. He was approaching the twilight of his career and had very strong habits that he didn't want disrupted. Many an hour was now spent sitting in a hickory split-bottomed chair on the porch of his little white office building, keeping an eye on the distillery. Come quitting time, he stuffed the *Nashville American* news-paper in his coat pocket and rode his buggy back to the farm, where he made the rounds, checking the fields and the livestock. Once sat-isfied, he settled on his back porch for a drink of whiskey, plunking a little ice and a small lump of sugar into the glass, as well as bruising some tansy for added flavor. As Jack sipped the refreshing drink, he relished the fragrant honeysuckle in the field and the odors drifting from the kitchen. On certain evenings, he enjoyed the company of his younger nephews and nieces, playfully bantering with them. Lem, on the other hand, was no longer interested in giggling at Uncle Jack's feet and playing a subservient role in his orderly life.

Sure enough, when Jack returned to the distillery after his fight with Lem, he discovered that his impetuous nephew had requisitioned the distillery's best craftsman, Mr. A. R. Hinkle, to build his brandy distillery. "Damn to Hell," Jack cursed, using his favorite oath. As far as Jack was concerned, they were in the whiskey business, period. Besides, it would be a foolish outlay of cash that could very well result in Lem overextending himself. Then again, Lem was crafty—he could get money from anywhere. Intent on having his say, Jack rode up to Lem's farm, but no blustery tirade was going to force Hinkle off the job or dissuade Lem. As his sons later noted at his funeral, Lem "loved his friends and despised his enemies. He asked no quar-ter and gave none. Like nearly all strong men, when once he took a position it was difficult to change him."[17] What became known as the Upper Distillery was built, and it churned out peach brandy.[18] Brandy wasn't necessarily a bad thing, for as the great poet and critic Samuel Johnson once said, "Claret is the liquor for boys; port, for men; but he who aspires to be a hero must drink brandy."

LEM'S MULE-TRADING BUSINESS also proved to be a headache for Jack and threatened his distillery's sterling reputation. It was 1906, and America was on the cusp of the age of the horseless carriage. Henry Ford had founded Ford Motors in 1903, and, in 1908, he would introduce the world to his affordable Model T, thus democratizing the motorcar. His Model T made for a far more mobile America; the countryside was suddenly accessible to the urban masses—or at least those masses who could afford the $825 sticker price. Meanwhile, in Lynchburg, a quality yearling mule with a longer lifespan than its mechanized brother could be had for under $200.

These beasts of burden were and would remain crucial for distributing Jack Daniel's sour mash whiskey. As of 1906, Jack had five teams of mules—driven by "negroes"—hauling whiskey twelve miles over deplorable roads to the Tullahoma railyard, as well as to Shelbyville and Fayetteville. In the winter, he shipped about 20 barrels a day, with 5 to 7 barrels, or 2,000 to 2,800 pounds, to a load. Twice as much was shipped in the colder winter months than at any other time. For the arduous job, Jack preferred to buy mature three-year-old mules, which were inevitably overworked. From the strains on their tendons, they would start walking on their toes and eventually come up lame. To keep his stable stocked, Jack threw most of his business Lem's way.

Lemmie, who now owned a number of stables, raised quality mules and had won the red ribbon at Lynchburg's Mule Day.[19] As the area's dominant mule trader, he was able to strike a hard bargain; however, according to some Lynchburg citizens, he was also a generous man at times. If a farmer couldn't afford to buy his mules, for example, Lem leased them for a nominal amount. Also, in years that crops failed, he gave flour and corn to widows and poverty-stricken families.[20] An inconsistent personality, he could also be very callous and impatient and would not always admit when he was wrong. It was his bullheaded business dealing that brought trouble and landed Jack in the courthouse.

One particular episode started with the local farmer Hugh Ledford, who came to Lem in search of a mule team capable of hauling by wagon two loads of 50 bushels of corn four miles each way daily. Relying on Lem's guarantee that his beasts were healthy, Ledford bought two three-year-old black mare mules for $385 in cash, a good chunk of change. Not long after, however, *both* mules came up lame, walking on their toes, strongly suggesting that they'd been overworked before Ledford ever bought them. When Lem refused to take back the mules and refund Ledford's money, Ledford took him to court. Subsequently, County Sheriff G. R. Stephenson subpoenaed Jack to testify at the behest of the defense—subpoenaed, because he wasn't voluntarily going to submit himself to a pair of jackal lawyers on behalf of nobody. One can only imagine the "Damn to Hell" that echoed through the Hollow that day.

Despite his best efforts to keep a low profile when it came to anything having to do with the government, Jack found himself in the lovely brick Moore County Courthouse on October 26, 1906, to testify on behalf of Lem. In the last few years, Jack had spent his fair share of time using legal means to protect his lands, but this was the first time he was placed in the uncomfortable situation of being questioned. This would prove to be one of the rare instances Jack Daniel was captured on record verbatim, his voice and vernacular unadulterated. Sitting in the witness chair behind the wood railing, Jack looked like a strangely wizened kid caught playing hooky. Fortunately for him, in addition to the pleasant smell of wood polish and autumn, there was the comforting odor of mash from his distillery vats wafting through the room.

When Lem's lawyer asked Jack his place of residence and occupation, Jack replied with a cocky, sly tone, "Two miles from town is where I live at. Well, hayseeder, mostly farming." Two miles was as specific as he would get, and everyone knew he was far more than a hayseeder. Only when asked what he hauled by mule did he admit his association with distilling: "Well, liquors and grain, barrel timber, you know, and wood and coal."

To nail down Jack's occupation, the lawyer said, "During this time, state whether or not you have been engaged in any other business besides farming."

"Yes, I have been engaged in the distillery business and right smart in the grain business." And he added that he'd been distilling "thirty odd years or more"–placing his entry into the business about the time he and Dan Call formed their partnership in 1875. Not a bad memory for a whiskey man.

Now came the questions concerning the mules. When asked if he ever had mules that walked on their toes, Jack again gave a slightly evasive answer, "Well, I have had a good many to walk on their toes. I never kept count of the number."

As evidence of a mule walking on its toes, the lawyer then wanted to know, would the hoof's heel grow faster than its toes?

"Well," said Jack, "the wearing off of the toe more or less, and not using the heel would cause it to grow faster."

The lawyer finally got to the heart of the matter; he asked Jack if he remembered seeing the mules. "Yes, sir, I remember of seeing them once. I saw them more than once I reckon, but one time in particular." It was when they had hauled whiskey from a Mr. Brinkley's distillery. The pair in question pulled one wagon of whiskey and a pair of Mr. Brinkley's mules pulled the second wagon's worth. "They were in very nice fix then," Jack said, "right purty pair of mules."

When asked if he hauled his whiskey to Tullahoma, Jack said, "I haul a portion of it there, the most of it, a great deal of it." That is, the majority of it. The mules hauling his whiskey, Jack explained, lasted three years and up, some even working ten or twelve years, "but they generally go two or three years before they commence walking on their toes, and never unless they are strained. I think it is bad driving and overloading that causes them to go to walking on their toes."

During the cross-examination, Ledford's lawyer said, "I suppose you all overload and overwork all of your mules, do you?"

"Well, yes, a great deal, most of them we do," Jack admitted. Beasts of burden were just another cost to be entered on the ledger– as were laborers in the factories–but at least Jack was talking mules, not men, women, and children.

A frustrated Jack kicked the rather weighty safe and paid the price.

The case of the two lame mules consumed dozens of pages of testimony and court records—seemingly overkill by lawyers looking to bill obscene hours, even in modest Lynchburg—which illustrated how important mules were to country farmers. For all the records, the verdict remains buried. One truth that emerged: Lem was now a powerful figure in the community who wasn't adverse to operating in a morally gray area. Also, Lem was clearly willing to oppose his mentor Jack Daniel, as demonstrated by his construction of the brandy distillery.

HOTHEADED LEM, the temperance movement, the revenuers, and the various aggravations of business all ripped away at Jack's patience and geniality. To soothe his nerves, he had started eating and drinking more. Unfortunately, his excessive consumption of rich food and drink took its toll; bluntly put, Jack was fat, which only added to his frustrations. A vicious cycle had begun. His aggravated mental state came to a head one morning when he arrived at the office before anyone else. Jack attempted to access the company safe—a waist-high, black iron monster on wheels—but couldn't get the combination to work. Out of frustration, he reared back and kicked it with his left foot. Well, it still didn't open—not that he thought it would—and he only succeeded in bruising his foot.[21]

While he didn't think anything of it at the time, that foot injury would have serious consequences. In the days after, Jack, now age fifty-seven, walked with a limp. Then he started to sport a cane. His health in general suddenly deteriorated, and, a month after he testified in the Ledford mule case, the *Lynchburg Falcon* noted that Jack was sick and confined to bed.[22] Over the next several years, he would have periodic bouts of illness that were caused more by his poor diet than by any natural infirmities brought on by age. The Gay Nineties had caught up with him. Not only was Jack's health suffering but so was the United States' economy; and as both man and country fell gravely ill, the legendary boy distiller would seriously consider retirement, even as his reputation continued to grow.

13

REBORN

꙳·꙳

The gods who are most interested in the human race preside over the tavern.
The tavern will compare favorably with the church. The church is the place
where prayers and sermons are delivered, but the tavern is where they are to
take effect, and if the former are good the latter cannot be bad.

—Henry David Thoreau

Throughout the Gilded Age, the United States had been suscep-
tible to financial panics and depressions, due to the lack of sound
monetary policies and reasonable regulation of private enterprise.
The new century brought more of the same chaos, and President
Theodore Roosevelt, claiming to carry a big stick, perpetuated it. His
bellicose attitude toward big business continually rattled Wall Street.
And when Wall Street wavered, so did the public's confidence. On
March 14, 1907, panic finally struck and investors scrambled to sell
their stocks. The Dow Jones Industrial Average plummeted 25 percent. In Lynchburg, the Farmers Bank board of directors convened
and noted that the bank should be proud of its affairs; only ten or
twelve customers "got scared and withdrew their money," while other
banks had to put a lid on withdrawals. A real credit to their money
management, Jack and his fellow directors were even able to declare
a 10 percent dividend.[1] However, the March panic was just a precur-
sor, a mere intimation, of what was to come.

In October 1907, two rapacious Wall Street speculators, F. Augustus Heinze and Charles W. Morse, attempted to corner the copper market and failed. The alarm sounded. Already-timorous investors made a run on the banks that had financed their ill-advised scheme, causing those banks to fail and the ex-president of the Knickerbocker Trust banking firm to kill himself. The stock market crashed to a new low, and the interest rate on short-term loans shot to 125 percent. J. Pierpont Morgan convened emergency meetings, at which he smoked cigars furiously and fell asleep from sheer exhaustion, and even John D. Rockefeller, a virtual recluse, offered to ante up half his fortune to thwart the panic. Wall Street financiers and the country's industrialists were not the only ones affected, as the panic sent shock waves rippling through the nation—even to Lynchburg.

Country bankers were dependent on powerful financiers like Morgan, who dictated the flow of money and interest rates. At Farmers Bank, cashier Tom Motlow was completely attuned to the October financial panic, which carried over into November despite Morgan's best efforts to save the day. Tom recalled,

> During the panic of November 1907, thousands of people were lined up in front of the New York banks, waiting to draw their money out. So some prominent financiers got together and agreed not to open the banks until the people calmed down. They sent telegrams urging every banker in America to remain closed until further notice. When I got my telegram I called New York to confirm the closing. Knowing that some of my depositors might become worried, I attempted to build up my cash reserve by drawing money from larger banks in the state. This I was unable to do, so I arranged to "buy" some money from a New York firm at the rate of $70 a thousand. That was on a Saturday. By Monday morning I had all the money I wanted, and our bank remained open. Our depositors knew their money was available if they wanted it.

To shore up confidence during that horrific November, legend has it that Jack, who remained a bank director despite his ailments, visited the Red Dog and the White Rabbit saloons to set everyone up with drinks and to announce that the Farmers Bank would remain open. Consequently, there was no mad dash by Moore County citizens.

Lynchburg's businessmen had to tip their hats to Tom Motlow, who was decidedly Jack's kind of banker; he scorned the Yankees and took care of his hometown people. Known to friends and acquaintances simply as Mr. Tom, he lived a modest life, boarding under Lem's roof for twenty-five years and then renting a room at the legendary Bobo Hotel, known later as Miss Mary Bobo's Boarding House. He would become the president of Farmers Bank in 1916 and remain at the helm for more than fifty years. For that entire span he served his customers devoutly, the bank closing but one business day. His dedication was inspired by a local farmer who didn't know his alphabet, a fact Tom was always quick to point out:

> I learned my first—and most important—lesson the second day after I came into the bank, I learned that the purpose of my life as a banker was not to make money for stockholders, but to be able to pay every depositor whenever he wanted his money. Why do I believe this? A 65-year old man who had worked all his life on his little farm walked into the bank that day and said, "Tom, I've sold my farm. I've got $1,500, and I want you to take care of it." He shoved the $1,500 through the window, and I told him to wait for a receipt. He said, "Don't give me a receipt. Whenever I want my money, I'm sure I can get it." And he walked out. I'd rather die than go back on anyone who trusts me like that.[2]

That's exactly how Jack felt about his whiskey business; however, he wasn't finding the business environment as trusting and friendly as Mr. Tom's clients.

DESPITE THE COUNTRY'S FINANCIAL WOES, Jack prospered in 1907. For the year he paid $43,218 in local and county taxes, indicative of a superlative income that had to be well over $100,000. He owned five sizable pieces of property, amounting to hundreds of acres, and two lots in town. And his fame continued to spread when Lem arranged a high-profile deal with the Maxwell House, a renowned and elegant Nashville hotel. The establishment also served a high-quality blend of coffee, which was immortalized when Teddy Roosevelt visited in 1907, ordered a cup, and reputedly said it was "good to the last drop."[3] Such an endorsement and that slogan would make it a national brand that remains on store shelves today. Lem, who had rented a suite of rooms in the Utopia Hotel on Church Street for conducting business, was more concerned about the whiskey the Maxwell House served, especially since the hotel catered to such illustrious men as Teddy Roosevelt.

To curry favor with the owner, Colonel John Overton, Lem had a special decanter designed in honor of the hotel and sent it, along with a letter requesting an interview. Overton was greatly impressed by the good taste of both Lem's overture and the whiskey. After a congenial meeting, he agreed to buy two hundred cases of Jack Daniel's, to be packaged in a special bottle that would be sold exclusively at the Maxwell House. At some point, he also offered Lem co-ownership of the Old Oak Bar, located in the hotel. Lem accepted, naturally. On July 3, 1907, he proudly informed Uncle Jack that Maxwell House customers were choosing Jack Daniel's whiskey two to one over the competitors' brands. "It is, Uncle Jack, a truly distinctive potable, with special appeal to the educated palate," he wrote, sounding rather educated himself.[4] At any other time prior, Jack would have been tickled, but now his elevated reputation and monetary prosperity were no longer priorities. Like Wall Street, his health had taken a serious hit.

Jack's unabated appetite for beef and pork, pies and pastries, and wine and whiskey not only caught up with him but passed him by. A young Lynchburg boy observed that the portly Uncle Jack, who was putting more and more weight on his cane as he hobbled along, looked like "a Mr. Five by Five." He now sported a long beard, rather than a trimmed goatee, and didn't bother dyeing it black—nothing would mask his failing health.[5] Many worried that he would suffer heart trouble. In the spring of 1907, just age fifty-seven, he fell deathly sick, and, like his father fifty years earlier, he was bedridden, unable to manage his daily affairs.[6] To prepare for death, Jack wrote his last will and testament, signed and dated April 20, 1907. But he didn't die. Instead, he was forced to contend with a living death: his impending retirement.

Jack had already been divesting some of his extensive land holdings. In the early 1900s, for example, he sold off some acreage, including sixteen acres to a James Baker for just a bag of maize. Obviously, Jack was in a generous mood, although Baker must have been a good man in some respect, too.[7] Jack's greatest gift was about to come, however. As he reviewed his dazzling accomplishments, he couldn't help but acknowledge that the world was a different place. Most notable, gone were the great distillers Jack had had such a strong kinship with. The pioneering Eaton clan had moved its operation to whiskey-friendly Memphis, the only Tennessee city more debauched than Nashville; the Tolley clan had completely closed up shop; the Spencers, the Hiles, and the Berrys—all gone. Of the regional powers, only Shwab's Cascade in Tullahoma and Bill Hughes in Winchester survived.[8] So many distillers had been done in by the passage of time, by the government, and by the temperance movement. When it came to the revenuers, Jack himself admitted that he no longer wanted to "fool with the signing of papers," day in and day out. When it came to the constant heckling and derision from the temperance leaders, Jack himself knew it was only a matter of time before the dry forces would completely wipe out distilling in Tennessee. Due to his deteriorating health and his lack of zest for tasting every barrel, Jack decided to quit the business.[9]

Imagine the surprise when Jack deeded the company—the whole shebang—to his "boys," his two nephews, Lem Motlow and Dick Daniel, for not a penny in return. Apparently, any disagreements with Lem were ultimately inconsequential. Jack's language in the deed said it all:

> For and in consideration of valuable services rendered me, extending over several years past, and for the love and affection I have for my two nephews Lem Motlow and Dick Daniel, I, Jack Daniel, of Moore County, Tennessee, do hereby transfer and convey unto the said Dick Daniel and Lem Motlow my entire distillery business and plant located at Lynchbug Tenn., together with the good will thereof, and trade name and trade marks, and all other rights. . . . I reserve full possession of said premises until first day of next January, when said Daniel and Motlow shall receive full possession of the premises and plant aforesaid.[10]

The transaction included 200 acres of land and a debt-free whiskey-making business, a credit to Jack's business acumen. The document

Closing in on retirement, Jack, second row third from the right, forever cultivated an esprit de corps among his still hands.

was dated April 16, 1907, but the nephews wouldn't take possession of the prized property until January 1, 1908.

BOTH LEM AND DICK WERE closing in on forty years of age, the prime of their business lives, and, like two mature wolves in a pack, they recognized that only one could remain. Although Dick had been the bookkeeper for the distilling business belonging to his father, Wiley, and had now served Jack for a number of years in the same capacity, Lem was none too happy that Dick received a share of the business. There wasn't much Lem could do about it, however. Jack had a strong affinity for his brother Wiley, as well as for his brother's eldest boy, who was Lem's senior by a year. Also, Dick, who lived adjacent to the old Calaway Daniel farm, had further strengthened the ties with the Motlow clan when he married Agnes Irene Motlow circa 1900.[11] It was a touchy situation. Regardless, Lem wanted Dick out of the way before they took possession of the business in eight months' time.

Dangling a big wad of cash was Lem's best option. He certainly had the money to buy out his unwanted partner; his income was prodigious enough and he owned such a substantial amount of land that he paid $42,700 in local and state taxes in 1907. As it turned out, Dick didn't have the enthusiasm required for owning a distillery anyway and that August accepted a lump sum of $10,000 from Lem to step aside and relinquish any claims on the business.[12] Considering the momentum the dry forces had and the distinct possibility that the distillery would be shuttered, it was a windfall for Dick. On the other hand, if the dry forces failed and the distillery prospered, then it was a steal for Lem.

THE HORIZON HAD BLACKENED considerably. Whereas the century had begun with close to a hundred registered distilleries in Tennessee, in Lem's first year as the proprietor of the Jack Daniel Distillery there were only forty-three remaining—the power of the industry in Tennessee cut in half.[13] All of the tax districts in the state had been combined into one, and Lem's reasonably local brethren included but three: the Cascade Distillery and B. B. Mitchell & Co. in Tullahoma, and Jones & Hughes in Winchester. Meanwhile, Lem himself had three distilleries registered: Jack Daniel, #514; Jack Daniel, Lem Motlow, proprietor, #524; and Lem Motlow, #596.[14] More headstrong than ever, he also owned saloons in Lynchburg (the White Rabbit Saloon being his favorite watering hole), Nashville, Shelbyville, and Alabama.

Either Lem was completely naïve and didn't believe that prohibition would become universal law, or he was planning to go down with guns blazing, because, in April 1908, he laid plans to build a larger brandy warehouse.[15] He also expanded the whiskey brand line. He created a No. 5 brand—called that simply because it was a younger whiskey than No. 7—and a Lem Motlow Tennessee Sour Mash Whiskey that was in the barrel for only one year. Due to the mellowing the whiskey underwent when filtered through the sugar maple charcoal, Lem believed that it was smooth enough after just a year in the barrel. Well, there was also the specter of prohibition, which pushed him hard to reap maximum profits now. To be within arm's length of his baby at all times, adjacent to the distillery Lem built a beautiful two-story, Greek Revival home with two pillars gracing the entrance. His wife, Ophelia—a strong personality in her own right, who never allowed liquor in the house except for medicinal purposes—had even become involved in his business. She was the proprietor of the Lynchburg Waterworks, the company formed to sell water from the Cave Spring to town residences—a good but very modest hedge in case the distillery was indeed closed.[16]

While Jack had always been a fatalist about the future of distilling and never had attempted to influence the politicians at the state capitol, Lem was intent on joining the fray personally. Over the years he had attended secret meetings held by the wet forces, at which they targeted those politicians they could ply with money and alcohol. More sophisticated tactics were now required, however. In 1907, an editor of a liquor trade journal, T. M. Gilmore, established the Model License League, the league's mission being to reform saloons, give licenses only to men of upstanding character, revoke licenses belonging to those who didn't follow the law, and do away with any other objectionable features of the liquor industry, among other activities. Their ultimate goal was to take the wind out of the prohibitionists' sails. Following Gilmore's lead, in the summer of 1908, Lem, along with other Tennessee distillers, brewers, and liquor dealers, attended a Nashville Model License League meeting. Offering an olive branch, they proclaimed that they would fight statewide prohibition through education, not politics, further stating that

> we emphatically repudiate any effort to induce the trade to violate the laws, and strongly condemn such actions, and as the retailers have been long sufferers from the corrupting influence of political factions, we are determined to remove the same from partisan politics, by demanding obedience to the laws on one side and enforcement of them on the other, under the true principles of good citizenship, as advocated by the Tennessee Model License League.

It appeared to be too little too late from a group of men whose incentives were in question.

That same summer the Anti-Saloon League and the WCTU aggressively pressed the campaign by organizing mass rallies across Tennessee. The *American Issue,* the Anti-Saloon League's mouthpiece, trumpeted: "The battle is on! On one side the Anti-Saloon League and other combined temperance forces fighting for a 'clean sweep of the liquor traffic from Tennessee in 1909.' On the other side, the saloon, the brewery, the distillery, hard pressed and desperate, making a fight for life."[17] In nearby Fayetteville, the WCTU held parades with horse-drawn floats, the women waving American flags and signs calling for prohibition.

Ongoing illicit activity in the region didn't help Lem's cause. In July 1907, IRS agents, a.k.a. revenue raiders, pounced on a moon-shining operation southwest of Fayetteville at the headwaters of Briar Fork, where they destroyed a still with a superlative daily capacity of 100 gallons and equipped with "a splendid boiler." The operators escaped. As the *Fayetteville Observer* wryly put it, "It seems that the persons engaged in the illicit distillation of spirits have a superior way of learning of the movements of the 'revenoos.'"[18] And, despite the proclamations of the Model License League, in July 1909, a wealthy distiller operating near Knoxville, J. H. Buckner, was arrested for trying to bribe a revenue officer. He was sentenced to eighteen months in jail, and his indiscretion made the papers across the state.[19] Such news fed prohibition, which was like a hurricane sucking energy and moisture from the warm ocean water and then roaring inland.

But if anyone could blockade the dry forces and grow the whiskey business, it was Lem. Broad shouldered and thick bodied, he still exuded a rough-and-tumble image with his open-collared white shirt and no necktie. Also, he was proving to have a tremendous capacity to function at a number of levels simultaneously. As one friend claimed, "He had four or five brains—and could talk to several people, add a column of figures as long as your arm in his head, and write checks, all at once."[20] Despite Lem's determination, it appeared that the prospects for the distillery were dimming, and, in parallel, so was Jack's life.

* * *

JACK'S HEALTH MIRRORED that of the whiskey industry. Having given himself completely to the business, it was his life force and he couldn't bear the thought of the distillery fire going out. Unfortunately, his immediate enemy was no longer the dry forces but the grippe, pneumonia, and inexplicable periods of utter exhaustion. On occasion, he experienced blurred vision, too, and, although he knew better, his appetite increased. Yes, he was overweight and his diet was both excessive and poor, but there was something else dragging his body down. It was time to see the family doctor, who quickly determined that Jack's case was too complex for him to handle. So, he sought medical advice in Nashville, but again, no cut-and-dry diagnosis was offered.

Yearning to recover his health, Jack checked himself into a sanitarium in Hot Springs, Arkansas. At the time, Palm Beach in Florida, Poland Springs in Maine, and Hot Springs, the latter a favorite of the steel titan Andrew Carnegie, were among the top spa towns catering to the wealthy. Located in west central Arkansas, Hot Springs lived up to its name: it boasted forty-seven thermal springs pumping out over a million gallons of 143-degree water a day, some of it piped into steam baths and cooled in reservoirs to a more tolerable temperature. Jack hoped that these springs, somewhat different in purpose than that of Cave Spring, would prove to be the elixir he now needed. Over the following days, he spent hours breathing in the steam and the minerals, silently praying that they would open his lungs and arteries. However, the steam baths, the restricted diet, and other treatments offered only temporary relief, nothing more. Jack would find himself confined to his room for much of the remainder of his life, a pathetic state of affairs for a man with such zest for living.[21] His once-beautiful farm began to deteriorate. In the near future, it would fall into disrepair, roofs would leak, windowsills rot, and fences collapse. Its value would depreciate precipitously.[22]

Sensing ever-encroaching death, Jack made preparations. With the will written and the distillery deeded, a remaining big decision was where to be buried. A family plot was the proper thing for a man of his standing, so Jack relocated his parents' graves to the Lynchburg Cemetery, where he could be reunited with them. On doing so, he gave them new headstones, but he recorded his mother's death year incorrectly as 1847–two years before her actual death.[23] Such inaccuracy was not expected from an "exactin'" man like Jack–clearly, his mind was wandering.

There was one other pressing issue: life after death, the great unknown. Because Jack had hosted so many church dinners over the years, the community assumed that he was a churchgoing believer. He was not. But he wasn't exactly going to publicize his agnosticism–it was a dangerous status, considering that the locals liked to think that if the Bible Belt had a buckle, they'd be on it. In this neck of the woods, the Primitive Baptist Association he had forsaken fifty years ago remained strong and active; brother Wiley had been a devout member for years, as were various and sundry Motlows, Waggoners, and Tolleys. Now, with death circling, Jack felt Jesus by his side. With no wife and no children, it was natural that he turned to the church for comfort. Yet in death, he knew that only the baptized could commune at the Lord's table–it was time for a conversion.

NO ONE HAD FORGOTTEN how Jack relished galloping up to the Primitive Baptist church and shouting brazenly through the door, "Hey, Elder Webster, you've talked long enough. Turn loose your congregation and come with me for dinner." The interim years had brought much humility, as the man now respectfully addressed as Major Jack Daniel was very discreet when he approached the church elder A. J. Willis to make a profession of religion. There would be no private baptism, however; he had to join the church in the presence of the members. So, on a Sunday morning in late April 1909, when Elder Willis invited all people who wished to become members of the church to come forward, Jack, at the age of sixty, rose gingerly from his pew and limped up to the front. The baptism was to be performed in Mulberry Creek. As members of the congregation walked through the narrow field, the flood plain, to the rather modest river, they sang hymns rejoicing in Jesus.

Two men assisted Jack into the waist-deep water. On the bank, Elder Willis said a prayer and then waded with great purpose into the river. Next to Jack, Elder Willis raised one hand, prayed over the ill

The Primitive Baptist church where Jack was baptized still stands.

man, and then, with the help of an assistant, he immersed Jack. He was submerged faceup, thus lying as he would in death, but then raised out of the water, signifying his rebirth. Jack rose from the pool, water dripping off his matted-down hair and drooping mustache, and, while clapping his hands, he cried, "Hallelujah, hallelujah, hallelujah." Despite the chill of the April water, it was a warm and happy moment. Elder Willis later observed that Jack's "conversion was one of the most earnest he had ever known."[24] He never did do anything half-assed, and, more so than ever, the broken man needed faith. Despite his earnestness, Jack remained low key and very private about his conversion. Only by accident was the story discovered by the newspapers, which, once printed, would set off a public outcry.

Not long after the baptism, Elder Willis happened to bump into a newspaper correspondent and innocently recounted Major Jack's joining the church. When people read of his conversion, they were shocked to learn he had not been a churchgoer all these years, apparently living as a heathen. This revelation created such a furor in the community that two weeks after first reporting his conversion, both the *Shelbyville Gazette* and the *Fayetteville Observer* felt it necessary to blunt the gossip: "We have known Major Daniel many years and have always known him as a genial, unobtrusive gentleman, neither seeking or desiring notoriety. Besides this, he has in a very wide sense, always been a noble-hearted, kind, generous, liberal man. He has always aided in building churches and school houses and has given liberally to the support of God's ministry. . . . He was a good man while out of the church, and will become a still better one in it."[25] While the newspapers were optimistic about his spiritual well-being, Jack was not. The year Major Jack Daniel was reborn, the liquor industry faced its ultimate challenge. It was a year of personal salvation and heartbreak for the wizened boy distiller.

14

THE FINAL BATTLE

☓·☓

When I'm dead and in my grave
No more whiskey will I crave
But on my tombstone shall be wrote,
They's many a jolt went down his throat.

–John Copeland

America's impressive consumption of alcohol was garnering more attention in the mainstream press. In April 1906, the *Nation* reported that annual per capita consumption had increased to an astounding 20 gallons of alcohol in 1905, from a mere 4 gallons in 1850. As for whiskey alone, it had increased to 1.5 gallons, from just 1 gallon eight years earlier, a big jump for hard liquor.[1] Even so, the whiskey men were concerned about America becoming a beer-drinking nation like Germany, forsaking its identity as the robust frontier liquor-drinking country it once was. Meanwhile, according to the likes of Carry Nation and the militant dry forces, this upward trend did not bode well for the American soul, and they redoubled their reform efforts.

The temperance movement now had a stranglehold on the South. "So absorbed has this country been for the last few years in the attempt to regulate corporations, check monopolies, and deal with the unprincipled rich," the *Nation* reported, "that a veritable revolution in the sentiment of the people upon a great social question has taken place practically unnoticed. Only when the Georgia Legislature voted almost unanimously for prohibition did the general public begin to learn that there is a great anti-saloon movement underway."[2] In addition to the horrific revolution in Georgia, almost two-thirds of Alabama's counties were dry; Mississippi was expected to go dry when the legislature convened in January 1908; the anti-saloon forces in Kentucky were victors, the state effectively dry; and in Tennessee, "only three towns and three cities and 5 out of 96 counties still tolerate the sale of liquor."[3] A demoralized Jack, dreaming of past glory, was isolated in Lynchburg, surrounded by an army almost as heinous as the Billy Yanks. Only Nashville and Memphis remained strongholds for the drinking man. In Nashville, the Men's Quarter was relatively vibrant, despite increased police activity; prostitutes worked the red light district known as "Hell's Half Acre"; and a defiant Nashville mayor declared that he himself patronized his city's saloons. Memphis took debauchery to another level. "Streetwalkers have been thick as wasps in summertime," the papers reported, and the city's red light district offered not only whores and booze but opium and cocaine.[4]

Refocusing their campaign, the dry forces blamed liquor for labor violence and anarchy in the North and black men raping white women in the South—all very convenient. The Anti-Saloon League went so far as to scrutinize court records and determined that whiskey was related to many black crimes.[5] Their claims appeared to be justified during the 1908 gubernatorial election in Tennessee when, in a high-profile case, a black man raped and murdered a fourteen-year-old girl. He was caught and lynched. In the aftermath, the pro-temperance newspaper *Nashville Tennessean* ran an interview with a Methodist minister, who blamed cheap gin on creating such monsters. He declared, "This gin, with its label, has made more black rape fiends, and has procured the outrage of more white women in the South than all other agencies combined. It is sold with the promise that it will bring white virtue into the black's brute power." It was so easy for the blind righteous to play the racial card.

The 1908 Tennessee gubernatorial election and its aftermath would prove to be a pivotal point in the great battle between wet and dry forces. If Tennessee went dry, it would kill Jack.

IN THE DEMOCRATIC PRIMARY, the incumbent Malcolm Patterson, a temperance moderate who supported the local option law, was challenged by Edward Ward Carmack, an intense man with a bushy walrus mustache who was a dry radical. Although Patterson defeated Carmack and then fended off the prohibitionist Republican candidate, Carmack was determined to push through legislation that would make Tennessee dry, once and for all. And Carmack, now the powerful editor of the *Nashville Tennessean,* had the weapons to do it. In what has been described as "exceptionally vitriolic editorials," he attacked Patterson and his allies, including his political adviser Colonel Duncan B. Cooper. In kind, Cooper threatened Carmack's life and both started packing pistols. On November 9, 1908, on the heels of another shrill editorial, the two men happened to encounter each other on a Nashville street in the late afternoon. Cooper ran at Carmack, shouting angrily. Carmack drew his pistol and fired twice. He accidentally hit Cooper's son Robin, who returned fire, killing Carmack. The prohibitionists immediately elevated Carmack to martyr status. The hysterical *Tennessean* called it "murder cold-blooded, deliberate, premeditated, with every detail planned out before hand; murder without justification; a dastardly crime without parallel in the annals of the state."[6] Lynching of blacks aside, apparently. Both Coopers were convicted of second-degree murder, but Robin's conviction was overturned on a technicality, and Governor Patterson issued a pardon for the elder Cooper. However, in death it did appear that Carmack would achieve his goal of prohibition, as this series of events served to galvanize the dry forces that had captured the state's Senate and House of Representatives.

When the Legislature convened in January 1909, the dry forces wasted no time in introducing a bill that would ban the sale of alcohol within four miles of a schoolhouse anywhere in the state, which effectively amounted to statewide prohibition. Such a bill, Governor

Patterson argued, would result in large-scale moonshining, crime, increased taxation, and social discord; therefore, he threatened to veto it. To derail the legislation, liquor lobbyists worked feverishly. They even brought in a carload of beautiful "fallen" women to seduce key legislators—according to claims made by a Methodist clergyman who was practiced in the art of propaganda.

On the day the vote was to take place, a snowstorm swept down upon Nashville, but still the capitol building's galleries were filled with hymn-singing prohibitionists who conducted themselves more like exhibitionists. Up until the final moments, debate was heated. The most eloquent speech on behalf of whiskey came from Caruthers Ewing, a representative from western Tennessee:

> In this sad hour when so many . . . are raving and rioting against the use of intoxicants, I desire to go on record as favoring the stuff. It may be driven from the haunts of men and exiled from the homes of those who love and long for it, but wheresoever it may be driven I want it to know that I entertain for it the liveliest affection and will never permit it to go unused and neglected, if I can avoid it. It has been my fortune to know its virtues, to feel its exhilarating embrace, to yield the response of blood and brain to its amorous touch, to learn its glory and its grief. . . . Intoxicants, discreetly used, have lightened many a burden, silver-rimmed many a cloud, dissipated many a friend of care, made roseate many an unhappy hour and converted many a wail of woe into a "rippling river of laughter."

Ewing went on to rail against the temperance-minded, who "think they are entitled to speak by the mere claim that they never took a drink. . . . The man who knows naught of the glory and the grief that lurks in a jug is not qualified to harangue about the liquor habit."[7] Such a stirring speech should have bred a whole generation of joyous alcoholics. The law passed in both houses anyway.

One cheery dry representative took the speaker's rostrum and played "Dixie" on a fife; another played "Good Bye, Whisky, Good Bye" on a Jew's harp. As promised, Patterson vetoed the bill. Subsequently, both houses overrode his veto, and, on January 20, 1909, the legislation banning the sale of alcohol within four miles of any schoolhouse was made law.[8] It was a dagger to Jack's heart, as his life's work was spit on and crushed under a heavy legislative foot. Symbolic of the disastrous year, on October 14, 1909, a cyclone roared through the Mulberry area, not far from Jack's farm. It ripped the second floors off area homes and uprooted trees.

AS A RESULT OF the heinous legislation, Lem, who could still keep the distillery fire burning, had to shutter his Lynchburg saloons. Other liquor dealers attempted to build saloons outside the four-mile radius of schools, where there were no local option laws, but this strategy failed miserably—there was hardly a customer in such desolate places. Fortunately, there were, and always would be, Blind Tigers, later known as speakeasies. While the Men's Quarter in Nashville would never be the same, the saloons did their best to sell soda over the counter and liquor under it to their favored patrons. In fact, it was relatively easy for saloons to pay off the right cops and judges and continue as merrily as before. Widespread violations by saloons were to be expected, and enforcement did indeed leave much to be desired. A full year later, in 1910, the editor of the *Baptist and Reflector,* E. E. Folk, decried the situation, "Crimes of all kinds are rampant. . . . The situation is becoming alarming, desperate. It is fast growing intolerable. Something must be done."[9] He had little reason for complaint, compared to the beleaguered distillers.

In early 1909, yet another blow was dealt the Jack Daniel Distillery: the State Legislature passed the Manufacturer's Bill, which banned the making of intoxicants in Tennessee. Once again Governor Patterson, claiming it was akin to destroying private property, vetoed it, and once again both houses overrode him. This second disastrous law went into effect on January 1, 1910—the squeamish lawmakers were good enough to allow distillers almost a year's window to make alternative plans, if they could. The grace period didn't help the scores of Moore County men who were thrown out of work but did reinvigorate the moonshiners and the bootleggers who were waiting in the wings. In the months before the law went into effect, Lem and his fellow distillers ran at full capacity and feverishly sold their whiskey at rock-bottom prices.

Any hope of overturning these laws was dashed when the Republican and prohibitionist Ben Wade Hooper was elected as Tennessee governor in 1910. Hooper believed that the state had a right to stop citizens from drinking "for the great and righteous purpose of protecting society."[10] Despite the laws and the blustery rhetoric, Jack Daniel could take some comfort in knowing that drinking in Nashville and Memphis continued unabated. Even on election day, drinking in Nashville's Men's Quarter was hardly discreet. A correspondent for the *Commercial Appeal* reported:

> Mainstreet and downtown saloons within a few doors of the polling places, where policemen were on duty, were running wide open and doing a land office business. A negro porter came out of a side door of the Climax Saloon, at Second Street and Monroe Avenue, with a tray of drinks and started to the voting booth a few doors below.
>
> "Say, nigger," said a large white man, who had been taking an active part in the voting, "for the Lord's sake, put a napkin or something over that tray."
>
> The negro returned a few minutes later with a cloth cover over the tray and there were no further suggestions.[11]

Both Nashville's and Memphis's mayors continued to allow their saloons to operate, in open defiance of the state's prohibition law. Finally, in 1915, the state passed a law that gave it the power to throw public officials out of office if they refused to enforce prohibition. Before a year had passed, both Ed Crump of Memphis and Hilary Howse of Nashville were expeditiously tossed out.

MEANWHILE, LEM MOVED QUICKLY in transporting most of his liquor to more friendly locales. By 1911, there were only twenty-five distillery warehouses hanging on in Tennessee, including Lem, his old friend Bill Hughes, and Cascade; by 1914, the number was down to thirteen and Hughes was gone.[12] The distillers' favorite new locations: Hopkinsville and Paducah, Kentucky; Evansville, Indiana; Cincinnati, Ohio; and St. Louis, Missouri. Lem chose the latter, where he would eventually haul his distilling equipment and build a new operation. Strategically located on the Mississippi River and the site of Jack's triumph at the 1904 Louisiana Exposition, St. Louis remained relatively friendly to business interests, including liquor, the cozy relationship dating back to St. Louis's days as the headquarters for the Whiskey Ring. From there, Lem was actually permitted by law to ship liquor back to individual Tennessee consumers via mail order, as individuals were still permitted to drink in the privacy of their homes. And, in a sweet moment among the sour, in May 1911, U.S. Secretary of War Jacob M. Dickinson declared his favorite whiskey to be Jack Daniel's and sent six bottles to President Taft, who acknowledged the receipt and noted that his wife "will appreciate it."[13] All was not lost—yet.

While Lem carried the torch bravely in St. Louis, it did little to relieve Jack's despair. The year the Tennessee legislators lay down like lambs before the dry forces, he was confined to his bedroom and, due to poor health, would rarely leave it again. The fire had gone out at his distillery and inside his soul. Trained nurses and his sisters Bette and Louisa cared for his needs. His vision began to fail considerably, the numbness in his extremities worsened, and then the foot he had damaged all those years ago from kicking the safe turned black. It became gangrenous. There was little choice but to leave the comforts of his farm for Nashville, to consult with the best physicians. They, in turn, had little choice but to remove his foot. The operation didn't halt what had to be the onset of severe diabetes, brought on by all the years of rich food and drink and being overweight.[14] In the summer of 1911, Jack, age sixty-two, was forced to return to Nashville to have his leg amputated at the upper thigh. The disease was relentless.[15]

The man who once lived like a prince was now emasculated. Friends and family despaired. When Dora Enochs Stephens, the daughter of Jack's half-sister Sena, and her daughter Carmie took a horsedrawn buggy out to Jack's farm to spend the day with him, they were taken aback by the shriveled man—now skin and bones—lying in bed.[16] Jack's hair was no longer the deceptive black, it was all ghostly white. In the weeks before his death, he was gravely ill and, in the final days, the pain unbearable. Jack Daniel welcomed the end on October 9, 1911, a Monday afternoon. It was expected; as a *Fayetteville Observer* reporter noted, "For the past seven years he has been in failing health and it was known that soon he would reach the river's brink and take passage for the further shore."[17]

ON TUESDAY AFTERNOON, it was standing room only at the Primitive Baptist church, as area residents paid tribute to Jack Daniel, the man who put Lynchburg on the map and embodied their traditional way of life. His sisters Louisa and Bette and his brother Wiley were the only direct blood relations to attend the funeral, which was presided over by Elder Willis, who had baptized Jack. Old Felix Waggoner, his hair still coal black, was there, too. Always quick to attribute his longevity to "eating hog-meat three times a day!" he would die the next year at age ninety-two.[18] After Jack was buried in the family plot, two cast-iron chairs mysteriously appeared next to his headstone—it was said they were for the women who mourned the passing of the county's most eligible bachelor. For some, he remained the most eligible bachelor even in death.

Ever since the oppressive dry forces had begun to gain irreversible momentum at the turn of the century, Jack received scant mention in a press that was, generally speaking, too timid to draw the ire of those raining fire and brimstone upon the liquor industry. Such was the case in death, too. The *Fayetteville Observer,* which had advocated prohibition for years, gave Jack a fleeting tribute: "The Captain was gifted with superior business qualifications and had accumulated a large estate. He was a pleasant and affable companion and every acquaintance was a warm friend."[19] The only recognition in the *Nashville Banner* was "Former Widely Known Distiller Succumbs to Long Illness at Lynchburg."[20]

At least, the hometown paper, the *Lynchburg Falcon,* provided a proper obituary. It mentioned that Jack had had the skin disease called white swelling as a boy and even directly referred to his whiskey business: "It is said that he ran it for 35 years without letting the fire go out, besides building two other distilleries at the same time." The *Falcon* then paid tribute to his local philanthropy: "Mr. Daniel acquired a great fortune, and was always ready with a helping hand for the distressed widows and orphans. He was ever ready to help build schoolhouses and churches, and there are but a few that have been built in this county but that have been built with the aid of this man, and they stand as monuments to his memory."[21] At his death, his estate was estimated at $250,000—the modest figure indicative that he had given away much in his lifetime.[22]

An editorial in the *Tennessee Democrat*—obviously, a Democratic paper—was kinder in terms of both space and accolades:

> No more charitable man lived than Jack Daniel. If charity is a cardinal virtue, he was its highest exponent in his section of the state. Many a poor minister of the gospel received donations from him when times were hard.
>
> No worthy charity sought him in vain. He made honest good whiskey, he stood erect among his fellowmen, and despised littleness. A warmer heart never beat in a human breast than the one that supplied the life current to Jack Daniel.[23]

In the twilight of his life, Jack had been generous with his money and indulged in local philanthropy, funding businesses, saving farms, and financing churches and schools. When an orphan, he had relied on the community; when a man, he felt compelled to give back to it. He was no Carnegie or Rockefeller, but his charitable ways made him a greater hero in Moore County than was any Gilded Age tycoon.

In addressing Jack's legacy, the *Memphis Herald* predicted that historians will take note of Moore County, as it will become renowned as the location of Jack Daniel's famous distillery. "The historians will do this because the excellence of the product of that old-time distillery has done more to give fame to" the county "than any other factor or set of factors." This prophecy would be fulfilled.

JACK'S UNDYING DEDICATION to his family was revealed when his will was unsealed—no one was forgotten. His nephews Lem Motlow and Dick Daniel, named co-executors, were instructed to "have a suitable monument erected at my grave not to exceed in cost the sum of one thousand dollars."[24] The two also realized the largest windfalls; both were bequeathed $10,000, with Dick receiving Jack's largest diamond ring as well. Jack bequeathed money to more than twenty-five nephews and nieces, including those belonging to half-sisters Sena and Belle, the amounts ranging from $1,000 to $3,000. These cash disbursements reached a total of $63,000, with more to come.

In further instructions, Jack directed that all his land, except the farm that his sister Bette lived on, all livestock farming implements, and all other personal property, except for his whiskies and brandies, be sold either publicly or privately. His whiskies and brandies—a substantial collection that he expected would take several years to dispose of—were to be sold privately and legally, meaning that his estate would pay any taxes due to the government. Proceeds from the sales and all other money were then to be divided among nephews and nieces of whole blood and of half blood, but half-blood relatives were to get half of what the others received; in other words, 50 cents on the dollar. If anything, Jack was also a square dealer in death. In his will, he left nothing to the Primitive Baptist church or any other institution. Family came first for all eternity.

As for his sister Bette, who had cared for him through his long illness, she not only was allowed to remain on the farm but received the parlor and kitchen furniture, the beautiful piano, the artwork, and other ornaments. However, Jack stipulated that these items and the farm were to be sold to the highest bidder on her death, and the proceeds to be divided among the nephews and nieces. Alone, Bette lived in Jack's house for the next two years. The property continued to fall into disrepair, soon reaching such a dilapidated state that she could hardly survive on the money it produced. According to Lem Motlow, Jack and then Bette had been "forced to rely on irresponsible negroes and other persons to manage and cultivate the farm, and in consequence it was not cultivated much." She attempted to buy it outright, hoping to induce her nephew Jack Daniel Motlow to come and manage the property, with him eventually taking ownership.[25] Death caught up with her first.

Six years after Jack's death, Fannie Blythe Enoch, once the apple of his eye, took her son Lee to see the old mansion that had been uninhabited since Bette's passing. The drawing room with the beautiful piano lay untouched, preserved just as it was when Jack had died, now an eerie mausoleum to another age. After a moment's hesitation, they walked into the room where Fannie had entertained Jack's guests with lively music. She approached the piano. "My mother raised the lid and touched a few keys," Lee Enoch recalled. "She stood back and just remained silent for awhile."[26]

EPILOGUE

꘎·꘎

LEM'S TRIALS

Logic, like whiskey, loses its beneficial effect when taken in too large quantities.
—Lord Dunsany

I n the years and the decades following Jack's death, Lem would have to contend with prohibition, gangsters, and accusations of murder; put bluntly, compared to what he was about to face, a dinner date with Carry Nation would have been a pleasure. These impending trials were forewarned not five years into his career as a St. Louis distiller, when a fire gutted his operation in 1913. Lem's fighting spirit was hardly extinguished, however; he built a larger, more technologically advanced distillery of concrete and steel. Life during this period was hectic, as he traveled by sleeper car between his home in Lynchburg and his business in St. Louis, as well as to Birmingham, Alabama, where he had a major warehouse. When in Lynchburg, he focused on expanding his mule-trading business and on hosting auctions and barbecues. There was big money in mule teams; those that worked well together would soon fetch as much as $1,200 a pair—far more than the $385 that farmer Ledford had paid in 1905. The cost was justified; mules were far more dependable than not just horses but politicians.

In one of the world's great sociopolitical blunders, on January 29, 1919, the United States Congress ratified the Eighteenth Amendment, the Prohibition Amendment, which would go into effect one year later. To his credit, Woodrow Wilson had vetoed it, only to be overridden. To provide for enforcement of the new amendment, Congress then passed the National Prohibition Act on October 28, 1919; however, the notion of enforcing prohibition would become a joke. Nevertheless, hounded like a fox, Lem had to finally douse the fire in the Jack Daniel Distillery. From sea to shining sea, there was no safe haven remaining that protected an individual's freedom.

The moonshiners from General Raum's era paled in comparison to the rapacious bootleggers who now made the most of prohibition, peddling bathtub gin and rotten whiskey, and indulging in cold-blooded murder on a vast scale, as these rapscallions battled over millions of dollars in booty. Prohibition made a few heroes, too, such as Eliot Ness, the unassuming agent with the Department of Justice, and his Untouchables, who were determined to bring down the likes of Al Capone, the Brooklyn-born mobster. Nicknamed Scarface after having been slashed across his cheek during a boyhood gang scrap, Capone moved to Chicago in 1919 and six years later became the crime czar. He was depicted by Ness as ruling "the city with an iron fist in a glove of steel"—specializing in gambling, prostitution, and bootlegging.[1] He also allegedly engineered the infamous 1929 St. Valentine's Day Massacre in Chicago, in which seven members of the rival Bugs Moran's gang were machine-gunned down in a garage. At the height of Capone's power, his consortium raked in over $100 million a year.[2]

As for the more pedestrian folks, prohibition hardly suppressed any partygoers who could easily purchase liquor for their homes or could support their local speakeasies with little fear of reprisal. Enforcement of prohibition varied greatly across the country, dependent on how the locals felt about it and how receptive federal agents were to bribery. Rest assured, the good people of Lynchburg were never in want of liquor, as enforcement was especially weak in rural areas and small towns. It wasn't called the Roaring Twenties for nothing—not with flappers, jitterbugs, speakeasies, and machine gun-toting gangsters all the rage. Prohibition, which meant no more prodigious excise tax on liquor, would cost the government an estimated $11 billion in lost revenue.[3]

WHEN PROHIBITION HIT, Lem was worth about $3 million, so he wasn't exactly going to go hungry or thirsty. Settled once again into a Lynchburg routine, he tended to his mule-trading business, which alone would make him a millionaire, and pursued his hobby of breeding champion-caliber Tennessee walking horses. His best-known horse was Chief Alton, a winner of blue ribbons and a prolific sire. A lover of nature, Lem became devoted to quail shooting and fox hunting.[4] He also added to his already extensive land holdings in the area, eventually owning about 7,000 acres, including the wooded valley at the headwaters of Hurricane Creek, located just east of Lynchburg, where he then built a dam to create a lake for fishing and boating. At one point he owned fifteen farms, including a portion of the original Calaway Daniel farmland, and spent hundreds of thousands of dollars on developing land for agricultural use, from clearing land to building concrete silos and feed troughs.[5]

Though Lem now sported an expensive broadcloth suit and a stylish wide-brimmed black hat with the crown uncreased, a necktie remained conspicuously missing from his wardrobe; as one acquaintance put it, Lem "refused to choke himself and his personality with a necktie."[6] Still quick tempered, he could have used some throttling. He was evolving into a tyrant, a controlling man who was hard on his four boys—Reagor, Evans, Conner, and Robert. He never wanted them to marry; they were to be lieutenants in his empire, without female distractions.[7] The empire was about to be seriously threatened, however, due to Lem's greed and volatile temper.

Lem now had whiskey—patiently stored for the day prohibition would end—warehoused in Birmingham, Cincinnati, and St. Louis, the latter his primary base, where he networked with fellow distillers and became a member of the Merchant's Exchange. In the spring of 1923, a business broker, R. A. Organ, approached Lem and offered to buy the whiskey in his St. Louis warehouse.[8] Considering that the whiskey was just sitting there, with the angels taking their daily portion, it seemed like a good idea at the time. Lem also offered his distillery and warehouse for a grand total of $400,000. Negotiations ensued, and Organ, who was supposedly representing a Don H. Robinson of Chicago, agreed to buy 893 barrels for $125,000 and lease the warehouse for $500 a month. The deal was inked in June; the Internal Revenue Service was informed; and everything appeared to be on the up and up.

What Lem didn't know was that Robinson's attorney, George Remus, was a successful Midwest bootlegger–the Lynchburg mule man was dealing with professional gangsters during the golden age of Al Capone. Back in 1922, Lem had already encountered the criminal element, when three masked thieves wielding revolvers tied up four government men and robbed the Jack Daniel's warehouse of sixteen barrels. It was December 2–clearly, someone was planning early for his holiday party.[9] Mr. Remus's scheme was a bit more ambitious. His plan was to whisk his recently purchased whiskey from Lem's warehouse–yes, steal from himself–cut it by 50 percent with water and then sell it at $30 a gallon, for a total street value of about $2 million. And so it was, on a hot August night in 1923, that Remus's men parked trucks loaded with empty barrels in a garage next door to the warehouse, into which they ran hoses and then, over the course of two weeks, pumped out the whiskey. To cover their tracks, they filled the emptied barrels with water. Shortly after the "milking job," carousers gleefully lifted glasses of Old No. 7 in St. Louis speakeasies.

Not until September, when the government watchmen decided to pour themselves a little illicit refreshment and, to their disgust, discovered soured water, was the crime stumbled upon. One of the biggest thefts since prohibition was enacted, it made front-page news. Immediately, the government suspected Lem of complacency, and, even though he offered to come to St. Louis and help in the investigation, the revenue department filed a suit against him to force him to pay for the future tax that would now go uncollected. For the next six months he shuttled back and forth between Lynchburg and St. Louis, to confer with his attorneys there. In March 1924, on one such trip, his trouble deepened dramatically.

* * *

AFTER DINING WITH SOME FRIENDS in St. Louis, on March 17, Lem walked into the St. Louis train station, as he had done so many times before. There was the typical hustle and bustle, the sounds of shrill whistles, and the oppressive smell of stale steam and smoke. As Lem approached the Pullman car, the train porter Ed Wallis noticed that he was a little unsteady, a bit disheveled—drunk, most likely. From the start, Lem and the porter, who was black, engaged in a running verbal battle that, once Lem was aboard the train, quickly escalated to a physical confrontation. Suddenly, Lem pulled a pistol and aimed it at Wallis. Just as he squeezed the trigger—the shot sounding sharp but flat—a conductor, C. T. Pullis, jumped into the fray. Pullis crumpled in the blue haze of the gun smoke. He was taken to a hospital in East St. Louis but died the next day.

Lem was thrown in jail, where, the next morning, his puffy face and generally unkempt appearance strongly suggested that he was hungover, recovering from a serious bender. It would take several days for the fifty-three-year-old former distiller to regain his composure. Not long after his arrest, his eldest son, Reagor, and a friend came to East St. Louis and made arrangements for Lem to be transferred to the women's side of the jailhouse because it was more comfortable, which drew a chortle from the press. Reagor and the lawyers then negotiated a quick release, which prompted the *St. Louis Globe-Democrat*'s sneering headline "Motlow Smilingly Gives $25,000 Bond as Victim is Buried." Lem did issue a statement of regret over the fatal shooting and gave the widow $10,000. His murder trial was set for December 1924. In the meantime, the Internal Revenue Service seized Lem's distillery and warehouse as collateral for the unpaid taxes on the stolen whiskey and was determined to try him, along with Remus, for violating prohibition laws. This involvement with gangsters wasn't going to help Lem in his upcoming murder trial. It was character assassination, or suicide, at its best. In these worst of times, it certainly appeared that Jack Daniel's whiskey would never again breathe in a snifter.

In December, Lem entered the St. Louis courtroom, dressed in a "natty" blue serge suit and his standard white shirt open at the collar.

The jury was all white, of course, which played to his advantage, considering that the black porter's testimony would be pivotal. When the defense presented its argument, Lem's legal eagle had nothing bad to say of the victim; his quarrel was with the black porter. As his attorney explained, Lem did indeed admit to having a drink with his friends, but he was hardly drunk. It was Wallis, the porter, who opened the hostilities by attempting to stop him from boarding the train because he had no ticket. Lem then appealed to the conductors at the gate, who, recognizing him, permitted him to board. Once in his berth, Lem asked Wallis to remake his bed so that his head would point toward the locomotive. The porter refused, but the conductor ordered him to. According to Lem, the porter again harassed him about not having a ticket. When Lem rose from his seat to respond, the porter attacked him with a rod he used to close the transoms and started choking him. It was then that Lem pulled the gun, but the porter struck it aside, causing it to discharge, the bullet hitting the conductor who had rushed over to break up the fight.

The prosecutor, seeking the death penalty, agreed with what had happened, except he argued that Lem was quite drunk and the aggressor. One witness, a clergyman, testified that Lem appeared staggering drunk, was mumbling to himself, and was arguing with both the conductor and the porter. When the porter asked him to sit down, Lem replied that "no damned nigger could tell him what to do." Another witness corroborated the drunken appearance. Others saw no bruises on Lem's face, to indicate that he had been attacked. More condemning, when the porter in question took the stand, he could not be rattled under cross-examination. It appeared that Lem's argument was crumbling.

To bolster their defense, Lem's lawyers paraded out a series of character witnesses, including former Tennessee governor Malcolm Patterson. Other witnesses threw doubt on the clergyman's testimony and claimed that Lem appeared sober. Lem himself took the stand on December 8. He did admit to having two drinks that made him feel "right smart" but not drunk. It was the porter who had attacked him, and, with his head twisted back while being choked, Lem could not see in what direction he fired the pistol. Lem, whose voice was described as "high-pitched and shrill but friendly," explained, "I was almost dead, I thought. I reached for my pistol—then somebody grabbed my hand from behind and the pistol was accidentally discharged twice." In closing arguments, Lem's lawyer concluded that his client was mistook for "po' white trash" by Wallis, the black porter. In a slick move, he played up the blackness for the all-white jury's benefit.

In his instructions to the jury, the judge explained the differences between first- and second-degree murder, manslaughter, and self-defense. He added that an accidental killing did not necessarily justify a verdict of not guilty. As the jury deliberated, Lem's lawyer paced the hallway, where, in front of one heat duct, he heard the jury singing, "going back to my Tennessee home tonight," a line from "Sunny Tennessee." The verdict: not guilty. The jury foreman explained, "We didn't believe the negro. We believed there was a fight and that Motlow was forced to defend himself. This was the opinion of us all and there was very little discussion among us."

Public opinion put a different spin on the verdict. There was a strong feeling that Lem had bought his way out with an "extraordinary array of lawyers" who had deftly appealed to racial prejudices and succeeded. The circuit attorney called it a "miscarriage of justice" and explained to reporters, "The jury did not really try the defendant Motlow. It tried Ed Wallis, the Pullman porter. It probably had its mind made up before speaking, but it enjoyed hearing the Tennessee lawyers fight the Civil War over and make speeches of the Ku Klux Klan type." The prosecutor blamed his weakened case on one key witness having died prior to the trial and another in North Carolina who refused to testify—all very suspicious.[10]

Some members of Lem's own family suspected that their patriarch had acted rashly and were greatly embarrassed by the event. Some even believed he was suffering from the effects of syphilis, which, at times, made him appear intoxicated and act crazy.[11] Shovelfuls of silence were used in an attempt to bury this unsavory bit of family history. Lem's children were so tight-mouthed that at least one of his grandchildren didn't find out about it until she was an adult—a friend told her—and even then her parents still refused to discuss it.[12] The story of the killing remains a juicy topic for local gossip today.

Now came Lem's battle to clear himself of violating prohibition laws. A week before the trial started, Lem appeared before United States Commissioner Harry A. Luck to plead his case. After reviewing the evidence, Luck determined that the government's case against Lem was weak, prompting federal prosecutors to not try him with Remus and the other conspirators but to wait until June 1926 to do so separately. The trial was conveniently held in the District Court of Middle Tennessee—Lem's home turf. The outcome was a given: the judge declared the evidence unconvincing and threw out the case.[13] But the next year brought more bad news. In 1927, a fire caused by a combustion of semivolatile flour reduced the old Jack Daniel's distillery in Lynchburg to ash. What had been a monument to Uncle Jack was now destroyed. With his house and his distillery now dust to dust, memories of Jack Daniel, the man, were slowly disappearing.

CATACLYSMIC EVENTS on the national stage eclipsed Lem's troubles, as the Roaring Twenties came to an inauspicious close with the stock market crash of 1929 and the subsequent Great Depression. But then, as the bread lines lengthened, there was a wee dram of good news to relieve the suffering: after fourteen years of hijinks, it appeared that national prohibition was an endangered constitutional amendment. As the 1920s had progressed, the fundamentalists who continued to fervently wave the dry flag began to wear out their welcome, to alienate the more moderate. And America in general was tiring of the corruption that prohibition had wrought. Seeking change, at their national convention in 1932, the Democrats adopted a platform calling for prohibition's repeal. That fall, the presidential election pitted the incumbent Republican Herbert Hoover, running on a dry ticket, against the Democrat Franklin D. Roosevelt. Roosevelt won. The people had spoken: they demanded their beer, their wine, and their liquor—legally. The Depression didn't help Hoover either.

After prohibition was repealed in 1933 with the introduction of the Twenty-first Amendment, some states elected to continue with statewide prohibition. Much of Tennessee leaned toward the dry side, and, somewhat surprisingly, the county made famous by its whiskey—

Moore County!—appeared content to remain dry. For Lem, this situation was intolerable; he was determined to bring the distillery back to
Lynchburg. Considering the stranglehold the Great Depression had
on the country, it was not an opportune time to start or restart a
business. However, working hard to resurrect his image, Lem ran for
public office, his sights set on becoming a representative in the Tennessee General Assembly, where he might effect legislation that would
allow him to bring the Jack Daniel Distillery back to Lynchburg.
Either he did indeed garner enough respect or scared enough people
or paid enough people that he was elected to the Tennessee House of
Representatives, serving there from 1933 to 1937, and then in the
state Senate from 1939 to 1941.

In 1937, Lem used his influence to win passage of a bill that
allowed liquor to be manufactured in Tennessee for sale outside the
state, which was later revised to permit the sale of liquor to wet terri-
tories inside the state. Still, the people of Moore County would have
to approve it, so Lem petitioned the county court to call an election.
It turned him down. Undeterred, Lem complained before the state
Supreme Court, which ordered the Moore County Chancery Court
to hold the vote. Although the local newspapers and the preachers
attacked him, Lem won the right to rebuild the distillery by a slim
margin—hardly an overwhelming vote of confidence. As the *Nashville
Tennessean* reported on June 26, 1938: "Moore County is showing little excitement over the fact that soon whiskey-manufacturing will be
resumed here after more than 35 years."[14] Apparently, the only happy
people—in addition to Lem—were a Mr. and Mrs. Buford Huskey, residents in the Hollow who were looking forward to a plethora of slop
to fatten their hogs.

In rebuilding the distillery, Lem didn't use an architect or an engi-
neer. Instead, he relied on old still hands and their know-how to con-
struct a new brick distillery and a mash room. It was a crude operation, with an old sawmill boiler supplying steam and an old threshing
machine grinding the grain, and the daily capacity was a mere 50
bushels or 150 gallons of whiskey.[15] It truly did hark back to the old
days. November 11, 1938, marked the day the first barrel of Jack
Daniel's rolled into the warehouse post-prohibition. To generate cash

flow, Lem waited but one year before he bottled some of the whiskey. About this time, having witnessed the reemergence of the legendary Jack Daniel's whiskey, Lem suffered a stroke that left his right arm and right leg paralyzed. He was always a tough bird, so it didn't slow him down. He had a driver take him around and worked from a wheelchair; as his younger brother Tom said, "Lem Motlow will direct his business from his bed should he become too disabled to be on his feet."[16]

To properly honor his Uncle Jack before he himself crossed the river, Lem commissioned a statue of the legendary boy distiller in his signature knee-length frock coat, planter's hat, vest, and broad bow tie and erected it in front of the hallowed cave in 1941. Made of Italian marble and weighing in at 1,800 pounds, it was a life-size replica, although the statue's feet were proportionately a little large so that he wouldn't topple off his base. Also honoring Uncle Jack's whiskey-making acumen, as well as that of other sour mash men, in 1941, the federal government officially recognized that whiskey made the Lincoln County way deserved its own legal designation, to distinguish it from bourbon; thereafter, it was labeled Tennessee Whiskey.[17] But these glowing moments were tempered by World War II, during which whiskey production was banned except for a few periods. Lem managed to bottle several hundred cases a month, but that was it. Not much of a hardship, considering that anywhere from 40 to 60 million people would lose their lives due to the war.

Lem, having been in poor health for about eight years, faced his maker in 1947. Still insistent that he be taken to the office every day, Lem, now age seventy-seven, was there on a Saturday in late August. The next morning, however, he wasn't feeling well and decided to stay home, resting on the couch. Later his family discovered him unconscious, and, on September 1, 1947, Lemuel Motlow died of a cerebral hemorrhage. "The death of Lem Motlow ends a long and colorful era in Tennessee's history," eulogized the *Nashville Tennessean*. "Colorful in his person as well as in his pursuits, Mr. Motlow exercised an almost fatal sway over nearly the whole of one of this state's counties."[18] As the largest landowner in Moore County, he held unrivaled power, and without his unbridled determination, there would be no Jack Daniel Distillery today.

* * *

NOW THE RESPONSIBILITIES FELL squarely on Lem's four boys, all graduates of Vanderbilt University and known as the "four shirt-sleeve brothers" because they were hands on; they didn't mind rolling up their sleeves and getting dirty. No Italian suit jackets for them. Reagor, chunky and chatty, was the president of the firm and, beginning in 1941, he would follow in his father's footsteps by serving twelve terms in both Tennessee houses. The family's recognized leader, he would, with their support, donate two hundred acres to help found Motlow State Community College in 1969. Rounding out the Jack Daniel's team, Conner was vice president; Robert, secretary-treasurer; Evans, sales manager; and their Uncle Jess, head distiller.

The four brothers became highly respected in their own right and continued to embody the old way of doing things. To a *Fortune* magazine reporter, Reagor explained, "With good straight whiskey, and not those fruit-salad concoctions, you can't substitute formulas and instruments for instinct and experience. There's no escape from the 'four unknowns' all whiskey has to go through—mashing, fermenting, distilling, and barreling. Each time, despite controls, any one of these reactions is liable to turn out differently. You have to be alert enough to spot something wrong about a batch, and then have the guts to do it over again until it's right. Why, Uncle Jess here never read a chemistry text in his life, but after fifty-four years of stillin' whiskey you can't fool his eye, his nose, or his tongue."

Uncle Jess chimed in, "Why, Lord a' mercy, I don't know nothin' about diastase and such things as Reagor talks about. All we was taught was how to take a bushel o' grain and get some whiskey out of it."[19] Clearly, they were practiced in the art of portraying that good ol' boy image. But they were sharp businessmen, too.

In the latter 1940s and early 1950s, the brothers increased production as much as 50 percent a year.[20] While they claimed to harbor no desire to be "Big Rich," they did decide to sell the company in 1956 for big money.[21] Their suitor: Louisville-based liquor powerhouse Brown-Forman. George Garvin Brown, a one-time pharmaceuticals salesman who started distilling Old Forester and became a pioneer in bottling whiskey, had founded the company back in the 1870s. He later formed a partnership with his accountant, George Forman, thus, Brown-Forman. After Forman died, Brown elected to keep the name as it was.[22] In the 1950s, Brown-Forman brands included Old Forester, Early Times, and King, with the firm later adding Canadian Mist, Southern Comfort, Korbel champagne, and Fetzer wines, among others, to their franchise. And on August 29, 1956, the *Nashville Tennessean* reported that the Motlow brothers sold the Jack Daniel Distillery to Brown-Forman for $20 million.[23]

To facilitate the transition and to ensure that their whiskey remained of high quality—as well as to benefit themselves, of course—Reagor Motlow remained the president and the other brothers officers of the Jack Daniel Distillery. Though a distant generation removed from their legendary founder, the Motlow brothers cherished Jack Daniel's legacy, and it was their duty to protect it for as long as they could. They succeeded. A genuine American-born and -bred gem, the little man from Lynchburg deservedly remains a treasured piece of our country's lore.

AFTERWORD

THE MAKING OF A LEGEND

During prohibition, the legendary status Jack Daniel had established for himself faded into the porous limestone of Lynchburg. But then, in 1951, almost twenty years after prohibition had been repealed, a reporter for the popular *Fortune* magazine opened his feature article with, "If you've never heard of Jack Daniel's whiskey, so much the better. Its relative obscurity is part of its charm. For this backwoods brand of spirits, which is scarcely advertised at all and amounts to the merest ripple in the oceans of whiskey produced and consumed in the U.S., has become the beneficiary of a wonderful whispering campaign."

The resurrection of Jack Daniel, the "boy distiller" decked out in high-rolled plantation hat and frock coat, had begun; indeed, the scarce advertising and being a mere "ripple in the oceans of whiskey produced" would, by the twenty-first century, explode into a proliferation of both. Today, a cult of personality surrounds Jack Daniel and his whiskey; the Jack Daniel's black No. 7 label is as recognizable as Budweiser or Harley Davidson. So, how is it that a backwoods man who preferred the dark, safe corner of a saloon when away from his home territory became such a global powerhouse? Since the early 1950s, what exactly has fueled the phenomenal success of Jack Daniel's?

First we must take a step backward to World War II and the immediately ensuing years, in which Lem Motlow's stubbornness actually contributed to the whiskey's charm. During the war, distillers could make only industrial alcohol, which obviously created a shortage of sipping whiskey. In the first years after the war, they could again make whiskey but were allowed to use only certain grains—namely, low-quality stuff used for chickenfeed, not the high-quality white corn that went into Jack Daniel's. Lem refused to do so, declaring, "Jack Daniel's has been made from No. 1 grain—the finest white corn money can buy—for seventy-five years, and so long as I live we're not going to use anything else."[1] The result: no whiskey was barreled until the government lifted those restrictions several years later. Certainly, Lem's righteous philosophy cost the company big money, but the scarcity of Jack Daniel's in the postwar boom years made its appeal all the more greater. As the reporter for *Fortune* magazine put it, "To the drinking elite there is a certain cachet to the rare, the quaint, the romantic Jack Daniel's." The elite included the vice president of the United States John N. Garner, who, serving under Franklin Delano Roosevelt, invited friends to his private chambers for a nip of Jack; the Nobel Prize–winning novelist William Faulkner, who preferred it on the rocks; Harry S. Truman, who sent the whiskey to Winston Churchill; and the FBI legend J. Edgar Hoover, who, after a grueling day of digging up dirt on politicos and Hollywood stars, relaxed with some television and a glass of Jack Daniel's.

IN SPITE OF THE FLASHY CELEBRITIES drinking Jack Daniel's, when Brown-Forman took over the company in 1956, it designed a brilliant marketing campaign to play up the backwoods charm that *Fortune* magazine had touched upon. The campaign included a grassroots movement and wholesome advertising. That year the company founded the Tennessee Squires, a fan club now open to anyone sponsored by an existing member, to generate goodwill. With membership, which includes a number of celebrities and public figures, you receive a little plot of Moore County land and a copy of the land deed itself. An official-looking document full of legalese, the deed reminds you that your plot is "near The Hollow, the site still used for charcoal mellowing Tennessee Whiskey drop by drop." A rather entertaining Tennessee Squire story centering on these deeds involves the former president of Russia Boris Yeltsin. When he was in the hospital, about to have heart surgery, and his death appeared imminent, Russian officials started going through his papers to put his affairs in order. They came across a document, a deed, that showed he owned land in Tennessee, apparently bought from a certain Jack Daniel. Red flags went up. The officials called the Russian embassy in the United States, which, in turn, called the Jack Daniel Distillery and demanded an explanation. The answer was simple: Yeltsin was a Tennessee Squire.[2] In addition to the land, squires receive sometimes corny but well-meaning communications. Prior to Halloween in 2002, I received an invitation to join a hunting party that was going to attempt to track down and spot "The Tennessee Wyooter," the state's bigfoot. It was scheduled for the evening of November 1, the time of year that the twelve-foot-tall Wyooter is known to be out and about. More down-home Happy Holidays cards to Tennessee Squires include such lines as, "Here in the hollow we've learned that good things come to those who wait." It's the classic grassroots marketing that Jack loved.

As for Jack Daniel's advertising, it didn't feature crooning cowboys like Gene Autrey and Roy Rogers; to the contrary, it was purposefully rustic to appeal to the common man. "Using a sort of reverse sophistication," observed a reporter for the *Nashville Magazine* in 1964, "the Jack Daniel ads draw the eye like an old photograph of Abraham Lincoln. The simple scenes of workmen in unaffected khakis and open collars, rustic mule-drawn wagons, and ducks waddling down the wide street by the stillhouse, etc., appeal to most of us considerably more than the jaded models, usually in a painfully posed social situation, who appear for Jack's competitors."[3] Indeed, the black-and-white ads, which first appeared in 1954, featured local folks, evoking a slower-paced, simple lifestyle with good old boys sittin' around, shootin' the breeze, whittlin' sticks, and watchin' the whiskey age. Some ads even flaunted the hillbilly culture.[4]

The folksy tone is ubiquitous. When I visited the distillery, which was listed on the National Register of Historic Places on September 14, 1972, I picked up a brochure that featured a photo of Jack in a planter's hat, accompanied by homespun prose: "If you were picking out a place to make whiskey the old-time way, slowly mellowing it drop by drop, you couldn't do better than the Jack Daniel's Hollow here in Lynchburg, Tennessee. Nothing changes very much in Mr. Jack's hometown. His spirit lives in the character of his whiskey and in life in Lynchburg." Other photos depicted an old flatbed truck loaded with twenty barrels, surrounded by classic good ol' boys in overalls or dungarees and flannel shirts; an old geezer in the warehouse built by Lem Motlow in 1938, sitting on a barrel and looking off into the distance; and a shot of Jimmy Bedford, the firm's sixth master distiller, with the caption "Still Made the Old Time Way." More of the same can be found in the 2003 and 2004 Jack Daniel's calendar. And the official distillery stationery is headlined with, "Whiskey made as our fathers made it."

But don't be fooled; these casual images were and continue to be carefully poised to have a very calculated effect. As the *Nashville Magazine* pointed out, "When you visit The Hollow, however, you get the impression that things aren't quite as simple as the ads would have you believe." The Jack Daniel Distillery was and is a modern, efficient business operation promoted by very sophisticated marketing. Almost thirty years after the *Nashville Magazine* article, the *Wall Street Journal* opened a 1990 story with, "The modern world worships hustle, energy and Beautiful People. But for thirty-six years, ads for Jack Daniel's Tennessee whiskey have evoked the slow-paced life of the rural South. And year after year, Jack Daniel's sales stay in the fast lane."[5] The same holds true today. As the distillery raconteur and P.R. man Roger Brashears says, "We ain't gonna kick a pulling mule"–a line he enjoys using.[6] In other words, if grassroots marketing and a down-home image worked for Jack Daniel and has continued to succeed, why change the advertising philosophy?

The ad campaign, however, has been changing, evolving, and expanding to include–heaven forbid–glitzier images. In a recent *Time* magazine, I came across a glossy color ad featuring a bar scene of young people with the slogan "In any bar in America, you know someone by name." That would be Jack Daniel. Clearly, the Jack Daniel Distillery is looking to attract the younger generations, while retaining that older customer (like my aunt and uncle–JD converts who once imbibed the enemy Jim Beam). In addition, these days the company peddles far more than Tennessee sour mash whiskey made the Lincoln County way. Yes, for years you've been able to purchase the usual Jack Daniel's trinkets and souvenirs—T-shirts, flags, mugs, snifters, key chains, belt buckles, posters, and so on—but now the company has plastered its label on a number of other consumable products. There's Jack Daniel's mustard, barbecue sauce, chocolates, cocktails, and hard cola, among others. This brand proliferation has its dangers.

In a recent article entitled "Brand Schizophrenia: Today's Epidemic," the magazine *Brandweek* warned that "companies all too often leave rationality by the wayside in their zeal to enter new markets and capture new customers." In Jack Daniel's defense, the article does hail the company's barbecue sauce, made in partnership with H.J. Heinz, as an example of a success, relying on Jack Daniel's "Southern heritage, original, high-quality craftsmanship and flavor" and "the fact that grilling and barbecue also have longstanding roots in the south. . . ."[7] As for the watering down of their brand, Brashears says they are "guarding against cheapening it."[8] Time will tell if Brown-Forman is prostituting its premier brand in a way that will lead to a tarnished image, or if it's another marketing coup that will reap millions of dollars.

IN OLD-TIME LYNCHBURG there is another sign of modernization: the Jack Daniel Distillery visitors' center that was opened in June 2000. A bright, modern facility, or a mausoleum, it houses various artifacts that celebrate the company's heritage, including the marble statue of Jack that Lem had commissioned and dedicated back in the 1940s. Out by the hallowed cave, in place of the marble statue, there now stands a bronze sculpture of Jack Daniel, which was unveiled in September 2000 to celebrate the 150th anniversary of his birth. Hat in hand and foot propped on a barrel of whiskey, Jack's shining pose captures his youthful energy. At the dedication, Lynne Tolley lifted a glass of Jack Daniel's Single Barrel whiskey in toast: "Here's to my Uncle Jack on his 150th birthday and to the new statue that stands

The thousands upon thousands of used whiskey barrels tucked away in several Lynchburg fields are mouthwatering sights.

To celebrate the 150th anniversary of Jack's birth, the distillery commissioned a bronze statue that captures his youthful vigor.

here in the Hollow. Like Mr. Jack's whiskey, this work of art has been carefully crafted by hand according to time-honored techniques. It is faithful to the original, full of character and looks good on the rocks."[9] While the visitors' center isn't quite Graceland over in Memphis, some 200,000 to 250,000 Jack Daniel's fans pass through annually to pay their respects.

In the summer months, Lynchburg's prim village square, preserved to invoke life of a century ago, is overrun by tourists and hardcore whiskey drinkers alike. While the crowds bring in money for local merchants, many of the area's residents are wary of the distillery's booming popularity and the commercialization of the town. With the town's idyllic appearance, carefully preserved by the distillery, comes a sense of falseness, a superficiality that also perturbs some locals who embody an old way that is more genuine than the lifestyle depicted in Jack Daniel's advertising. So, while they might brag that every road in Moore County is paved (in part, due to the wealth Jack Daniel's brings to the area), they complain fervently about the hideous Dollar store on the pike and other signs of today's Wal-Mart society. In fact, as of November 2002, there was a motel under construction on the pike, whereas only a couple of bed and breakfasts once served any overnight guests. Fueling the concerns of those more paranoid is the possibility that the Motlow family, which still owns sizable tracts of land in the Lynchburg area, might sell its extensive properties off to developers. As the residents of this relatively isolated area struggle with their popular big brother Jack, it makes for an interesting case study for sociologists.

Over the years, the brilliant marketing conducted by Brown-Forman has not only brought a troubling prosperity to Lynchburg but has imbued the story of Jack Daniel with a fictional quality, the distortion part intentional and part accidental. The Jack Daniel's brand itself has become so dominant that you can easily forget there was actually a man by the same name—maybe that's why I am often asked, "There was a real Jack Daniel?" Once again, I answer, "Yes." And his life and times are dynamic enough that they need no embellishment. Still, I suspect, in another decade or two, legend will have it that the boy distiller nursed on white dog whiskey, cut down legions of Yankee soldiers with but a broken square bottle, and, becoming as giant a figure in American lore as Davy Crockett, single-handedly blazed the whiskey trail, inventing sour mash, charred oak barrels, and charcoal leaching. Personally, I want to be able to return to the Tucker Inn in the village of Lois without seeing fast-food joints lining the pike and neon signs on the old Dan Call farm, flashing: Jack Distilled Here.

NOTES

❧·❧

Introduction

1. Author interview with Lynne Tolley, April 23, 2002; author interviews with Roger Brashears, April 24 and November 18, 2002.

2. *New York Times,* April 3, 2003.

1. The Cursed Child

1. The Book of Job, 1:6–7.

2. Jim Murray, *The Complete Guide to Whiskey* (Chicago: Triumph Books, 1997), p. 28.

3. Joseph Earl Dabney, *Mountain Spirits* (Asheville, N.C.: Bright Mountain Books, 1974), p. 36.

4. R. J. Dickson, *Ulster Immigration to Colonial America 1718–1775* (London: Routledge and Kegan Paul, 1996), p. 70.

5. Dabney, p. 48.

6. Dickson, p. 207.

7. Dabney, pp. 50–51.

8. H. G. Jones, *North Carolina Illustrated* (Chapel Hill: University of North Carolina Press, 1983), p. 54.

9. Felix W. Motlow, Motlow Family History typed manuscript and collected documents (hereafter Motlow Family History), pp. 6–7, Moore County Library. Whether they eloped to America is uncertain, as their names do not appear in David Dobson's *The Original Scots Colonists of early America, 1612–1783* (Baltimore: Genealogical Publishing Co., 1989). It is possible they traveled under assumed names to hide from the Calaway family.

10. Motlow Family History, p. 7.

11. Richard Erdoes, *Saloons of the Old West* (New York: Alfred A. Knopf, 1979), p. 28.

12. Oscar Getz, *Whiskey: An American Pictorial History* (New York: David McKay, 1978), p. 41.

13. Motlow Family History, Exhibit A. Elizabeth Daniel told her grandchildren this story.

14. Motlow Family History, p. 4.

15. J. B. Killebrew, *Information for Immigrants Concerning Middle Tennessee* (Nashville: Marshall & Bruce Co., 1898), pp. 8–11.

16. Dabney, p. 52.

17. Paul H. Bergeron, Stephen Ash, and Jeanette Keith, *Tennesseans and Their History* (Knoxville: University of Tennessee Press, 1999), pp. 7–11.

18. John M. Bright, "Pioneers of Lincoln County," *The Volunteer* (Spring/Summer 1996). *The Volunteer* is published by the Lincoln County Historical Society.

19. Wilma Dykeman, *Tennessee: A Bicentennial History* (New York: W. W. Norton, 1975), p. 136.

20. Federal Writer's Project of the Work Projects Administration for the State of Tennessee, *Tennessee: A Guide to the State* (New York: Viking Press, 1939), p. 134.

21. Motlow Family History, pp. 5 and 134.

22. Roberta Motlow Ostrom, "The Whitaker Family of Mulberry," *The Volunteer* (Spring 1982); and Rufus Alonzo Parks, "The Parkes Family" (www.knology.net/~jparkes/genealogy/parkes/papers/histrap.htm).

23. *Goodspeed's Histories of Giles, Lincoln, Franklin & Moore Counties of Tennessee* (Chicago: Goodspeed Publishers, 1886), p. 806.

24. For more information, see James L. Peacock and Ruel W. Tyson Jr., *Pilgrims of Paradox: Calvinism and Experience among the Primitive Baptists of the Blue Ridge* (Washington, D.C.: Smithsonian Institution Press, 1989).

25. Erdoes, p. 124.

26. According to the Bible of Louisa Daniel Rutledge (Jack's sister), their mother Lucinda died on January 27, 1849. Considering that Jack was listed as a one year old in the 1850 census, he must have been born immediately prior to her death. Census workers were from the area in which they gathered the information, so one has to assume that the information is fairly accurate.

27. Lant Wood, "Notes on Early Grist Mills of Moore County," typed manuscript, 1965, located in the Moore County Library. For more descriptions of early industry, see Goodspeed, pp. 804–805.

28. See Lincoln County Census 1850 and 1860.

29. According to the Bible of Louisa Daniel Rutledge (Jack's sister), their mother Lucinda died on January 27, 1849.

30. Federal Writer's Project of the Work Projects Administrator for the State of Tennessee, p. 135.

31. Reverend Silas Emmett Lucas Jr. and Ella Lee Sheffield, editors, *35,000 Tennessee Marriage Records and Bonds, 1783–1870,* Vol. I (Easley, S.C.: Southern Historical Press, 1981); Motlow Family History, p. 3.

32. Ben A. Green, *Jack Daniel's Legacy* (Nashville: Rich Printing Co., 1967), pp. 7–10; Lincoln County Census 1860; Bergeron, et al., p. 129.

33. *Fayetteville Observer,* January 28 and February 11, 1851.

34. Chase C. Mooney, *Slavery in Tennessee* (Bloomington: Indiana University Press, 1957), pp. 104–105, 122.

35. Stephen V. Ash, *Middle Tennessee Transformed 1860–1870* (Baton Rouge: Louisiana State University Press, 1988), p. 11.

36. Ash, pp. 66 and 68.

37. Stanley J. Folmsbee, Robert E. Corlew, and Enoch L. Mitchell, *Tennessee, a Short History* (Knoxville: University of Tennessee Press, 1969), p. 317.

38. James M. McPherson, *Battle Cry of Freedom* (New York: Ballantine Books, 1988), p. 259.

39. *Lynchburg Falcon,* November 30, 1906; "The Cholera Epidemic of 1854," *The Volunteer* (Spring/Summer 1996).

40. *Lynchburg Falcon,* May 17, 1907.

41. Ash, p. 74.

2. Everything Gone but the Dirt

1. James Lee McDonough, *Stones River: Bloody Winter in Tennessee* (Knoxville: University of Tennessee Press, 1980), p. 12.

2. McPherson, pp. 342, 442, and 454.

3. Service information comes from *Tennesseans in the Civil War* (Nashville: Civil War Centennial Commission, 1964); and www.tngennet.org/civilwar/csainf/csa23.html.

4. Lincoln County Census 1860; Motlow Family History, pp. 4–6, and 9.

5. *Lynchburg Falcon,* May 17, 1907.

6. Lester C. Lamon, *Blacks in Tennessee, 1791–1970* (Knoxville: University of Tennessee Press, 1981), p. 23.

7. Brian Steel Wills, *A Battle from the Start: The Life of Nathan Bedford Forrest* (New York: HarperCollins, 1992), p. 71.

8. Steven E. Woodworth, *Six Armies in Tennessee* (Lincoln: University of Nebraska Press, 1998), p. 44.

9. Wills, p. 64.

10. Ash, pp. 84–85.

11. Folmsbee, et al., p. 344.

12. Wills, p. 69.

13. www.tngennet.org/civilwar/csainf/csa8.html. For a detailed account of the Stones River battle, see *Stones River* by James Lee McDonough.

14. McDonough, p. 23.

15. McDonough, p. 58.

16. McDonough, p. 50; Gerald Carson, *The Social History of Bourbon* (New York: Dodd, Mead, 1963), p. 71.

17. Carson, p. 75.

18. Getz, p. 91.

19. Woodworth, p. 42.

20. McPherson, p. 670.

21. Mabel Abbott Tucker and Jane Warren, compilers, *Lincoln County Tennessee Bible Records, Vol. 4* (Lincoln County, Tennessee, Volunteers). In this compilation, the editors include the Bible of Louisa Rutledge, in which she stated that Lemuel died on August 6, 1864; however, it's clear from family stories that he died on the eve of Chickamauga, which was in 1863.

22. Ash, p. 157.

23. Stephen V. Ash, "Sharks in an Angry Sea: Civilian Resistance and Guerrilla Warfare in Occupied Middle Tennessee, 1862–1865," *Tennessee Historical Quarterly* XLV, no. 3 (Fall 1986): 220.

24. Sarah Dickey Holland, "Mulberry, Lincoln, Tennessee," *The Volunteer* (November 1982); Ash, "Sharks in an Angry Sea," pp. 147–148.

25. www.knology.net/~jparkes/genealogy/parkes/papers/histrap.htm, March 3, 2002.

26. McPherson, p. 440.

27. Folmsbee, et al., p. 347.

28. Ash, "Sharks in an Angry Sea," p. 87.

29. Ibid, pp. 85–86.

30. *Lincoln County Tennessee Bible Records, Vol. 4*, Bible of Louisa Rutledge.

31. See *Samuel Rutledge et al. vs. Samuel Arbor et al. and Wiley B. Daniel et al.*, Lincoln County Chancery Court Minutes, Reel 12, pp. 71–80 and pp. 553–556.

32. Melvin Elliott Brewer, "Ancestors of Melvin Elliott Brewer" (members .aol.com/_ht_a/elliott233/mel/d430.htm).

33. *Samuel Rutledge et al. vs. Samuel Arbor et al. and Wiley B. Daniel et al.*

34. Byron Sistler and Barbara Sistler, *Early Middle Tennessee Marriages, Vol. I* (Nashville: Byron Sistler & Associates, 1988), Lincoln County Census 1860.

35. Lincoln County Census 1860 and 1870.

36. See records listed in Helen and Timothy Marsh, compilers, *Deed Genealogy of Lincoln County Tennessee 1828–1834, Vol. 3* (Greenville, S.C.: Southern Historical Press, 1996); Helen C. and Timothy Marsh, compilers, *Early*

Unpublished Court Records of Lincoln County, Tennessee (Greenville, S.C.: Southern Historical Press, 1993).

37. Tom Wiseman, "Early Churches of Lois Community," *Moore County News*, March 28, 1968.

38. L. Richard Bradley, "The Lutheran Church and Slavery," *Concordia Historical Quarterly* (February 1971): 33.

39. Douglas C. Stange, "Our Duty to Preach the Gospel to Negroes: Southern Lutherans and American Slavery," *Concordia Historical Institute Quarterly* (November 1969). See Stange's article for more details on southern Lutheran attitudes toward slavery.

40. Ibid, p. 180.

41. Hugh George Anderson, *Lutheranism in the Southeastern States, 1860–1886, a Social History* (Paris: Mouton, 1969). See Anderson's book for more details on southern Lutheran attitudes.

42. Anderson, p. 55.

43. Green, p. 50.

44. See undated newspaper clipping in Joan Crutcher Ferguson, *Reminiscing about Lynchburg* (Privately printed), p. 87.

45. McPherson, p. 854.

46. Bergeron, et al., p. 158.

47. *Samuel Rutledge et al. vs. Samuel Arbor et al. and Wiley B. Daniel et al.*

3. Legend of the Boy Distiller

1. Betty Anderson Bridgewater, editor, "Coffee County's Stockholders in the Nashville & Chattanooga Rail Road Co.," *Tullahoma: Episodes from Its Past* VI, nos. 3 and 4 (1975): 42.

2. Motlow Family History, p. 6.

3. Federal Writer's Project of the Work Projects Administrator for the State of Tennessee, p. 135.

4. See the *Gadsen Times*, September 5, 1971. An article entitled "Famous Daniel's Distillery Once Located in Gadsen" states that Jack didn't enter the whiskey business until after the Civil War, when he was eighteen years of age. There is other evidence, which I will present, that clearly indicates Jack started distilling after the war.

5. William C. Davis, *Look Away! History of the Confederate States of America* (New York: Free Press, 2002), p. 311.

6. Davis, p. 312.

7. William Downard, *Dictionary of the History of American Brewing and Distilling Industries* (Westport, Conn.: Greenwood Press, 1980), p. xxi.

8. Wilbur R. Miller, *Revenuers and Moonshiners: Enforcing Federal Liquor Law in the Mountain South, 1865–1900* (Chapel Hill: University of North Carolina Press, 1991), p. 37.

9. For local history see, *Moore County Review* 9, no. 2 (July 1998); and *Moore County Review* 8, no. 1 (January 1997).

10. Goodspeed, p. 807; Danny Smith to author, July 18, 2002–Danny Smith is a great-grandnephew of Dan Call; interview with Jack Daniel employee Richard "Booger" Grant, *Nashville Banner,* January 30, 1975.

11. Erdoes, p. 29.

12. Moore County Census 1880. Ben Green misspells Nearis as Nearest.

13. Federal Writer's Project of the Work Projects Administrator for the State of Tennessee, pp. 143–144; and Dykeman, pp. 138–141.

14. Erdoes, p. 86.

15. Dabney, *Mountain Spirits,* p. 43.

16. Erdoes, p. 91.

17. Carson, p. 43.

18. Miller, p. 32.

19. Esther Kellner, *Moonshine: Its History and Folklore* (New York: Weathervane Books, 1971), p. 56.

20. Kellner, p. 58.

21. Carson, p. 42.

22. Dabney, p. 8.

23. Stephen E. Ambrose, *Nothing Like It in the World* (New York: Simon & Schuster, 2000), p. 357.

24. David Cruise and Alison Griffiths, *The Great Adventure: How the Mounties Conquered the West* (New York: St. Martin's, 1996), pp. 104–108.

25. Erdoes, p. 98.

26. Getz, p. 89.

27. Edward Chambers Bette, *Early History of Huntsville, Alabama 1804–1870* (Montgomery, Ala.: Brown Printing Co., 1916), p. 112.

28. Undated Lem Motlow obituary clipping from the *Tennessean,* Ferguson, p. 115. It mentions Jack carting his whiskey to Alabama to sell to the soldiers.

29. Ash, pp. 193, 203; Bergeron, et al., p. 173.

30. Ash, pp. 194, 198, 197.

31. Allen W. Trelease, *White Terror: The Ku Klux Klan Conspiracy and Southern Reconstruction* (New York: Harper & Row, 1971), p. 5.

32. Folmsbee, et al., p. 361.

33. Lawrence Edwards, *The Primitive Baptists* (thesis, University of Tennessee, May 1940), p. 67.

34. For more information on the Freedmen's Bureau, see Paul David Phillips, *A History of the Freedmen's Bureau in Tennessee* (Ph.D. thesis, Vanderbilt University, 1964).

35. Trelease, p. 22.

36. Folmsbee, et al., p. 362.

37. See *Coffee County Historical Quarterly* XIII, nos. 3–4 (1982).

38. Trelease, p. 35; and *Report of Evidence Taken before the Military Committee in Relation to Outrages Committed by the Ku Klux Klan* (Nashville, S.C.: Mercer, 1868).

39. *Fayetteville Observer,* January 12, 1871.

40. Lee A. Enoch, *Memories around Lynchburg* (Nashville: Privately printed, 1989), p. 87.

4. The Nomad

1. Green, pp. 40–46. According to Green, he gleaned the Huntsville information during interviews with Tom Motlow and Lee Baldwin, who knew "Button" Waggoner.

2. Miller, p. 63.

3. For when Jack first entered the distilling business legally, see Daniel H. Call to Jack Daniel, September 27, 1877, Moore County Deed Book, Vol. 1, p. 257. In this deed it specifically states that Dan Call and Jack Daniel entered into partnership on November 27, 1875. Prior to 1875, Jack Daniel did not own a distillery, and it is fairly clear that in the first several years after the Civil War, moonshining in the South was rampant.

4. Miller, p. 31.

5. *Coffee County Historical Society Quarterly* II, nos. 2 and 3 (1971): 7.

6. Miller, p. 63.

7. Carson, p. 97; Miller, p. 148.

8. Downard, p. 237; Carson, pp. 95–96; *Fayetteville Observer,* August 6, 1866.

9. 1870 Lincoln County Census.

10. Green, pp. 61–62. Green details some of Hughes's Civil War exploits, which may or may not be true.

11. For more details–the facts–on John Mason Hughes's military service, see www.tngennet.org/civilwar/crosters/inf/inf25/hnames.html; www.tcarden.com/tree/ensor/SwallTN.html; www.rootsweb.com/~tnjames/regthist.htm#25tncreg; and www.kycourts.net/Counties/Allen.asp?County=Allen.

12. 1870 Lincoln County Census.

13. Hughes, Eaton & Co. of Mary A. Green, April 15, 1869, Lincoln County Deed Book, Vol. E-2, p. 207; W. R. Call and D. H. Call to Hughes

& Tolley, March 25, 1869, Lincoln County Deed Book, Vol. 1, p. 98; for information on William R. Call, see Lincoln County Census 1860, as well as tax assessment lists.

14. Ben Green provides his version of their partnership on pp. 67–70.

15. See "Introduction to the Motley Family," Motlow Family History.

16. Lincoln County Census 1870; the Lincoln County Census 1870 lists Jack as living with Felix and Finetta Motlow; the 1872 Moore County tax assessment listing for Felix Motlow.

17. *Samuel Rutledge et al. vs. Samuel Arbor et al. and Wiley B. Daniel et al.,* Lincoln County Chancery Court Minutes, Reel 12, February 10, 1870, pp. 553–556, and August 10, 1870, pp. 71–80.

18. Wiley Daniel and Susan Elizabeth Waggoner family information taken from the Felix W. Motlow family manuscript, Moore County Public Library.

19. *Samuel Rutledge et al. vs. Samuel Arbor et al. and Wiley B. Daniel et al.* Note: When the papers were filed in court, Felix was listed as Jack's guardian. Jack never went to court to have the guardianship lifted prior to his twenty-first birthday, as legend would have it.

20. Bergeron, et al., p. 160.

21. Address of J. B. Killebrew, Esq., Delivered before the Montgomery Farmers' Club, March 12, 1870, Tennessee State Library, Killebrew Papers, pamphlet no. 2.

22. 1872–1874 Moore County tax assessment lists. No property is listed for Jack Daniel, and he paid only $2 in taxes annually for those years.

23. Marjorie Hood Fischer, *Tennessee Tidbits* (Greenville, S.C.: Southern Historical Press, 1986), p. 111.

24. *Lynchburg Falcon,* October 12, 1911.

25. *Lynchburg Sentinel,* February 1876; Green, p. 72.

5. Reunion and Challenge

1. The sales revenue is based on making 100 gallons of whiskey for 240 days and then selling it at $3 a gallon for net sales revenue of $2.10 a gallon after backing out the 90 cents per gallon in federal taxes; Daniel H. Call to Jack Daniel, September 27, 1877, Moore County Deed Book, Vol. 1, p. 257. In this deed it specifically states that Dan Call and Jack Daniel entered into partnership on November 27, 1875. Also see *Hugh Ledford versus Lem Motlow,* October 26, 1906, Moore County Chancery Court Minutes, Reel 70, pp. 309–718. In this court case, Jack states that he had been in the distilling business "thirty odd years or more," which is circa 1875. And *Goodspeed's Histories of Giles, Lincoln, Franklin & Moore Counties of Tennessee* (p. 926)

states that Jack, in partnership with Dan Call, built his first distillery in 1876–not in 1866, as legend has it.

2. For details concerning the Jack Daniel farm, see Moore County Chancery Court Minutes, Reel 71, pp. 1026–1097.

3. J. B. Killebrew, *Introduction to the Resources of Tennessee,* p. 862; J. B. Killebrew, *Tennessee: Agricultural Resources and Mineral Wealth* (Nashville: Tavel, Eastman & Howell, 1874), p. 67.

4. *Lynchburg Sentinel,* February 11, 1876.

5. *Lynchburg Sentinel,* March 24, 1876.

6. *Lynchburg Sentinel,* June 3, 1875.

7. *Lynchburg Sentinel,* March 24, 1876.

8. *Lynchburg Sentinel,* February 23, 1877.

9. *Lynchburg Sentinel,* November 11, 1875; *Lynchburg Sentinel,* April 14, 1876; *Lynchburg Sentinel,* July 14, 1876.

10. *Lynchburg Sentinel,* June 28, 1876;

11. *Lynchburg Sentinel,* March 16, 1877, and March 23, 1877.

12. Mary O. Motlow, "Lynchburg," a typed manuscript, Moore County Library, Motlow Papers, Box 9, Folder 2.

13. *Moore County Pioneer,* Friday, June 6, 1873.

14. *Lynchburg Sentinel,* July 22, 1875.

15. *Lynchburg Sentinel,* December 28, 1875.

16. *Lynchburg Sentinel,* March 8, 1877.

17. Edwin G. Burrows and Mike Wallace, *Gotham* (New York: Oxford University Press, 1999), pp. 1020–1030.

18. *Lynchburg Sentinel,* May 14, 1875.

19. *Lynchburg Sentinel,* July 14, 1876; August 11, 1876; August 18, 1876.

20. Burrows and Wallace, pp. 1034–1035.

21. Getz, p. 97

22. *Lynchburg Falcon,* November 30, 1906.

23. *Fayetteville Observer,* January 12, 1871.

24. *Lynchburg Sentinel,* April 14, 1876; June 9, 1876; June 28, 1876; December 1, 1876; and June 17, 1875.

25. Anderson, p. 148.

26. *Fayetteville Observer,* January 12, 1871, and January 5, 1871; *Lynchburg Sentinel,* September 22, 1876.

27. Miller, pp. 97–99. Miller provides biographical material on Raum.

28. Dabney, p. 59; Carson, p. 12.

29. Getz, p. 58.

30. Carson, p. 12.

31. Dabney, p. 72.

32. Miller, p. 70.

33. Miller, p. 73.

34. Miller, p. 73.

35. Miller, p. 64.

36. Carson, pp. 116 and 119.

37. Carson, p. 123.

38. *Lynchburg Sentinel,* November 11, 1875.

6. A Rebellion against the Government

1. *Lynchburg Sentinel,* January 26, 1877.

2. *Lynchburg Sentinel,* June 3, 1875.

3. *Lynchburg Sentinel,* March 16, 1877.

4. Ibid.

5. *Lynchburg Sentinel,* February 16, 1877.

6. "The Sour Mash Distillers," *Lynchburg Sentinel,* March 23, 1877.

7. *Lynchburg Sentinel,* February 16, 1877.

8. Kay Baker Gaston, "Tennessee Distillers: Their Rise, Fall, and Re-Emergence," *Border States: Journal of the Kentucky-Tennessee American Studies Association,* no. 12 (1999). The calculation is based on the assumption of distilling 26 days per month for 9 months.

9. Kay Baker Gaston, "Robertson County Distillers, 1796–1909," *Tennessee Historical Quarterly* XLIII, no. 1 (Spring 1984).

10. *Lynchburg Sentinel,* March 2, 1877. As of March 1877, the prices of whiskey sold on the market in Memphis were: Common $1.00 at 1.15; Robertson County $1.75 at 3.00; Bourbon $5.00 at 5.50; and Lincoln County $1.75 at 3.00.

11. All quotes in this paragraph are from the *Lynchburg Sentinel,* February 16, 1877.

12. *Annual Report of the Commissioner of Internal Revenue,* year ending June 30, 1877 (Washington, D.C.: Government Office of Publications), p. XXX.

13. *Annual Report of the Commissioner of Internal Revenue,* year ending June 30, 1877, p. XXXI.

14. Getz, p. 123.

15. From Wilson to Hon. Green B. Raum, December 21, 1882, National Archives and Records Administration (NARA), Record Group 56, Entry 355, Box 4.

16. Miller, p. 116.

17. Miller, pp. 102–103.

18. Miller, p. 133.

19. 1880 Moore County Tax Assessment List. Daniel owned 140 acres in District One and 66 acres in District Six.

20. Leonidas Hubbard Jr. "The Moonshiners at Home," *Atlantic Monthly* (August 1902): 235.

21. Young E. Allison. "Moonshine Men," *Southern Bivouac* (February 1887): 528–531.

22. *Annual Report of the Commissioner of Internal Revenue,* year ending June 30, 1880, p. V.

23. Miller, p. 136.

24. *Lynchburg Sentinel,* March 30, 1877.

25. Carson, pp. 99–100.

7. Identity Crisis

1. *Lynchburg Sentinel,* April 13, 1877.

2. Newspaper clipping dated March 5, 1880, from Tennessee State Library, Killebrew papers, Scrapbook, Box 3, Folder 3.

3. *Annual Report of the Commissioner of Internal Revenue,* year ending June 30, 1880, p. VI. There were 469 licensed distilleries in 1880 versus 177 in 1878, in collection districts where illicit distilling was prevalent.

4. *Annual Report of the Commissioner of Internal Revenue,* year ending June 30, 1880, p. 67; *Annual Report of the Commissioner of Internal Revenue,* year ending June 30, 1897, p. 67.

5. U.S. Bureau of the Census.

6. *Nashville Banner* clipping, July 8, 1879, from Tennessee State Library, Killebrew papers, Scrapbook, Box 3, Folder 3.

7. The assumption is that Daniel and Call distilled 240 days a year and sold their whiskey for $3 a gallon; Moore County 1880 tax assessment listing for Jack Daniel.

8. S. J. Kleinberg, *The Shadow of the Mills: Working Class Families in Pittsburgh, 1870–1907* (Pittsburgh: University of Pittsburgh Press, 1989), p. 26.

9. 1880–1882 Moore County tax assessment listing for Jack Daniel; 1881 Moore County tax assessment listing for Dan Call.

10. This calculation assumes that each bushel weighs 60 pounds.

11. www.knology.net/~jparkes/genealogy/mooretn/jdaniel/web/d746.htm, March 8, 2002.

12. Moore County Census 1880.

13. J. B. Killebrew, *April 1879 Crop and Statistical Report,* Tennessee State Library, Killebrew papers, Pamphlet no. 29.

14. F. Motlow to W. B. and J. N. Daniel, December 14, 1880, Moore County Deed Book, Vol. 2, p. 50.

15. F. Motlow to J. Daniel, July 21, 1881, Moore County Deed Book, Vol. 2, p. 65.

16. Carson, p. 62.

17. Don H. Doyle, *Nashville in the New South, 1880–1930* (Knoxville: University of Tennessee Press, 1985), pp. 3–12.

18. Bergeron, et al., p. 192.

19. Ernest Hurst Cherrington, *The Evolution of Prohibition in the United States of America* (Westerville, Ohio: American Issue Press, 1920), p. 208.

20. Anderson, p. 150.

21. Moore County Census 1880.

22. Moore County Deed Book, Vol. 1, p. 257. Green states that Dan Call quit the business prior to the Civil War, and another story has Dan Call quitting just after the Civil War; for this latter version, see Jeanne Ridgway Bigger, "Jack Daniel Distillery and Lynchburg: A Visit to Moore County, Tennessee," *Tennessee Historical Quarterly* 31, no. 1 (Spring 1972): 4–5. The Green and the Bigger versions are false.

23. Danny Smith to author, July 18, 2002.

24. Tom Wiseman, "Land, Labor Donated for Lois School." *Moore County News*, February 22, 1968.

25. *Moore County Review* 8, no. 1 (January 1997).

26. Green, pp. 77–78.

27. Lem Motlow's obituary, *Nashville Tennessean*, September 2, 1947; see the bottle picture in Mitchamore, p. 57.

28. "Uncle Jack's Famous Legacy," *Old Tennessee Valley Magazine and Mercantile Advertiser*, no. 92 (2001).

29. www.jackdaniels.com/stories.asp, October 31, 2002.

30. "The Sour Mash Distillers," *The Sentinel*, March 23, 1877. In their collective letter to Green B. Raum, commissioner of the Internal Revenue Service, the old fourth district distillers noted that all the numbers from the fourth district "remain the same except No. 7 in the Fourth is changed to No. 16 in the Fifth." It was stated in Lem Motlow's obituary, *Nashville Tennessean*, September 2, 1947, that some distant relatives of Jack once claimed that his distillery was the seventh registered in the United States, thus No. 7—so they were close to the source of the brand name.

8. Seizing the Legendary Hollow

1. Miller, pp. 97–98. Miller gives a brief biographical sketch of Raum.

2. Miller, pp. 147–148.

3. Bergeron, et al., p. 193.

4. Cherrington, p. 211.

5. Paul E. Isaac, *Prohibition and Politics in Tennessee* (Knoxville: University of Tennessee Press, 1965), p. 28.

6. Isaac, pp. 16–17.

7. Goodspeed, p. 807.

8. Kay Baker Gaston, "Tennessee Distillers"; *Annual Report of the Commissioner of Internal Revenue,* year ending June 30, 1887, p. LXXIX.

9. *Nashville American,* March 8, 1896; *Lynchburg Sentinel,* March 23, 1877; Goodspeed, p. 926.

10. Wilburn Hiles & Berry to Jack Daniel, June 17, 1884, Moore County Deed Book, Vol. 3, pp. 130–131.

11. Jasper N. Daniel to Tolley & Eaton, October 11, 1884, Moore County Deed Book, Vol. 3, p. 180.

12. Goodspeed, pp. 807, 926.

13. Goodspeed, pp. 816–817.

14. The year after Jack bought the Hollow, twenty-one men were prosecuted for carrying pistols, noted in Goodspeed, p. 811.

15. See Motlow Family History.

16. "Rare Jack Daniel's," *Fortune* (July 1951).

17. William "Bill" Hughes information is taken from the 1880 Moore County Census and Green, pp. 78–79. In 1880, he was working at a distillery.

18. *Hugh Ledford versus Lem Motlow,* October 26, 1906, Moore County Chancery Court Minutes, Reel 70, p. 638. In his testimony in this case, Jack provides some insight into his business.

19. Frank B. Williams Jr., "893 Barrels of Jack Daniel's Old No. 7: The Troubles and Trials of Lem Motlow, 1923–1930," *Tennessee Historical Quarterly* 58, no. 1 (Spring 1999). Williams's description of Lem is based on newspaper accounts.

20. Green, p. 135.

21. Jeanne Ridgway Bigger, "Jack Daniel Distillery and Lynchburg: A Visit to Moore County, Tennessee," *Tennessee Historical Quarterly* 31, no. 1 (Spring 1972): 6.

22. Per the 1885 Moore County tax listing, Lem Motlow lived with Jack. He then moved in with Bill Hughes. For information on the Hughes wedding, see Green, p. 118.

23. www.knology.net/~jparkes/genealogy/mooretn/jdaniel/web/d2961.htm.

24. For a more colorful and somewhat fabricated description, see Green, pp. 139–140.

25. Peter Krass, *Carnegie* (New York: John Wiley & Sons, 2002), pp. 218–219.

26. Jean Strouse, *Morgan: American Financier* (New York: Random House, 1999), p. 236.

27. *History of the Farmers Bank of Lynchburg, Tennessee,* a pamphlet published by the Farmers Bank; Farmers Bank, Lynchburg, Farmers Bank minutes book, 1889–1911; Strouse, p. 216.

28. Farmers Bank Minutes, April 22, 1890; April 25, 1893, minutes, and others that show a 10 percent dividend was declared.

29. Strouse, p. 215.

9. Taking On Nashville

1. 1890 and 1895 Moore County tax assessment listings for Jack Daniel.

2. *Lynchburg Daily Falcon,* June 18, 1892.

3. *Lynchburg Daily Falcon,* June 21, 1892.

4. Franklin County Census 1900 and Moore County Census 1900. I could not find the Green brothers in Tennessee as of 1900.

5. Green, p. 104.

6. Moore County Chancery Court Minutes, Reel 64, Case 265, pp. 1556–1566.

7. Contract entered into between John L. Tolley and Jack Daniel, Moore County Library, Motlow Papers, Box 6, Folder 18.

8. Downard, p. 244; Kay Baker Gaston, "Robertson County Distilleries, 1796–1909." The number of Robertson County distilleries was five as of 1894.

9. Jill Bruss, "A Long Run," *Beverage Industry* 92, no. 6 (June 2001); James B. Beam Distilling Company documents, www.jimbeam.com/jb_web/content/Heritage/default.asp, April 1, 2002.

10. Mark H. Waymack and James F. Harris, *The Book of Classic American Whiskeys* (Chicago: Open Court, 1995), p. 109.

11. Waymack and Harris, pp. 131–132.

12. Carson, p. 129.

13. Werner Troesken, "Exclusive Dealing and the Wiskey Trust, 1890–1895," *Journal of Economic History* 58, no. 3 (September 1998): 770–771.

14. Troesken, p. 759.

15. *New York Daily Tribune,* July 19, 1899; and *New York Daily Tribune,* January 6, 1899.

16. Kay Baker Gaston, "George Dickel Tennessee Sour Mash Whiskey: The Story behind the Label," *Tennessee Historical Quarterly* 57, no. 2 (Fall 1998).

17. Erdoes, p. 55.

18. *Lynchburg Falcon,* November 25, 1892.

19. "The Wallflowers and Third Eye Blind Rock Lynchburg, Tenn. in Honor of Jack Daniel's 150th Birthday," *PR Newswire* (October 5, 2000).

20. Jack Daniel Distillery documents on display in the distillery visitors' center, Lynchburg, Tennessee.

21. "Whiskey, Cornet Band Flourished Together," *Nashville Banner,* February 14, 1975.

22. *Lynchburg Sentinel,* November 25, 1892.

23. Doyle, pp. 83–84.

24. Doyle, p. 142.

25. Philip Thomason, "The Men's Quarter of Downtown Nashville," *Tennessee Historical Quarterly* XLI, no. 1 (Spring 1982): 52.

10. Big Man, Lonely Man

1. *Nashville American,* March 8, 1896.

2. "Memories of Jack," *Moore County Review* 10, no. 1 (January 1999): 18.

3. *United States Internal Revenue, List of Distillery Warehouses in the United States in which Spirits Were Held on Deposit in the Fiscal Year Ended June 30, 1898,* Government Printing Office, 1898, NARA, Box T568, Document No. 2074.

4. *Lynchburg Daily Falcon,* June 16, 1892.

5. *Nashville American,* March 8, 1896.

6. Ibid.

7. Moore County Chancery Court Minutes, Reel 68, Case 417, pp. 859–875. This case discusses Jack taking possession of the property.

8. Lincoln County Chancery Court Minutes, Reel 65, Case 299, pp. 1163–1183.

9. 1895 Moore County tax assessment listings for Jack Daniel.

10. Elizabeth W. White, compiler, *Giles County Chancery Court, Woodruff Files A through G, 1830–1900,* Vol. I (Privately printed, 1987), pp. 143 and 145.

11. See Giles County Chancery Court Records, Cases 5540, 5541, and 5549.

12. Lee A. Enoch Jr., "The Jack Daniel Story," reprinted in Lee A. Enoch, *Memories around Lynchburg* (Nashville: privately printed, 1989), p. 13.

13. Motlow Family History.

14. Motlow Family History; Green, pp. 119–120.

15. Green, p. 122.

16. *Lynchburg Falcon,* October 12, 1911.

17. Billy Enochs Sparks Akin, "First Money," reprinted in Lee A. Enoch, *Memories around Lynchburg* (Nashville: privately printed, 1989), p. 93.

18. Green, pp. 118–119.

19. *Nashville American,* March 8, 1896; using the excise tax per proof gallon of 90 cents for 1875 through August of 1894 and then $1.10 from September

1894 onward, and multiplying it against Jack's approximate daily capacity of 100 gallons from the last two months of 1875 to 1884, 150 gallons from 1885 to 1894, 300 gallons for 1895, and then 450 gallons for two months in 1896, it's possible to estimate his total revenue over the 22 years.

20. Federal Writer's Project of the Work Projects Administration for the State of Tennessee, pp. 318–319.

21. Mary Bobo, *Memoirs of Mary Bobo,* Moore County Library, Motlow Papers, Box 10, Folder 6.

22. Joan Crutcher Ferguson, *Reminiscing about Lynchburg* (Privately printed, 1987), pp. 88–89.

23. Strouse, p. 358.

24. Moore County Census 1900.

25. Lant Wood interview in the *Nashville Tennessean,* undated clipping in Moore County Library scrapbook.

26. See Motlow Family History, p. 9.

27. "Memories of Jack," *Moore County Review* 10, no. 1 (January 1999): 18.

28. Tim and Helen Marsh, compilers, *Cemetery Records of Moore County, Tennessee.*

29. *Moore County Marriages,* Vol. 5, Record 277. Fannie Blythe married on January 8, 1906.

30. Lee A. Enoch Jr., "The Jack Daniel Story," p. 14.

31. Green, p. 122.

11. Brand Magic

1. Waymack and Harris, p. 97.

2. Henry Adams, *The Education of Henry Adams* (Boston: Houghton Mifflin Company, 1918), p. 380.

3. Folmsbee, et al., pp. 430–432.

4. Carson, p. 156.

5. Carson, p. 157; Getz, p. 124.

6. Getz, p. 140.

7. Getz, p. 134.

8. Getz, pp. 127, 129, 130–131, and 133.

9. Pat Mitchamore, *A Tennessee Legend* (Nashville: Rutledge Hill Press, 1992), p. 71.

10. Green, p. 105.

11. 1895 Moore County tax assessment listing for Dan Call; *Fayetteville Observer,* September 8, 1904.

12. *Rules and Regulations Governing the System of Awards,* a Louisiana Exposition Pamphlet, May 1904, NARA, Record Group 56, Entry 589, Box 1.

13. www.jackdaniels.com/oldno7/awards.asp, March 6, 2002; Tom Motlow's interview with Ben Green, Green, pp. 110–114.

14. *Fayetteville Observer,* December 8, 1904.

12. Enemies

1. Kellner, pp. 77–79; Getz, pp. 113–121.

2. Getz, p. 114.

3. Kellner, p. 79. Kellner is related to the family of David Nation, Carry's husband.

4. Getz, p. 110.

5. Getz, p. 111.

6. Isaac, p. 78.

7. Isaac, pp. 82–83.

8. Isaac, p. 94.

9. *Fayetteville Observer,* February 4, 1904.

10. Isaac, p. 95.

11. Getz, p. 97. I don't know Getz's source for the figures; however, according to the U.S. Bureau of the Census, the population was 76 million in 1900 and 92 million in 1910. Clearly, the consumption of alcohol increased much faster than the population did.

12. www.knology.net/~jparkes/genealogy/mooretn/jdaniel/web/d518.htm, March 8, 2002; Felix W. Motlow family history.

13. *Lynchburg Falcon,* September 25, 1903.

14. "Consider this ... A Trip to Lynchburg." Nashville Public Radio, September 22, 1996. The radio program includes an old interview with Tom Motlow.

15. *Gadsden Times,* September 5, 1971.

16. See *Hugh Ledford versus Lem Motlow,* October 26, 1906, Moore County Chancery Court Minutes, Reel 70, pp. 309–718.

17. Eulogy for Lem Motlow, signed by the Jack Daniel Distillery board of directors (which included his sons), undated.

18. Green, pp. 137–138.

19. *Lynchburg Falcon,* September 25, 1903.

20. "Memories of Jack," *Moore County Review* 10, no. 1 (January 1999): 18.

21. According to legend, the incident reportedly happened in April 1905.

22. *Lynchburg Falcon,* November 30, 1906.

13. Reborn

1. Farmers Bank Board Meeting Minutes, April 25, 1908, Farmers Bank, Lynchburg, Tennessee.

2. Undated obituary clipping for T. G. Motlow, Ferguson, p. 113; interview with Thomas Motlow, Farmers Bank company documents, Lynchburg, Tennessee; Green, pp. 95–97; and "Consider This . . . A Trip to Lynchburg." Nashville Public Radio, September 22, 1996. The radio program includes an old interview with Tom Motlow.

3. Doyle, p. 43.

4. Mitchamore, p. 68.

5. Green, p. 120.

6. Moore County Chancery Court Minutes, Reel 71, Case 517, February 21, 1913, pp. 1026–1097.

7. Moore County Deed Book, Vol. 8, p. 294; Moore County Deed Book, Vol. 7, p. 92.

8. *Annual Report of the Commissioner of Internal Revenue,* 1908.

9. *Lynchburg Falcon,* October 12, 1911; Green, p. 127.

10. Moore County Deed Book, Vol. 9, pp. 340–341, April 16, 1907.

11. Rufus Alonzo Parks, "The Parkes Family" (www.knology.net/~jparkes/genealogy/parkes/papers/histrap.htm); Moore County Deed Book, Vol. 7, p. 332.

12. Dick Daniel to Lem Motlow, August 12, 1907, Moore County Deed Book, Vol. 9, pp. 375–376.

13. *Annual Report of the Commissioner of Internal Revenue,* 1897, 1901, and 1908.

14. NARA, Box T568; *Annual Report of the Commissioner of Internal Revenue,* 1908.

15. *Lynchburg Falcon,* April 30, 1908.

16. Undated obituary clipping for Mrs. Lem Motlow, Ferguson, p. 114.

17. Isaac, pp. 135–137.

18. *Fayetteville Observer,* August 1, 1907.

19. *Fayetteville Observer,* July 22, 1909.

20. Green, p. 136.

21. Moore County Chancery Court Minutes, Reel 71, Case 517, February 21, 1913, pp. 1026–1097.

22. Ibid.

23. Jack Daniel listed his mother's death as January 27, 1847.

24. *Fayetteville Observer,* April 29, 1909.

25. *Fayetteville Observer,* May 13, 1909.

14. The Final Battle

1. "Consumption in the U.S.," *Nation* (April 19, 1906): 313.

2. "The War on the Saloon," *Nation* (November 21, 1907): 460.

3. Ibid.

4. Bergeron, et al., p. 220.

5. Thomas H. Winn, "Liquor, Race and Politics: Clarksville during the Progressive Period," *Tennessee Historical Quarterly* XLIX, no. 4 (Winter 1990): 209.

6. Isaac, pp. 157–158.

7. Dabney, p. 105.

8. See Isaac, pp. 142–169, for more details on the successful drive for statewide prohibition in Tennessee.

9. Isaac, p. 173.

10. Bergeron, et al., p. 219.

11. Isaac, p. 175.

12. NARA, Box T568.

13. Williams, "893 Barrels of Jack Daniel's Old No. 7: The Troubles and Trials of Lem Motlow, 1923–1930," p. 35.

14. The most plausible explanation for the gangrene is that Jack Daniel suffered from diabetes, not from an incredibly delayed reaction from kicking a safe years earlier.

15. *Lynchburg Falcon,* October 12, 1911; Moore County Chancery Court Minutes, Reel 71, Case 517, February 21, 1913, pp. 1026–1097. Jack's health is discussed in detail.

16. Akin, p. 93.

17. *Fayetteville Observer,* October 12, 1911.

18. Melvin Elliott Brewer, "Ancestors of Melvin Elliott Brewer," www .members.aol.com/_ht_a/elliott233/mel/d430.htm.

19. *Fayetteville Observer,* October 12, 1911.

20. *Nashville Banner,* October 10, 1911.

21. *Lynchburg Falcon,* October 12, 1911.

22. *Maury Democrat,* September 28, 1911.

23. Green, p. 132.

24. Will of Jack Daniel, Moore County Chancery Court Minutes Book, Vol. 8, April 20, 1907, pp. 194–200.

25. Moore County Chancery Court Minutes, Reel 71, Case 517, February 21, 1913, pp. 1026–1097.

26. Lee A. Enoch Jr., "The Jack Daniel Story," p. 13.

Epilogue: Lem's Trials

1. Eliot Ness, with Oscar Fraley, *The Untouchables* (Mattituck, N.Y.: American Reprint Company, 1976, 1947), p. 94.

2. Laurence Bergreen, *Capone: The Man and the Era* (New York: Simon & Schuster, 1994), p. 236.

3. Getz, p. 180.

4. See Eulogy for Lem Motlow, signed by the Jack Daniel Distillery board of directors, undated.

5. Green, p. 154; Lem Motlow's obituary, *Nashville Tennessean,* September 2, 1947.

6. Green, p. 193.

7. Author interview with a Motlow family friend.

8. For more information, see Williams, "893 Barrels of Jack Daniel's Old No. 7: The Troubles and Trials of Lem Motlow, 1923–1930"; and *Nashville Tennessean,* December 9, 10, 11, and 12, 1924.

9. Green, p. 149.

10. Williams, "893 Barrels of Jack Daniel's Old No. 7: The Troubles and Trials of Lem Motlow, 1923–1930"; and *Nashville Tennessean,* December 9, 10, 11, and 12, 1924.

11. Author interview with a Motlow family friend.

12. Author interview with a Motlow family member.

13. Williams, "893 Barrels of Jack Daniel's Old No. 7: The Troubles and Trials of Lem Motlow, 1923–1930"; and *Nashville Tennessean,* December 9, 10, 11, and 12, 1924.

14. Green, p. 168.

15. "Rare Jack Daniel's," *Fortune* (July 1951).

16. Green, p. 166.

17. Stewart Berkshire to Jack Daniel Distillery, March 28, 1941, Green, p. 184.

18. *Nashville Tennessean,* September 3, 1947.

19. "Rare Jack Daniel's," *Fortune* (July 1951).

20. Ibid.

21. Ibid.

22. www.brown-forman.com/b-f_hist.htm, April 3, 2002. The corporate Web site provides company history.

23. Green, p. 175.

Afterword: The Making of a Legend

1. "Rare Jack Daniel's," *Fortune* (July 1951).
2. Victoria Moore, "All Right, Jack," *New Statesman* (October 16, 2000).
3. Green, p. 197.
4. "Old & New Superbrands." *Marketing,* London (March 20, 2003).
5. *Wall Street Journal,* May 18, 1990.
6. Author interview with Roger Brashears, November 18, 2002.
7. Lisa Marchese, "Brand Schizophrenia: Today's Epidemic," *Brandweek* (October 21, 2002).
8. Author interview with Roger Brashears, November 18, 2002.
9. "Jack Daniel Distillery Celebrates Founder's 150th Birthday with Unveiling of New Statue in the Hollow," *PR Newswire* (September 7, 2000).

BIBLIOGRAPHY

Adams, Henry. *The Education of Henry Adams*. Boston: Houghton Mifflin, 1918.

Ambrose, Stephen E. *Nothing Like It in the World*. New York: Simon & Schuster, 2000.

Anderson, Hugh George. *Lutheranism in the Southeastern States, 1860–1886, A Social History*. Paris: Mouton, 1969.

Ash, Stephen V. *Middle Tennessee Society Transformed 1860–1870*. Baton Rouge: Louisiana State University Press, 1988.

Bergeron, Paul H., Stephen Ash, and Jeanette Keith. *Tennesseans and Their History*. Knoxville: University of Tennessee Press, 1999.

Bergreen, Laurence. *Capone: The Man and the Era*. New York: Simon & Schuster, 1994.

Bette, Edward Chambers. *Early History of Huntsville, Alabama 1804–1870*. Brown, 1916.

Burrows, Edwin G., and Mike Wallace. *Gotham*. New York: Oxford University Press, 1999.

Carson, Gerald. *The Social History of Bourbon*. New York: Dodd, Mead, 1963.

Cherrington, Ernest Hurst. *The Evolution of Prohibition in the United States of America*. Westerville, Ohio: American Issue, 1920.

Cruise, David, and Alison Griffiths. *The Great Adventure: How the Mounties Conquered the West*. New York: St. Martin's, 1996.

Dabney, Joseph Earl. *Mountain Spirits*. Asheville, N.C.: Bright Mountain Books, 1974.

Davis, William C. *Look Away! History of the Confederate States of America*. New York: Free Press, 2002.

Dickson, R. J. *Ulster Immigration to Colonial America 1718–1775*. London: Routledge and Kegan Paul, 1996.

Downard, William. *Dictionary of the History of American Brewing and Distilling Industries*. Westport, Conn.: Greenwood, 1980.

Doyle, John H. *Nashville in the New South, 1880–1930*. Knoxville: University of Tennessee Press, 1985.

257

Dykeman, Wilma. *Tennessee: A Bicentennial History*. New York: W. W. Norton, 1975.

Edwards, Lawrence. *The Primitive Baptists*. A thesis, University of Tennessee, May 1940.

Enoch, Lee A. *Memories around Lynchburg*. Privately printed, 1989.

Erdoes, Richard. *Saloons of the Old West*. New York: Alfred A. Knopf, 1979.

Federal Writer's Project of the Work Projects Administration for the State of Tennessee. *Tennessee: A Guide to the State*. New York: Viking, 1939.

Ferguson, Joan Crutcher. *Reminiscing about Lynchburg*. Privately printed, 1987.

Folmsbee, Stanley J., Robert E. Corlew, and Enoch L. Mitchell. *Tennessee, a Short History*. Knoxville: University of Tennessee Press, 1969.

Getz, Oscar. *Whiskey: An American Pictorial History*. New York: David McKay, 1978.

Goodspeed's Histories of Giles, Lincoln, Franklin & Moore Counties of Tennessee. Chicago: Goodspeed, 1886.

Green, Ben. *Jack Daniel's Legacy*. Nashville: Rich, 1967.

Isaac, Paul E. *Prohibition and Politics in Tennessee*. Knoxville: University of Tennessee Press, 1965.

Jones, H. G. *North Carolina Illustrated*. Chapel Hill: University of North Carolina Press, 1983.

Kellner, Esther. *Moonshine: Its History and Folklore*. New York: Weathervane Books, 1971.

Killebrew, J. B. *Information for Immigrants Concerning Middle Tennessee*. Nashville: Marshall & Bruce, 1898.

Killebrew, J. B. *Tennessee: Agricultural Resources and Mineral Wealth*. Nashville: Tavel, Eastman & Howell, 1874.

Lamon, Lester C. *Blacks in Tennessee, 1790–1970*. Knoxville: University of Tennessee Press, 1981.

Lucas, Jr., Reverend Silas Emmett, and Ella Lee Sheffield, editors. *35,000 Tennessee Marriage Records and Bonds, 1783–1870,* Vol. 1. Easley, S.C.: Southern Historical Press, 1981.

Marsh, Helen C., and Timothy Marsh, compilers. *Deed Genealogy of Lincoln County Tennessee 1828–1834,* Vol. 3. Greenville, S.C.: Southern Historical Press, 1996.

Marsh, Helen C., and Timothy Marsh, compilers. *Early Unpublished Court Records of Lincoln County, Tennessee*. Greenville, S.C.: Southern Historical Press, 1993.

McDonough, James Lee. *Stones River: Bloody Winter in Tennessee*. Knoxville: University of Tennessee Press, 1980.

McPherson, James M. *Battle Cry of Freedom*. New York: Ballantine Books, 1988.

Miller, Wilbur R. *Revenuers and Moonshiners: Enforcing Federal Liquor Law in the Mountain South, 1865–1900*. Chapel Hill: University of North Carolina Press, 1991.

Mitchamore, Pat. *A Tennessee Legend*. Nashville: Rutledge Hill, 1992.

Mooney, Chase C. *Slavery in Tennessee*. Bloomington: Indiana University Press, 1957.

Murray, Jim. *The Complete Guide to Whiskey*. Chicago: Triumph Books, 1997.

Ness, Eliot, with Oscar Fraley. *The Untouchables*. Mattituck, N.Y.: American Reprint Company, 1976, 1947.

Sistler, Byron, and Barbara Sistler. *Early Middle Tennessee Marriages,* Vol. 1. Nashville: Byron Sistler & Associates, 1988.

Strouse, Jean. *Morgan: American Financier*. New York: Random House, 1999.

Trelease, Allen W. *White Terror: The Ku Klux Klan Conspiracy and Southern Reconstruction*. New York: Harper & Row, 1971.

Wills, Brian Steel. *A Battle from the Start: The Life of Nathan Bedford Forrest*. New York: HarperCollins, 1992.

Woodworth, Steven E. *Six Armies in Tennessee*. Lincoln: University of Nebraska Press, 1998.

INDEX

⁂

Page numbers in italics refer to illustrations.